The Tanner Lectures on Human Values

THE TANNER LECTURES
ON HUMAN VALUES

25

2005

de Waal, Dawkins, Korsgaard,
Benhabib, Frankfurt

Grethe B. Peterson, *Editor*

THE UNIVERSITY OF UTAH PRESS
Salt Lake City

♾ The paper used in this publication meets the minimum requirements of American National Standard for Information Sciences—Permanence of Paper for Printed Library Materials, ANSI Z39.48–1992

THE TANNER LECTURES ON HUMAN VALUES

The purpose of the Tanner Lectures is to advance and reflect upon scholarly and scientific learning that relates to human values.

To receive an appointment as a Tanner lecturer is a recognition of uncommon capabilities and outstanding scholarly or leadership achievement in the field of human values. The lecturers may be drawn from philosophy, religion, the humanities and sciences, the creative arts and learned professions, or from leadership in public or private affairs. The lectureships are international and intercultural and transcend ethnic, national, religious, or ideological distinctions.

The Tanner Lectures were formally founded on July 1, 1978, at Clare Hall, Cambridge University. They were established by the American scholar, industrialist, and philanthropist, Obert Clark Tanner. In creating the lectureships, Professor Tanner said, "I hope these lectures will contribute to the intellectual and moral life of mankind. I see them simply as a search for a better understanding of human behavior and human values. This understanding may be pursued for its own intrinsic worth, but it may also eventually have practical consequences for the quality of personal and social life."

Permanent Tanner lectureships, with lectures given annually, are established at nine institutions: Clare Hall, Cambridge University; Harvard University; Brasenose College, Oxford University; Princeton University; Stanford University; the University of California; the University of Michigan; the University of Utah; and Yale University. Other international lectureships occasionally take place. The institutions are selected by the Trustees.

The sponsoring institutions have full autonomy in the appointment of their lecturers. A major part of the lecture program is the publication and distribution of the Lectures in an annual volume.

The Tanner Lectures on Human Values is a nonprofit corporation administered at the University of Utah under the direction of a self-perpetuating, international Board of Trustees. The Trustees meet annually to enact policies that will ensure the quality of the lectureships.

The entire lecture program, including the costs of administration, is fully and generously funded in perpetuity by an endowment to the University of Utah by Professor Tanner and Mrs. Grace Adams Tanner.

Obert C. Tanner was born in Farmington, Utah, in 1904. He was educated at the University of Utah, Harvard University, and Stanford University. He served on the faculty at Stanford University and was a professor of philosophy at the University of Utah for twenty-eight years. Mr. Tanner was also the founder and chairman of the O. C. Tanner Company, the world's largest manufacturer of recognition award products.

Harvard University's former president Derek Bok once spoke of Obert Tanner as a "Renaissance Man," citing his remarkable achievements in three of life's major pursuits: business, education, and public service.

Obert C. Tanner died in Palm Springs, California, on October 14, 1993, at the age of eighty-nine.

GRETHE B. PETERSON
University of Utah

CONTENTS

PREFACE TO VOLUME 25

Volume 25 of the Tanner Lectures on Human Values includes lectures delivered during the academic year 2003–2004.

The Tanner Lectures are published in an annual volume.

In addition to the Lectures on Human Values, the Trustees of the Tanner Lectures have funded special international lectureships at selected colleges and universities which are administered independently of the permanent lectures.

Morality and the Social Instincts: Continuity with the Other Primates

FRANS B. M. DE WAAL

THE TANNER LECTURES ON HUMAN VALUES

Delivered at

Princeton University
November 19–20, 2003

FRANS B. M. DE WAAL is C. H. Candler Professor of Primate Behavior at Emory University and director of the Living Links Center at the Yerkes Regional Primate Research Center. He was educated at three Dutch universities—Nijmegen, Groningen, and Utrecht—and received a Ph.D. from the University of Utrecht. He has conducted research on the world's largest captive colony of chimpanzees at the Arnhem Zoo, did both observational and experimental studies of reconciliation behavior in monkeys at the Wisconsin Regional Primate Research Center, and worked with bonobos at the San Diego Zoo. He is a foreign associate of the National Academy of Sciences. In addition to many scientific papers, he is the author of *Chimpanzee Politics: Power and Sex among Apes* (1982); *Peacemaking among Primates* (1989), which was awarded the *Los Angeles Times* Book Award; *Bonobo: The Forgotten Ape* (1997); *The Ape and the Sushi Master* (2001); *Tree of Origin: What Primate Behavior Tells Us about Human Social Evolution* (2001), and *My Family Album: Thirty Years of Primate Photography* (2003).

ABSTRACT

The *Homo homini lupus* view of our species is recognizable in an influential school of biology, founded by Thomas Henry Huxley, which holds that we are born nasty and selfish. According to this school, it is only with the greatest effort that we can hope to become moral. This view of human nature is discussed here as "Veneer Theory," meaning that it sees morality as a thin layer barely disguising less noble tendencies. Veneer Theory is contrasted with the idea of Charles Darwin that morality is a natural outgrowth of the social instincts, hence continuous with the sociality of other animals.

Veneer Theory is criticized at two levels. First, it suffers from major unanswered theoretical questions. If true, we would need to explain why humans, and humans alone, have broken with their own biology, how such a feat is at all possible, and what motivates humans all over the world to do so. The Darwinian view, in contrast, has seen a steady stream of theoretical advances since the 1960s, developed out of the theories of kin selection and reciprocal altruism, but now reaching into fairness principles, reputation building, and punishment strategies. Second, Veneer Theory remains unsupported by empirical evidence. Given that it views morality as a recent addition to human behavior, it would predict that morality resides entirely in the newest parts of our enlarged brain and leads to behavior that deviates from anything other animals do. Modern neuroscience, however, has demonstrated that ethical dilemmas activate ancient emotional centers in the brain that originated long before our species. Moreover, studies of nonhuman primates hint at continuity in many areas considered relevant for an evolved morality. Human moral decisions often stem from emotionally driven "gut" reactions, some of which we share with our closest relatives. These animals may not be moral beings, but they do show signs of empathy, reciprocity, a sense of fairness, and social regularities that—like the norms and rules governing human moral conduct—promote a mutually satisfactory *modus vivendi*.

We approve and we disapprove because we cannot do otherwise.
Can we help feeling pain when the fire burns us?
Can we help sympathizing with our friends?

EDWARD WESTERMARCK (1912 [1908]: 19)

Why should our nastiness be the baggage of an apish past and our kindness
uniquely human? Why should we not seek continuity with other animals for
our "noble" traits as well?

STEPHEN JAY GOULD (1980: 261)

Homo homini lupus—"man is a wolf to man"—is an old Roman proverb popularized by Thomas Hobbes. Even though it permeates large parts of law, economics, and political science, the proverb contains two major errors. First, it fails to do justice to canids, which are among the most gregarious and cooperative animals on the planet (Lorenz 1954; Schleidt and Shalter 2003). But even worse, the saying denies the inherently social nature of our own species.

Social contract theory, and Western civilization with it, seems saturated with the assumption that we are asocial, even nasty creatures rather than the *zoon politikon* (political animal) that Aristotle saw in us. Hobbes explicitly rejected the Aristotelian view by proposing that our ancestors started out autonomous and combative, establishing community life only when the cost of continual strife became unbearable. Social life did not come naturally to us: the step was taken reluctantly, or in the words of Hobbes (1991 [1651]: 120), "by covenant only, which is artificial." More recently, John Rawls (1972) has proposed a milder version of this view, adding that humanity's step toward sociality hinged on conditions of fairness, that is, the prospect of mutually advantageous cooperation among equals.

These ideas about the origin of the well-ordered society remain popular even though the underlying assumption of a rational decision by inherently asocial creatures is untenable in light of what we know about the evolutionary background of our species. It creates the illusion of human society as a voluntary arrangement with self-imposed rules assented to by free and equal persons. Yet there never was a point at which we became social: descended from highly social ancestors, the monkeys and apes, we have been group-living forever. Free and equal people never existed. Humans started out—if a starting point is discernible at all—as interdependent, bonded, and unequal. We come from a long lineage of hierarchical animals for which life in groups is not an option but a survival strategy. Having companions offers advantages in locating food and avoiding predators (Wrangham 1980; van Schaik 1983). Inasmuch as group-oriented, gregarious individuals left more offspring than those less socially inclined (e.g., Silk et al. 2003), sociality became ever deeper ingrained in primate biology and psychology. If any decision to establish societies was made at all, therefore, credit should go to Mother Nature instead of ourselves.

This is not to dismiss the heuristic value of Rawls's "original position" as a way of getting us to reflect on what kind of society we would *prefer* to live in. The original position refers to a "purely hypothetical situation characterized so as to lead to certain conceptions of justice" (Rawls 1972: 12). But even if we do not take the original position literally, adopting it only for the sake of argument, it still distracts from the more pertinent argument that we should be pursuing instead about how we actually became what we are today. What parts of human nature have led us down this or that path, and how have these parts been shaped by evolution? Addressing a real rather than hypothetical past, such questions are bound to bring us closer to the truth. The truth is that we are born intensely social.

A good illustration of the social nature of our species is that, second to the death penalty, solitary confinement is the most extreme punishment we can think of. It works this way only, of course, because we are not born as loners. Our bodies and minds are not designed for life without others. We become hopelessly depressed in the absence of company. Without social support, our health deteriorates. In one recent experiment, healthy volunteers deliberately exposed to cold and flu viruses got sick more easily if they had fewer friends and family around (Cohen et al. 1997). While the primacy of connectedness is naturally understood by women—perhaps because mammalian females with caring tendencies have outreproduced those without for 180 million years—it applies equally to men. In modern society, there is no more effective way for men to expand their age horizon than to get and stay married: it increases their chance of living past the age of sixty-five from 65 to 90 percent (Taylor 2002).

Our social makeup is so obvious that there would be no need to belabor this point were it not for its conspicuous absence from origin stories within the disciplines of law, economics, and political science. A tendency

in the West to see emotions as soft and social attachment as messy has
made theoreticians turn to cognition and rationality as the preferred
guides of human behavior. This is so despite the fact that psychological
research suggests the primacy of affect: that is, that human behavior
derives above all from fast, automated emotional judgments and only
secondarily from slower conscious processes (e.g., Zajonc 1980, 1984;
Bargh and Chartrand 1999). Humans seem, in fact, about as emotional
in their dealing with each other as any other social animal.

Unfortunately, the overemphasis on rationality and downplaying of
emotions is not restricted to the humanities and social sciences. Within
evolutionary biology, too, some have embraced the illusion that we are a
self-invented species. A parallel debate pitting reason against emotion
has been raging regarding the origin of morality, a hallmark of human
society. One school views morality as a cultural innovation achieved by
our species alone. This school does not see moral tendencies as part and
parcel of human nature. Our ancestors, it claims, became moral by
choice. The second school, in contrast, views morality as growing out of
the social instincts that we share with many other animals. In this view,
morality is neither unique to us nor a conscious decision taken at a specific point in time: it is the product of gradual social evolution.

The first standpoint assumes that deep down we are not truly moral.
It views morality as a cultural overlay, a thin veneer hiding an otherwise
selfish and brutish nature. Perfectibility is what we should strive for.
Until recently, this was the dominant view within evolutionary biology
as well as among science writers popularizing this field. I use the term
"Veneer Theory" to denote these ideas, tracing their origin to Thomas
Henry Huxley. After treating these ideas, I review Charles Darwin's
quite different standpoint of an evolved morality, which was inspired by
the Scottish Enlightenment. I further discuss the views of Mencius and
Edward Westermarck, which agree with those of Darwin.

Given these two schools' contrasting opinions about continuity versus discontinuity with other animals, I build upon an earlier treatise (de
Waal 1996) in paying special attention to parallels between the behavior
of human and nonhuman primates.

1. VENEER THEORY

In 1893, for a large audience in Oxford, England, Huxley publicly reconciled his dim view of the natural world with the kindness occasionally
encountered in human society. Huxley realized that the laws of the phys-

ical world are unalterable. He felt, however, that their impact on human existence could be softened and modified if people kept nature under control. Huxley compared us with a gardener who has a hard time keeping weeds out of his garden. He declared human ethics a cultural victory over the evolutionary process (Huxley 1989 [1894]).

This was an astounding position for two reasons. First, it deliberately curbed the explanatory power of evolution. Since many consider morality the essence of our species, Huxley was in effect saying that what makes us human could not be handled by the evolutionary framework. This was an inexplicable retreat by someone who had gained a reputation as "Darwin's Bulldog" owing to his fierce advocacy of evolutionary theory. Second, Huxley gave no hint whatsoever where humanity might have unearthed the will and strength to go against its own nature. If we are indeed born competitors, who don't care about the feelings of others, how did we decide to transform ourselves into model citizens? Can people for generations maintain behavior that is out of character, like a shoal of piranhas that decides to turn vegetarian? How deep does such a change go? Are we the proverbial wolves in sheep's clothing: nice on the outside, nasty on the inside?

This was the only time Huxley visibly broke with Darwin. As Huxley's biographer, Adrian Desmond (1994: 599), put it: "Huxley was forcing his ethical Ark against the Darwinian current which had brought him so far." Two decades earlier, in *The Descent of Man,* Darwin (1982 [1871]) had unequivocally stressed morality as part of human nature. The reason for Huxley's departure has been sought in his suffering at the cruel hand of nature, which had taken the life of his beloved daughter, as well as his need to make the ruthlessness of the Darwinian cosmos palatable to the general public. He had depicted nature as so thoroughly "red in tooth and claw" that he could maintain this position only by dislodging human ethics, presenting it as a separate innovation (Desmond 1994). In short, Huxley had talked himself into a corner.

His curious dualism, which pits morality against nature and humans against other animals, was to receive a respectability boost from Sigmund Freud's writings, which throve on contrasts between the conscious and subconscious, the ego and superego, Love and Death, and so on. As with Huxley's gardener and garden, Freud was not just dividing the world in symmetrical halves: he saw struggle everywhere. He explained the incest taboo and other moral restrictions as the result of a violent break with the freewheeling sexual life of the primal horde, culminating in the collective slaughter of an overbearing father by his sons (Freud 1913). He let civilization arise out of the renunciation of instinct, the gaining of control over the forces of nature, and the building of a cultural superego.

Man's heroic combat against forces that try to drag him down remains a dominant theme within biology today, as illustrated by quotes from outspoken Huxleyans. Declaring ethics a radical break with biology, George Williams has written extensively about the wretchedness of nature, culminating in his claim that human morality is a mere by-product of the evolutionary process: "I account for morality as an accidental capability produced, in its boundless stupidity, by a biological process that is normally opposed to the expression of such a capability" (Williams 1988: 438).

Having explained at length that our genes know what is best for us, programming every little wheel of the human survival machine, Richard Dawkins waits until the last sentence of *The Selfish Gene* to reassure us that, in fact, we are welcome to chuck all of those genes out of the window: "We, alone on earth, can rebel against the tyranny of the selfish replicators" (Dawkins 1976: 215). The break with nature is obvious in this statement, as is the uniqueness of our species. Dawkins explicitly endorses Huxley: "What I am saying, along with many other people, among them T. H. Huxley, is that in our political and social life we are entitled to throw out Darwinism, to say we don't want to live in a Darwinian world" (Roes 1997: 3; see also Dawkins 2003).

Darwin must be turning in his grave, because the implied "Darwinian world" is miles removed from what he himself envisioned (see below). What is lacking in these statements is any indication of how we can possibly negate our genes, which the same authors at other times don't hesitate to depict as all-powerful. Like the views of Hobbes, Huxley, and Freud, the thinking is thoroughly dichotomous: we are part nature, part culture, rather than a well-integrated whole. Morality is a thin crust underneath which boil human passions that are invariably antisocial, amoral, and egoistic. This idea of morality as a veneer is best summarized by Michael Ghiselin's famous quip: "Scratch an 'altruist,' and watch a 'hypocrite' bleed" (Ghiselin 1974: 247; figure 1).

Veneer Theory has been popularized by countless science writers, such as Robert Wright (1994), who went so far as to claim that virtue is absent from people's hearts and souls, that our species is potentially but not naturally moral. But what, one might ask, about the many people

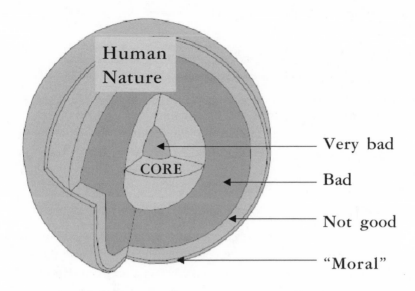

FIGURE 1. The popular view of morality among biologists during the past quarter of a century was best summarized by Ghiselin (1974: 247): "Scratch an 'altruist,' and watch a 'hypocrite' bleed." Accordingly, people are thoroughly competitive, and morality is no more than a last-minute, artificial addition. Summarized as "Veneer Theory," this idea goes back not to Charles Darwin but to his contemporary Thomas Henry Huxley. It is visualized here tongue-in-cheek as a human nature that is bad and selfish to its core.

who occasionally experience in themselves and others a degree of sympathy, goodness, and generosity? Echoing Ghiselin, Wright answers that the "moral animal" is essentially a hypocrite:

> ...the pretense of selflessness is about as much part of human nature as is its frequent absence. We dress ourselves up in tony moral language, denying base motives and stressing our at least minimal consideration for the greater good; and we fiercely and self-righteously decry selfishness in others. (Wright 1994: 344)

To explain how we manage to live with ourselves despite this travesty, theorists have called upon self-deception. If people think they are at times unselfish, so the argument goes, they must be hiding their true motives from themselves (e.g., Badcock 1986). In the ultimate twist of irony, anyone who fails to believe that we are fooling ourselves, and feels that genuine kindness actually exists in the world, is considered a wishful thinker, hence accused of fooling him- or herself. Some scientists have objected, however:

> It is frequently said that people endorse such hypotheses [about human altruism] because they *want* the world to be a friendly and hospitable place. The defenders of egoism and individualism who advance this criticism thereby pay themselves a compliment; they pat themselves on the back for staring reality squarely in the face. Egoists and individualists are objective, they suggest, whereas proponents of altruism and group selection are trapped by a comforting illusion. (Sober and Wilson 1998: 8–9)

All of these back-and-forth arguments about how to reconcile everyday human kindness with evolutionary theory seem an unfortunate legacy of Huxley, who had a poor understanding of the theory that he so zealously defended (Mayr 1997). It should be pointed out that in Huxley's time there was already opposition to his ideas (Desmond 1994), some of which came from Russian biologists, such as Petr Kropotkin. Given the harsh climate of Siberia, Russian scientists traditionally were far more impressed by the battle of animals against the elements than against each other, resulting in an emphasis on cooperation and solidarity that contrasted with Huxley's dog-eat-dog perspective (Todes 1989). Kropotkin's (1972 [1902]) *Mutual Aid* was a direct attack on Huxley, but written with great deference for Darwin.

Although Kropotkin never formulated his theory with the precision and evolutionary logic available to Robert Trivers (1971) in his seminal paper on reciprocal altruism, both pondered the origins of a cooperative, and ultimately moral, society without invoking false pretense, Freudian denial schemes, or cultural indoctrination. In this they proved the true followers of Darwin.

2. Darwin on the Evolution of Ethics

Evolution favors animals that assist each other if by doing so they achieve long-term benefits of greater value than the benefits derived from going it alone and competing with others. Unlike cooperation resting on simultaneous benefits to all parties involved (known as mutualism), reciprocity involves exchanged acts that, while beneficial to the recipient, are costly to the performer (Dugatkin 1997). This cost, which is generated because there is a time lag between giving and receiving, is eliminated as soon as a favor of equal value is returned to the performer (for treatments of this issue since Trivers 1971, see Axelrod and Hamilton 1981; Rothstein and Pierotti 1988; Taylor and McGuire 1988). It is in these theories that we find the germ of an evolutionary explanation that escaped Huxley.

It is important to clarify that these theories do not conflict by any means with popular ideas about the role of selfishness in evolution. It is only recently that the concept of "selfishness" has been plucked from the English language, robbed of its vernacular meaning, and applied outside of the psychological domain. Even though the term is seen by some as synonymous with being self-serving, English does have different terms for a reason. Selfishness implies the *intention* to serve oneself, hence knowledge of what one stands to gain from a particular behavior. A vine may be self-serving by overgrowing and suffocating a tree; but since plants lack intentions, they cannot be selfish except in a meaningless, metaphorical sense. Unfortunately, in complete violation of the term's original meaning, it is precisely this rather empty sense of "selfish" that has come to dominate debates about human nature. If our genes are selfish, we must be selfish, too, is the argument one often hears, despite the fact that genes are mere molecules, and hence cannot be selfish (Midgley 1979).

It is fine to describe animals (and humans) as the product of evolutionary forces that promote self-serving behavior so long as one realizes that this by no means precludes the evolution of altruistic and sympathetic tendencies. Darwin recognized this, explaining the evolution of these tendencies by group selection instead of the individual and kin selection favored by modern theoreticians (but see, e.g., Sober and Wilson 1998; Boehm 1999). Darwin firmly believed his theory capable of accommodating the origins of morality and did not see any conflict between the harshness of the evolutionary process and the gentleness of some of its products. Rather than presenting the human species as outside of the laws of biology, Darwin emphasized continuity with animals even in the moral domain:

> Any animal whatever, endowed with well-marked social instincts, the parental and filial affections being here included, would inevitably acquire a moral sense or conscience, as soon as its intellectual powers had become as well developed, or nearly as well developed, as in man. (Darwin 1982 [1871]: 71–72)

It is important to dwell on the capacity for sympathy hinted at here and expressed more clearly by Darwin elsewhere (e.g., "Many animals certainly sympathize with each other's distress or danger" [Darwin 1982 (1871): 77]), because it is in this domain that striking continuities exist between humans and other social animals. To be vicariously affected by the emotions of others must be very basic, because these reactions have been reported for a great variety of animals and are often immediate and uncontrollable. They undoubtedly derive from parental care, in which vulnerable individuals are fed and protected, but in many animals stretch well beyond this domain, extending to relations among unrelated adults (section 4 below).

In his view of sympathy, Darwin was inspired by Adam Smith, the Scottish moral philosopher and father of economics. It says a great deal about the distinctions we need to make between self-serving behavior and selfish motives that Smith, best known for his emphasis on self-interest as the guiding principle of economics, also wrote about the universal human capacity of sympathy:

> How selfish soever man may be supposed, there are evidently some principles in his nature, which interest him in the fortune of others, and render their happiness necessary to him, though he derives nothing from it, except the pleasure of seeing it. (Smith 1937 [1759]: 9)

The evolutionary origin of this inclination is no mystery. All species that rely on cooperation—from elephants to wolves and people—show group loyalty and helping tendencies. These tendencies evolved in the context of a close-knit social life in which they benefited relatives and companions able to repay the favor. The impulse to help was therefore never totally without survival value to the ones showing the impulse. But, as so often, the impulse became divorced from the consequences that shaped its evolution. This permitted its expression even when payoffs were unlikely, such as when strangers were beneficiaries. Personally, I am unconvinced that we need group selection to explain the origin of these tendencies—we seem to be able to get quite far with the theories of kin selection and reciprocal altruism. Moreover, there is so much intergroup migration (hence gene-flow) in primates that the conditions for group selection do not seem to be fulfilled. In all of the primates, the younger generation of one sex or another (males in many monkeys, females in the case of chimpanzees and bonobos) tends to leave the group to join neighboring groups (Pusey and Packer 1987). This means that primate groups are far from genetically isolated.

In discussing what constitutes morality, the actual behavior is less important than the underlying capacities. For example, instead of arguing that food-sharing is a building block of morality, it is rather the capacities thought to underlie food-sharing (e.g., high levels of tolerance, sensitivity to others' needs, reciprocal exchange) that are relevant. Ants, too, share food, but likely based on quite different urges than those that make chimpanzees or people share food (de Waal 1989a). This distinction was understood by Darwin, who looked beyond the actual behavior at the underlying motivations, intentions, and capacities. In other words, whether animals are nice to each other is not the issue; nor does it matter much whether their behavior fits our moral preferences or not. The relevant question is whether they possess the capacities for reciprocity and revenge, for the enforcement of social rules, for the settlement of disputes, and for sympathy and empathy (Flack and de Waal 2000).

This also means that calls to reject Darwinism in our daily lives so as to build a moral society are based on a misreading of Darwin. Since Darwin saw morality as a logical evolutionary product, he envisioned an eminently more livable world than the one proposed by Huxley and his followers. The latter believe in a culturally imposed, artificial morality that seems impossible to maintain, given that human nature is offering no helping hand. Huxley's world seems by far the colder and more terrifying place.

3. Edward Westermarck

Edward Westermarck, a Swedish Finn who lived from 1862 until 1939, deserves a central position in any debate about the origin of morality, since he was the first scholar to promote an integrated view including both humans and animals and both culture and evolution. That his ideas were underappreciated at the time is understandable, because they flew in the face of the Western dualistic tradition that pits body against mind and culture against instinct.

Westermarck's books are a curious blend of dry theorizing, detailed anthropology, and secondhand animal stories. The author was eager to connect human and animal behavior, but his own work focused entirely on people. Since in his days little systematic research on animal behavior existed, he had to rely on anecdotes, such as the one of a vengeful camel that had been excessively beaten on multiple occasions by a fourteen-year-old "lad" for loitering or turning the wrong way. The camel passively took the punishment; but a few days later, finding itself unladen alone on the road with the same conductor, "seized the unlucky boy's head in its monstrous mouth, and lifting him up in the air flung him down again on the earth with the upper part of the skull completely torn off, and his brains scattered on the ground" (Westermarck 1912 [1908]: 38).

We should not discard such unverified reports out of hand: stories of delayed retaliation abound in the zoo world, especially about apes and elephants. We now have systematic data on how chimpanzees punish negative actions with other negative actions (called a "revenge system" by de Waal and Luttrell 1988), and how a macaque attacked by a dominant member of its troop will turn around to redirect aggression against a vulnerable younger relative of its attacker (Aureli et al. 1992). These reactions fall under Westermarck's *retributive emotions*, but for him the term "retributive" went beyond its usual connotation of getting even. It also covered positive emotions, such as gratitude and the repayment of services. Depicting the retributive emotions as the cornerstone of morality, Westermarck weighed in on the question of its origin while antedating modern discussions of evolutionary ethics.

Westermarck is part of a long tradition, going back to Aristotle and Thomas Aquinas, which firmly anchors morality in the natural inclinations and desires of our species (Arnhart 1998, 1999). Emotions occupy a central role; it is well known that, rather than being the antithesis of rationality, emotions aid human reasoning. People can reason and deliberate as much as they want: neuroscientists have found that if there are no emotions attached to the various options in front of them, they will never reach a decision or conviction (Damasio 1994). This is critical for moral choice, because if anything morality involves strong convictions. These convictions don't—or rather can't—come about through a cool rationality: they require caring about others and powerful "gut feelings" about right and wrong.

Westermarck (1912 [1908], 1917 [1908]) discusses, one by one, a whole range of what philosophers before him, most notably David Hume (1978 [1739]) and Adam Smith (1937 [1759]), called the "moral sentiments." He classified the retributive emotions into those derived from resentment and anger, which seek revenge and punishment, and those that are more positive and prosocial. Whereas in his time few animal examples existed of the moral emotions—hence his reliance on

Moroccan camel stories—we know now that there are many parallels in primate behavior. He also discusses "forgiveness," and how the turning of the other cheek is a universally appreciated gesture. Chimpanzees kiss and embrace after fights, and these so-called reconciliations serve to preserve peace within the community (de Waal and van Roosmalen 1979). A rapidly growing literature exists on conflict resolution in primates and other mammals (de Waal 1989b, 2000; Aureli and de Waal 2000; Aureli et al. 2002). Reconciliation may not be the same as forgiveness, but the two are obviously related.

Westermarck also sees protection of others against aggression as resulting from what he calls "sympathetic resentment," thus implying that this behavior rests on identification and empathy with the other. Protection against aggression is common in monkeys and apes and in many other animals, who stick up for their kin and friends. The primate literature offers a well-investigated picture of coalitions and alliances, which some consider the hallmark of primate social life and the main reason that primates have evolved such complex, cognitively demanding societies (e.g., Byrne and Whiten 1988; Harcourt and de Waal 1992; de Waal 1998 [1982]).

Similarly, the retributive kindly emotions ("desire to give pleasure in return for pleasure": Westermarck 1912 [1908]: 93) have an obvious parallel in what we now call reciprocal altruism, such as the tendency to repay in kind those from whom assistance has been received. Westermarck adds moral approval as a retributive kindly emotion, hence as a component of reciprocal altruism. These views antedate the discussions about "indirect reciprocity" in the modern literature on evolutionary ethics, which revolve around reputation building within the larger community (e.g., Alexander 1987). It is truly amazing to see how many issues brought up by contemporary authors are, couched in somewhat different terms, already present in the writings of this Swedish Finn of one century ago.

The most insightful part of Westermarck's work is perhaps where he tries to come to grips with what defines a moral emotion as moral. Here he shows that there is more to these emotions than raw gut feeling, as he explains that they "differ from kindred non-moral emotions by their disinterestedness, apparent impartiality, and flavour of generality" (Westermarck 1917 [1908]: 738–39). Emotions, such as gratitude and resentment, directly concern one's own interests—how one has been treated or how one wishes to be treated—hence they are too egocentric to be moral. Moral emotions ought to be disconnected from one's immediate situation: they deal with good and bad at a more abstract, disinterested level. It is only when we make general judgments of how *anyone* ought to be treated that we can begin to speak of moral approval and disapproval. It is in this specific area, famously symbolized by Smith's (1937 [1759]) "impartial spectator," that humans seem to go radically further than other primates.

Section 4 discusses continuity between the two main pillars of human morality and primate behavior. Empathy and reciprocity have been described as the chief "prerequisites" (de Waal 1996) or "building blocks" of morality (Flack and de Waal 2000), meaning that whereas they are by no means sufficient to produce morality as we know it, they are indispensable.

4. ANIMAL EMPATHY

4a. Emotional Linkage

When Carolyn Zahn-Waxler visited homes to find out how children respond to family members instructed to feign sadness (sobbing), pain (crying), or distress (choking), she discovered that children a little over one year of age already comfort others. This is a milestone in their development: an aversive experience in another person draws out a concerned response. An unplanned sidebar to her classical study, however, was that household pets appeared as worried as the children by the "distress" of family members. They hovered over them or put their heads in their laps (Zahn-Waxler et al. 1984).

Intersubjectivity has many aspects apart from emotional linkage, such as an appraisal of the other's situation, experience-based predictions about the other's behavior, extraction of information from the other that is valuable to the self, and an understanding of the other's knowledge and intentions. When the emotional state of one individual induces a matching or related state in another, we speak of *emotional contagion* (Hatfield et al. 1993). With increasing differentiation between self and other, and an increasing appreciation of the precise circumstances underlying the emotional states of others, emotional contagion develops into empathy. Empathy encompasses—and could not possibly exist without—emotional contagion, yet goes beyond it in that it places filters between the other's state and the own, adding a cognitive layer. In empathy, the subject does *not* confuse its own internal state with the other's. These various levels of empathy, including personal distress and sympathetic concern, are defined and discussed by Nancy Eisenberg (2000).

Empathy is a social phenomenon with great adaptive significance for animals in groups. That most modern textbooks on animal cognition do not index empathy or sympathy does not mean that these capacities are not essential; it only means that they have been overlooked by a science traditionally focused on individual rather than interindividual capacities. Inasmuch as the survival of many animals depends on concerted action, mutual aid, and information transfer, selection must have favored proximate mechanisms to evaluate the emotional states of others and quickly respond to them in adaptive ways. Even though the human empathy literature often emphasizes the cognitive side of this ability, proposing complex simulations or evaluations of the other's state, Martin Hoffman (1981b: 79) rightly notes that "humans must be equipped biologically to function effectively in many social situations without undue reliance on cognitive processes."

Empathy, which allows us to relate to the emotional states of others, seems critical for the regulation of social interactions, such as coordinated activity, cooperation toward a common goal, social bonding, and care of others. It would be strange indeed if such an essential survival mechanism, which arises so early in life in all members of our species, would totally lack animal parallels.

4b. Early Experiments

An interesting older literature by experimental psychologists (reviewed by Preston and de Waal 2002a and 2002b and de Waal 2003) placed the words "empathy" and "sympathy" between quotation marks. In those days, talk of animal emotions was all but taboo. In a paper provocatively entitled "Emotional Reactions of Rats to the Pain of Others," R. M. Church (1959) established that rats that had learned to press a lever to obtain food would stop doing so if their response was paired with the delivery of an electric shock to a visible neighboring rat. Even though this inhibition habituated rapidly, it suggested something aversive about the pain reactions of others. Perhaps such reactions arouse negative emotions in rats that see and hear them.

Monkeys show a stronger inhibition than rats. The most compelling evidence for the strength of empathy in monkeys came from S. Wechkin et al. (1964) and J. Masserman et al. (1964). They found that rhesus monkeys refuse to pull a chain that delivers food to themselves if doing so shocks a companion. One monkey stopped pulling for five days, and another one for twelve days after witnessing shock-delivery to a companion. These monkeys were literally starving themselves to avoid inflicting pain upon another. Such sacrifice relates to the tight social system and emotional linkage among macaques, as supported by the finding that the inhibition to hurt another was more pronounced between familiar rather than unfamiliar individuals (Masserman et al. 1964).

4c. Consolation Behavior

Qualitative accounts of great ape temperament support the view that these animals show strong emotional reactions to others in pain or need. Thus, Robert Yerkes (1925: 246) reports how his bonobo was so extraordinarily concerned and protective toward his sickly chimpanzee companion, Panzee, that the scientific establishment might not accept his claims: "If I were to tell of his altruistic and obviously sympathetic behavior towards Panzee I should be suspected of idealizing an ape."

Nadezhda Ladygina-Kohts (2001 [1935]: 121) noticed similar empathic tendencies in her young chimpanzee, Joni, whom she raised at the beginning of the previous century in Moscow. Kohts, who analyzed Joni's behavior in the minutest detail, discovered that the only way to get him off the roof of her house after an escape (much better than any reward or threat of punishment) was by appealing to his sympathy:

> If I pretend to be crying, close my eyes and weep, Joni immediately stops his plays or any other activities, quickly runs over to me, all excited and shagged, from the most remote places in the house, such as the roof or the ceiling of his cage, from where I could not drive him down despite my persistent calls and entreaties. He hastily runs around me, as if looking for the offender; looking at my face, he tenderly takes my chin in his palm, lightly touches my face with his finger, as though trying to understand what is happening, and turns around, clenching his toes into firm fists.

These are just two out of many reports gathered and discussed by de Waal (1996, 1997a) that suggest that apart from emotional connectedness apes have an appreciation of the other's situation and a degree of perspective-taking. Another striking report in this regard concerns a bonobo female empathizing with a bird at Twycross Zoo, in England:

> One day, Kuni captured a starling. Out of fear that she might molest the stunned bird, which appeared undamaged, the keeper urged the

ape to let it go.... Kuni picked up the starling with one hand and climbed to the highest point of the highest tree where she wrapped her legs around the trunk so that she had both hands free to hold the bird. She then carefully unfolded its wings and spread them wide open, one wing in each hand, before throwing the bird as hard she could towards the barrier of the enclosure. Unfortunately, it fell short and landed onto the bank of the moat where Kuni guarded it for a long time against a curious juvenile. (de Waal 1997a: 156)

Obviously, what Kuni did would have been totally inappropriate toward a member of her own species. Having seen birds in flight many times, she seemed to have a notion of what would be good for a bird, thus giving us an anthropoid illustration of the empathic capacity so enduringly described by Smith (1937 [1759]: 10) as "changing places in fancy with the sufferer."

Primate empathy is such a rich area that Sanjida O'Connell (1995) was able to conduct a content analysis of thousands of qualitative reports. The investigator counted the frequency of three types of empathy, from emotional contagion to more cognitive forms, including an appreciation of the other's situation and aid-giving that is tailored to the other's needs. Understanding the emotional state of another was particularly common in the chimpanzee, with most outcomes resulting in the subject comforting the object of distress. Monkey displays of empathy were far more restricted but did include the adoption of orphans and reactions to illness, handicaps, and wounded companions.

This difference between monkey and ape empathy has been confirmed by systematic studies of behavior known as "consolation," first documented by de Waal and Angeline van Roosmalen (1979). Consolation is defined as reassurance and friendly contact directed by an uninvolved bystander to one of the combatants in a preceding aggressive incident. For example, a third party goes over to the loser of a fight and gently puts an arm around her shoulders (figure 2). Consolation is not to be confused with reconciliation, which seems mostly self-interested, such as by the imperative to restore a disturbed social relationship (de Waal 2000). The advantages of consolation for the actor remain unclear. The actor could probably walk away from the scene without any negative consequences.

Information on chimpanzee consolation is well quantified. De Waal and van Roosmalen (1979) based their conclusions on an analysis of hundreds of postconflict observations, and a replication study by de Waal

FIGURE 2. A typical instance of consolation in chimpanzees in which a juvenile puts an arm around a screaming adult male who has just been defeated in a fight with his rival. Photograph by the author.

and Filippo Aureli (1996) included an even larger sample in which the authors sought to test two relatively simple predictions. If third-party contacts indeed serve to alleviate the distress of conflict participants, these contacts should be directed more at recipients of aggression than at aggressors, and more at recipients of intense rather than mild aggression. Comparing third-party contact rates with baseline levels, the investigators found support for both of these predictions (figure 3).

Consolation has thus far been demonstrated in great apes only. When de Waal and Aureli (1996) set out to apply exactly the same observation methodology as used on chimpanzees to detect consolation in macaques, they failed to find any (reviewed by Watts et al. 2000). This came as a surprise, because reconciliation studies, which employ essentially the same design, have shown reconciliation in species after species. Why, then, would consolation be restricted to apes?

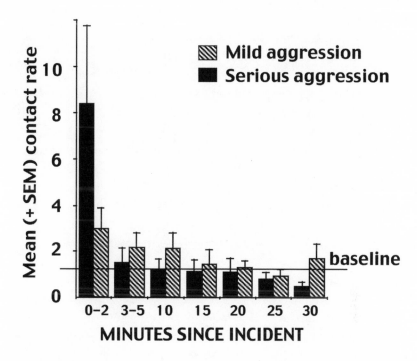

FIGURE 3. The rate with which third parties contact victims of aggression in chimpanzees, comparing recipients of serious and mild aggression. Especially in the first few minutes after the incident, recipients of serious aggression receive more contacts than baseline. After de Waal and Aureli (1996).

Targeted help in response to specific, sometimes novel, situations may require a distinction between self and other that allows the other's situation to be divorced from one's own while maintaining the emotional link that motivates behavior. Possibly, one cannot achieve cognitive empathy without a high degree of self-awareness. In other words, in order to understand that the source of vicarious arousal is not oneself but the other and to understand what caused the other's state, one needs a clear distinction between self and other. Based on these assumptions, Gordon Gallup (1982) was the first to speculate about a possible connection between cognitive empathy and mirror self-recognition (MSR). This view is supported both developmentally, by a correlation between the emergence of MSR in young children and their helping tendencies (Bischof-Köhler 1988; Zahn-Waxler et al. 1992), and phylogenetically, by the presence of complex helping and consolation in hominoids, such as humans and apes, but not in monkeys. Hominoids are also the only primates with MSR.

I have argued before that, apart from consolation behavior, targeted helping reflects cognitive empathy. Targeted helping is defined as altruistic behavior tailored to the specific needs of the other in novel situations, such as the previously described reaction of Kuni to the bird or the highly publicized case of Binti-Jua, a gorilla female who rescued a boy who had fallen into her enclosure at the Brookfield Zoo in Chicago (de Waal 1996, 2001). These responses require an understanding of the specific predicament of the individual needing help. Targeted helping is common in the great apes, but also striking in dolphins (Caldwell and Caldwell 1966). The recent discovery of MSR in dolphins (Reiss and Marino 2001) thus fits the proposed connection between increased self-awareness, on the one hand, and cognitive empathy, on the other.

4d. Russian Doll

Stephanie Preston and de Waal (2002b) propose that at the core of the empathic capacity is the reactivation of the subject's stored representations of previously experienced states similar to those perceived in the object. This process relies on the subject's experience with these particular states as well as its closeness to the object. As a result, bonded individuals will respond more strongly to each other than socially distant individuals. This Perception-Action Model (PAM) fits Antonio Damasio's (1994) somatic marker hypothesis of emotions as well as recent evidence for a link at the cellular level between perception and action (e.g., "mirror neurons": di Pellegrino et al. 1992). The idea that perception and action share representations is anything but new: it goes as far back as the first treatise on *Einfühlung,* the German concept later translated into English as "empathy" (Wispé 1991). When T. Lipps (1903) introduced *Einfühlung*, which literally means "feeling into," he speculated about *innere Nachahmung* (inner mimicry) of another's feelings along the same lines as proposed by the PAM.

Empathy is often an insuppressible, unconscious process, as demonstrated by electromyographic studies of invisible muscle contractions in people's faces in response to pictures of human facial expressions that have been shown so briefly that subjects are unaware of them (e.g., Dimberg et al. 2000). Accounts of empathy as a higher cognitive process of simulation or perspective-taking, such as theory-of-mind, neglect these automatic "gut level" reactions, which are too rapid to depend on higher

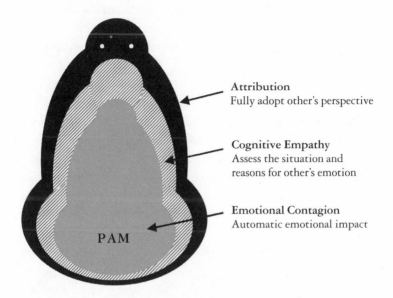

FIGURE 4. According to the Russian Doll Model, empathy covers all processes leading to related emotional states in subject and object; at its core are the perception-action mechanism (PAM) and emotional contagion: immediate, often unconscious state matching between individuals. Higher levels of empathy build on this hard-wired socio-affective basis, such as cognitive empathy (requiring an understanding of the reasons for the other's emotions) and mental state attribution (fully adopting the other's perspective). The Russian Doll Model proposes that these outer layers cannot exist without the inner ones. After de Waal (2003).

processes. This is not to say that more complex cognitive levels of empathy are irrelevant, yet they are built on top of this firm, hard-wired basis without which we would be at a loss about what moves others. This bottom-up view of empathy has led me to formulate a Russian doll model of empathy with a simple PAM-like mechanism at its core (figure 4).

Evolution never replaces anything: it works with existing structures and capacities, elaborating them and taking off from them. It has added to the PAM core a series of additions with increasingly complex components, such as emotional contagion, cognitive empathy, and attribution. Cognitive empathy implies appraisal of another's predicament or situation (cf. de Waal 1996). The subject not only responds to the signals emitted by the object but seeks to understand the reasons, looking for clues in the other's behavior and circumstances. Cognitive empathy makes it possible to furnish targeted help that takes the needs of the other into account. These responses go well beyond emotional contagion, yet they would be hard to explain without an emotional motivational component.

Whereas monkeys (and most other social mammals) clearly seem to possess emotional contagion and some forms of targeted helping, the latter phenomenon is more strikingly developed in the great apes. That monkeys lack this capacity is evident from an example at Jigokudani Park in Japan, where first-time mother macaques are kept out of warm-water springs by park wardens because of their experience that these females tend to drown their infants accidentally. They fail to pay attention to them when submerging themselves in the ponds. This is some-

FIGURE 5. Cognitive empathy (i.e., empathy combined with appraisal of the other's situation) allows for aid tailored to the other's needs. In this case, a mother chimpanzee reaches out to help her son out of a tree after he has screamed and begged (see hand gesture). Targeted helping may require a distinction between self and other, an ability that may also underlie mirror self-recognition, as found in humans, apes, and dolphins. Photograph by the author.

thing they apparently learn over time, showing that they do not automatically take their offspring's perspective. De Waal (1996) speaks of "learned adjustment" to differentiate these acquired adaptive reactions from the immediate understanding shown by ape mothers, which tend to respond appropriately to specific needs of their offspring (figure 5).

In conclusion, empathy is not an all-or-nothing phenomenon: it covers a wide range of emotional linkage patterns, from the very simple and automatic to the very sophisticated. It seems logical first to try to understand the more basic forms, which are widespread indeed, before addressing the interesting variations that cognitive evolution has constructed on top of this foundation.

5. RECIPROCITY AND FAIRNESS

Chimpanzees and capuchin monkeys—the two species I work with most—are special, because they are among the very few primates that share food outside the mother-offspring context (Feistner and McGrew 1989). The capuchin is a small, easy primate to work with, as opposed to the chimpanzee, which is many times stronger than we are. Both species are interested in each other's food and will share food on occasion—sometimes even hand over a piece to another. Most sharing, however, is passive, where one individual will reach for food owned by another, who will let go. But even passive sharing is special compared to most animals, in which a similar situation would result in a fight or assertion by the dominant, without any sharing at all.

5a. Chimpanzee Gratitude

We studied sequences involving food sharing to see how a beneficial act by individual A toward B would affect B's behavior toward A. The prediction was that B would show beneficial behavior toward A in return. The problem with food sharing is, however, that after a group-wide feeding session as used in our experiments the motivation to share changes (the animals are more sated). Hence, food sharing cannot be the only variable measured. A second social service unaffected by food consumption was included. For this, grooming between individuals prior to food sharing was used. The frequency and duration of hundreds of spontaneous grooming bouts among our chimpanzees were measured in the morning. Within half an hour after the end of these observations, starting around noon, the apes were given two tightly bound bundles of leaves and branches. Nearly 7,000 interactions over food were carefully recorded by observers and entered into a computer according to strict definitions described by de Waal (1989a). The resulting database on spontaneous services exceeds that for any other nonhuman primate.

It was found that adults were more likely to share food with individuals who had groomed them earlier. In other words, if A had groomed B in the morning, B was more likely than usual to share food with A later in the day. This result, however, could be explained in two ways. The first is the "good mood" hypothesis according to which individuals who have received grooming are in a benevolent mood, leading them to share indiscriminately with all individuals. The second explanation is the direct-exchange hypothesis, in which the individual who has been groomed responds by sharing food specifically with the groomer. The data indicated that the sharing increase was specific to the previous groomer. In other words, chimpanzees appeared to remember others who had just performed a service (grooming) and respond to those individuals by sharing more with them. Also, aggressive protests by food possessors to approaching individuals were directed more at those who had not groomed them than at previous grooming partners. This is compelling evidence for partner-specific reciprocal exchange (de Waal 1997b).

Of all existing examples of reciprocal altruism in nonhuman animals, the exchange of food for grooming in chimpanzees appears to be the most cognitively advanced. Our data strongly suggest a memory-based mechanism. A significant time delay existed between favors given and received (from half an hour to two hours); hence the favor was acted upon well after the previous interaction. Apart from memory of past events, we need to postulate that the memory of a received service, such as grooming, triggered a positive attitude toward the individual who offered the service, a psychological mechanism known as "gratitude" in humans. Gratitude in relation to the evolution of reciprocal exchange (cf. Trivers 1971) has been discussed at length by Kristin Bonnie and de Waal (2004) and is classified by Westermarck (1912 [1908]) as one of the "retributive kindly emotions" deemed essential for morality.

5b. Monkey Fairness

During the evolution of cooperation it may have become critical for actors to compare their own efforts and payoffs with those of others. Negative reactions may ensue in case of violated expectations. A recent theory proposes that aversion to inequity can explain human cooperation within the bounds of the rational choice model (Fehr and Schmidt 1999). Similarly, cooperative nonhuman species seem guided by a set of expectations about the outcome of cooperation and access to resources. De Waal (1996: 95) proposed a *sense of social regularity,* defined as: "A set of expectations about the way in which oneself (or others) should be treated and how resources should be divided. Whenever reality deviates from these expectations to one's (or the other's) disadvantage, a negative reaction ensues, most commonly protest by subordinate individuals and punishment by dominant individuals."

The sense of how others should or should not behave is essentially egocentric, although the interests of individuals close to the actor, especially kin, may be taken into account (hence the parenthetical inclusion of others). Note that the expectations have not been specified: they are species-typical. To explore expectations held by capuchin monkeys we made use of their ability to judge and respond to value. We knew from previous studies that capuchins easily learn to assign value to tokens. Furthermore they can use these assigned values to complete a simple barter. This allowed a test to elucidate inequity aversion by measuring the reactions of subjects to a partner receiving a superior reward for the same tokens.

We paired each monkey with a group mate and watched their reactions when their partners got a better reward for doing the same bartering task. This consisted of an exchange in which the experimenter gave the subject a token that could immediately be handed back for a reward (figure 6). Each session consisted of twenty-five exchanges by each individual, and the subject always saw the partner's exchange immediately before its own. Food rewards varied from lower-value rewards (e.g., a cucumber piece), which they are usually happy to work for, to higher value rewards (e.g., a grape), which were preferred by all individuals tested. All subjects were subjected to (a) an Equity Test, in which subject and partner did the same work for the same low-value food, (b) an Inequity Test, in which the partner received a superior reward (grape) for the same effort, (c) an Effort Control Test, designed to elucidate the role of effort, in which the partner received the higher-value grape for free, and (d) a Food Control Test, designed to elucidate the effect of the presence of the reward on subject behavior, in which grapes were visible but not given to another capuchin.

Individuals who received lower-value rewards showed both passive negative reactions (e.g., refusing to exchange the token, ignoring the

FIGURE 6. A capuchin monkey in the test chamber returns a token to the experimenter with her right hand while steadying the human hand with her left hand. Her partner looks on. Drawing by Gwen Bragg and Frans de Waal after a video still.

reward) and active negative reactions (e.g., throwing out the token or the reward). Compared to tests in which both received identical rewards, the capuchins were far less willing to complete the exchange or accept the reward if their partner received a better deal (figure 7; Brosnan and de Waal 2003). Capuchins refused to participate even more frequently if their partner did not have to work (exchange) to get the better reward but was handed it for "free." Of course, there is always the possibility that subjects were just reacting to the presence of the higher-value food and that what the partner received (free or not) did not affect their reaction. However, in the Food Control Test, in which the higher-value reward was visible but not given to another monkey, the reaction to the presence of this high-valued food decreased significantly over the course of testing, which is a change in the opposite direction from that seen when the high-value reward went to an actual partner. Clearly our subjects discriminate between higher-value food being consumed by a conspecific and such food being merely visible, intensifying their rejections only to the former (Brosnan and de Waal 2004).

Capuchin monkeys thus seem to measure reward in relative terms, comparing their own rewards with those available and their own efforts with those of others. Although our data cannot elucidate the precise motivations underlying these responses, one possibility is that monkeys, like humans, are guided by social emotions. These emotions, known as "passions" by economists, guide human reactions to the efforts, gains, losses, and attitudes of others (Hirschleifer 1987; Frank 1988; Sanfey et

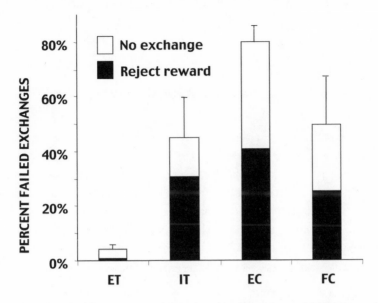

FIGURE 7. Mean percentage ± Standard Error of the Mean of failures to exchange for females across the four test types. Black bars represent the proportion of nonexchanges due to refusals to accept the reward; white bars represent nonexchanges due to refusals to return the token. ET = Equity Test, IT = Inequity Test, EC = Effort Control, FC = Food Control. The Y-axis shows the percentage of nonexchanges.

al. 2003). As opposed to primates marked by despotic hierarchies, tolerant species with well-developed food-sharing and cooperation, such as capuchin monkeys, may hold emotionally charged expectations about reward distribution and social exchange that lead them to dislike inequity.

Before we speak of "fairness" in this context it is good to point out a difference from human fairness. A full-blown sense of fairness would entail that the "rich" monkey shared with the "poor" one, as she would have felt she was getting excessive compensation for her efforts. Such behavior would have betrayed interest in a higher principle, one that Westermarck (1917 [1908]) called "disinterested," hence a truly moral notion. This is not the sort of reaction our monkeys showed, though; hence their sense of fairness, if we call it that, was more egocentric. They rather showed an expectation about how they themselves should be treated, not about how everybody around them should be treated. At the same time, it cannot be denied that the full-blown sense of fairness must have started somewhere and that the self is the logical place to look for its origin. Once the egocentric form existed, it was expanded to include others.

6. MENCIUS AND THE PRIMACY OF AFFECT

There is never much new under the sun. Westermarck's emphasis on the retributive emotions, whether friendly or vengeful, reminds one of the reply of Confucius to the question whether there is any single word that may serve as prescription for all of one's life. Confucius proposed "reciprocity" as such a word. Reciprocity is of course also at the heart of the Golden Rule, which remains unsurpassed as a summary of human morality. To know that some of the psychology behind this rule may exist in other species, along with the required empathy, bolsters the idea that morality, rather than being a recent invention, is part of human nature.

A follower of Confucius, Mencius, wrote extensively about human goodness during his life, from 372 to 289 BC. Mencius lost his father when he was three, and his mother made sure he received the best possible education. The mother is at least as well known as her son: she still serves as a maternal model to the Chinese for her absolute devotion to her son. Called the "second sage" because of his immense influence, second only to Confucius, Mencius had a revolutionary, subversive bent in that he stressed the obligation of rulers to provide for the common people. Recorded on bamboo clappers and handed down to his descendants and their students, his writings show that the debate about whether we are naturally moral or not is ancient indeed. In one exchange, Mencius (372–289 BC: 270–71) reacts against Kaou Tsze's views, which are astonishingly reminiscent of Huxley's gardener and garden metaphor:

> Man's nature is like the *ke* willow, and righteousness is like a cup or a bowl. The fashioning of benevolence and righteousness out of man's nature is like the making of cups and bowls from the *ke* willow.

Mencius replied:

> Can you, leaving untouched the nature of the willow, make with it cups and bowls? You must do violence and injury to the willow, before you can make cups and bowls with it. If you must do violence and injury to the willow, before you can make cups and bowls with it,

on your principles you must in the same way do violence and injury to humanity in order to fashion from it benevolence and righteousness! Your words alas! would certainly lead all men on to reckon benevolence and righteousness to be calamities.

Mencius believed that humans tend toward the good as naturally as water flows downhill. This is also evident from the following remark, in which he seeks to exclude the possibility of the Freudian double-agenda on the grounds that the immediacy of the moral emotions, such as sympathy, leaves little room for cognitive contortions:

> When I say that all men have a mind which cannot bear to see the suffering of others, my meaning may be illustrated thus: even nowadays, if men suddenly see a child about to fall into a well, they will without exception experience a feeling of alarm and distress. They will feel so, not as a ground on which they may gain the favor of the child's parents, nor as a ground on which they may seek the praise of their neighbors and friends, nor from a dislike to the reputation of having been unmoved by such a thing. From this case we may perceive that the feeling of commiseration is essential to man. (Mencius 372–289 BC: 78)

This example from Mencius reminds us of the above epigraph from Westermarck ("Can we help sympathizing with our friends?") and the earlier quotation from Smith ("How selfish soever man may be supposed..."). The central idea underlying all three statements is that distress at the sight of another's pain is an impulse over which we exert no control: it grabs us instantaneously, like a reflex, without time to weigh the pros and cons. Remarkably, all alternative motives listed by Mencius occur in the modern literature, usually under the heading of reputation-building. The big difference is, of course, that Mencius rejected these explanations as too contrived, given the immediacy and force of the sympathetic impulse. Manipulation of public opinion is entirely possible at other times, he said, but not at the very instant that a child falls into a well.

I could not agree more. Evolution has produced species that follow genuinely cooperative impulses. I don't know if people are deep down good or evil, but I do know that to believe that each and every move is selfishly calculated while being hidden from ourselves and from others grossly overestimates human mental powers, let alone those of other animals. Apart from the already discussed animal examples of consolation of distressed individuals and protection against aggression, there exists a rich literature on human empathy and sympathy that, generally, agrees with the assessment of Mencius that impulses in this regard come first and rationalizations later (e.g., Batson 1990; Wispé 1991).

7. CONCLUSION

In this lecture, I have drawn a stark contrast between two schools of thought on human goodness. One school sees people as essentially evil and selfish, and hence morality as a cultural overlay. This school of thought, personified by T. H. Huxley, is still very much with us even though I have noticed that no one (not even those explicitly endorsing this position) wants to be labeled a "veneer theorist." This is perhaps due to something about the wording itself, but also because once the assumptions of Veneer Theory are laid bare, it becomes obvious that the theory (a) lacks any sort of explanation of the transition from an amoral animal to a moral human being and (b) is at odds with empirical evidence bearing on moral judgment. If human morality truly operated entirely on the basis of calculations and rational decisions, without much emotional involvement, we would come close to being psychopaths, who indeed do not mean to be kind when they act kindly. Most of us hope to be slightly better than psychopaths; hence the widespread aversion to my black-and-white contrast between Veneer Theory and the other school, which seeks to ground morality in human nature.

This school sees morality arise naturally in our species and believes that there are sound evolutionary reasons for the capacities involved, even though it must be said that the theoretical framework to explain the transition from social to moral animal thus far consists of bits and pieces only. Its foundation is kin selection theory and reciprocal altruism, but other elements will need to be added. If one reads up on reputation building, fairness principles, empathy, and conflict resolution (disparate literatures that cannot be reviewed here in detail), there seems a promising movement toward a more integrated theory (for discussions, see Katz 2000).

According to this view of morality, the child is not going against its own nature by developing a caring, moral attitude any more than civil society is an out-of-control garden subdued by a sweating gardener. Moral attitudes have been with us from the beginning, and the gardener rather is, as John Dewey aptly put it, an organic grower. The successful gardener creates conditions and introduces plant species that may not be normal for this particular plot of land "but fall within the wont and use of nature as a whole" (Dewey 1993 [1898]: 109–10). In other words we are not subduing the proverbial wolf within us or hypocritically fooling everyone around us when we act morally: we are taking decisions that flow from social instincts far older than our species, even though we add to these the perhaps uniquely human complexity of a disinterested concern for others and the society at large.

Following Hume (1978 [1739]), who saw reason as the slave of the passions, Jonathan Haidt (2001) has called for a thorough reevaluation of the role played by rationality in moral judgment, arguing that most human justification seems to occur *post hoc*, that is, after moral judgments have been reached on the basis of quick, automatic intuitions. A range of studies indicates the unconscious mirroring of others' emotional displays (Dimberg et al. 2000) and provides evidence for the PAM mechanism (i.e., activation of brain areas identical to those activated in the people with whom we empathize: see Preston and de Waal 2000b; Carr et al. 2003; Decety and Chaminade 2003; Wicker et al. 2003; Singer et al. 2004). Whereas Veneer Theory (which emphasizes human uniqueness in the domain of morality) would predict that moral considerations take place in evolutionarily recent additions to our brain, such as the neocortex, neuroimaging shows that moral judgments in fact involve a wide variety of brain areas, some rather ancient (Greene and Haidt 2002). In short, neuroscience is lending support to human morality as a relatively automated process closely tied to mammalian social instincts.

Additional evidence comes from child research. Developmental psychologists used to believe that the child learns its first moral distinctions through fear of punishment and a desire for praise. Similar to veneer theorists, they conceived morality as coming from the outside, imposed by adults upon a passive, naturally selfish child. Children were thought to adopt parental values to construct a superego, the moral agency of the self. Left to their own devices, children would never arrive at anything close to morality. We now know, however, that at an early age children understand the difference between moral principles ("do not steal") and cultural conventions ("no pajamas at school"). They apparently appreciate that the breaking of certain rules distresses and harms others, whereas the breaking of other rules merely violates expectations about what is appropriate. Their attitudes don't seem based purely on reward and punishment. Whereas many pediatric handbooks still depict young children as self-centered monsters, it has become clear that by one year of age they spontaneously comfort people in distress (Zahn-Waxler et al. 1992) and that soon thereafter they begin to develop a moral perspective through interactions with other members of their species (Killen and Nucci 1995).

Instead of us doing "violence to the willow," as Mencius called it, to create the cups and bowls of an artificial morality, we rely on natural growth in which simple emotions, like those encountered in young children and social animals, develop into the more refined, other-including sentiments that we recognize as moral. My own argument obviously revolves around the continuity between human social instincts and those of our closest relatives, the monkeys and apes (de Waal 1996), but I feel that we are standing at the threshold of a much larger shift in theorizing that will end up positioning morality firmly within the emotional core of human nature.

Why did evolutionary biology stray from this path during the final quarter of the previous century? This is probably due to the conviction of some prominent figures, inspired by Huxley, that there is no way natural selection could have produced anything other than nasty organisms. No good could possibly have come from such a blind process. This belief, however, represents a monumental confusion between process and outcome. Natural selection is indeed a merciless process of elimination, yet it has the capacity to produce an incredible range of organisms, from the most asocial and competitive to the kindest and gentlest. If we assume that the building blocks of morality are among its many products, as Darwin did, then morality, instead of being a human-made veneer, should be looked at as an integral part of our history as group-living animals, hence an extension of our primate social instincts.

REFERENCES

Alexander, R. A. 1987. *The Biology of Moral Systems.* New York: Aldine de Gruyter.

Arnhart, L. 1998. *Darwinian Natural Right: The Biological Ethics of Human Nature.* Albany, N.Y.: SUNY Press.

———. 1999. E. O. Wilson Has More in Common with Thomas Aquinas Than He Realizes. *Christianity Today International* 5 (6): 36.

Aureli, F., M. Cords, and C. P. van Schaik. 2002. Conflict Resolution Following Aggression in Gregarious Animals: A Predictive Framework. *Animal Behaviour* 64: 325–43.

Aureli, F., R. Cozzolino, C. Cordischi, and S. Scucchi. 1992. Kin-Oriented Redirection among Japanese Macaques: An Expression of a Revenge System? *Animal Behaviour* 44: 283–91.

Aureli, F., and F. B. M. de Waal. 2000. *Natural Conflict Resolution.* Berkeley: University of California Press.

Axelrod, R., and W. D. Hamilton. 1981. The Evolution of Cooperation. *Science* 211: 1390–96.

Badcock, C. R. 1986. *The Problem of Altruism: Freudian-Darwinian Solutions.* Oxford: Blackwell.

Bargh, J. A., and T. L. Chartrand. 1999. The Unbearable Automaticity of Being. *American Psychologist* 54: 462–79.

Baron-Cohen, S. 2000. Theory of Mind and Autism: A Fifteen Year Review. In *Understanding Other Minds*, ed. S. Baron-Cohen, H. Tager-Flusberg, and D. J. Cohen, pp. 3–20. Oxford: Oxford University Press.

Batson, C. D. 1990. How Social an Animal?: The Human Capacity for Caring. *American Psychologist* 45: 336–46.

Bischof-Köhler, D. 1988. Über den Zusammenhang von Empathie und der Fähigkeit sich im Spiegel zu erkennen. *Schweizerische Zeitschrift für Psychologie* 47: 147–59.

Boehm, C. 1999. *Hierarchy in the Forest: The Evolution of Egalitarian Behavior.* Cambridge, Mass.: Harvard University Press.

Bonnie, K. E., and F. B. M. de Waal. 2004. Primate Social Reciprocity and the Origin of Gratitude. In *The Psychology of Gratitude*, ed. R. A. Emmons and M. E. McCullough, pp. 213–29. Oxford: Oxford University Press.

Brosnan, S. F., and F. B. M. de Waal. 2003. Monkeys Reject Unequal Pay. *Nature* 425: 297–99.

———. 2004. Reply to Commentators. *Nature* 428: 140.

Byrne, R. W., and A. Whiten. 1988. *Machiavellian Intelligence: Social Expertise and the Evolution of Intellect in Monkeys, Apes, and Humans.* Oxford: Oxford University Press.

Caldwell, M. C., and D. K. Caldwell. 1966. Epimeletic (Care-Giving) Behavior in Cetacea. In *Whales, Dolphins, and Porpoises,* ed. K. S. Norris, pp. 755–89. Berkeley: University of California Press.

Carr, L., M. Iacoboni, M.-C. Dubeau, J. C. Mazziotta, and G. L. Lenzi. 2003. Neural Mechanisms of Empathy in Humans: A Relay from Neural Systems for Imitation to Limbic Areas. *Proceedings of the National Academy of Sciences* 100: 5497–5502.

Church, R. M. 1959. Emotional Reactions of Rats to the Pain of Others. *Journal of Comparative & Physiological Psychology* 52: 132–34.

Cohen, S., W. J. Doyle, D. P. Skoner, B. S. Rabin, and J. M. Gwaltney. 1997. Social Ties and Susceptibility to the Common Cold. *Journal of the American Medical Association* 277: 1940–44.

Damasio, A. 1994. *Descartes' Error: Emotion, Reason, and the Human Brain.* New York: Putnam.

Darwin, C. 1982 [1871]. *The Descent of Man, and Selection in Relation to Sex.* Princeton: Princeton University Press.

Dawkins, R. 1976. *The Selfish Gene.* Oxford: Oxford University Press.

———— 2003. *A Devil's Chaplain: Reflections on Hope, Lies, Science, and Love.* New York: Houghton Mifflin.

de Waal, F. B. M. 1989a. Food Sharing and Reciprocal Obligations among Chimpanzees. *Journal of Human Evolution* 18: 433–59.

————. 1989b. *Peacemaking among Primates.* Cambridge, Mass.: Harvard University Press.

————. 1996. *Good Natured: The Origins of Right and Wrong in Humans and Other Animals.* Cambridge, Mass.: Harvard University Press.

————. 1997a. *Bonobo: The Forgotten Ape.* Berkeley: University of California Press.

————. 1997b. The Chimpanzee's Service Economy: Food for Grooming. *Evolution & Human Behavior* 18: 375–86.

————. 1998 [1982]. *Chimpanzee Politics: Power and Sex among Apes.* Baltimore, Md.: Johns Hopkins University Press.

————. 2000. Primates—A Natural Heritage of Conflict Resolution. *Science* 289: 586–90.

————. 2001. *The Ape and the Sushi Master: Cultural Reflections by a Primatologist.* New York: Basic Books.

————. 2003. On the Possibility of Animal Empathy. In *Feelings and Emotions: The Amsterdam Symposium,* ed. T. Manstead, N. Frijda, and A. Fischer, pp. 379–99. Cambridge: Cambridge University Press.

de Waal, F. B. M., and F. Aureli. 1996. Consolation, Reconciliation, and a Possible Cognitive Difference between Macaque and Chimpanzee. In *Reaching into Thought: The Minds of the Great Apes,* ed. A. E. Russon, K. A. Bard, and S. T. Parker, pp. 80–110. Cambridge: Cambridge University Press.

de Waal, F. B. M., and L. M. Luttrell. 1988. Mechanisms of Social Reciprocity in Three Primate Species: Symmetrical Relationship Characteristics or Cognition? *Ethology & Sociobiology* 9: 101–18.

de Waal, F. B. M., and A. van Roosmalen. 1979. Reconciliation and Consolation among Chimpanzees. *Behavioral Ecology & Sociobiology* 5: 55–66.

Decety, J., and T. Chaminade. 2003. Neural Correlates of Feeling Sympathy. *Neuropsychologia* 41: 127–38.

Desmond, A. 1994. *Huxley: From Devil's Disciple to Evolution's High Priest.* New York: Perseus.

Dewey, J. 1993 [1898]. Evolution and Ethics. Reprinted in *Evolutionary Ethics,* ed. M. H. Nitecki and D. V. Nitecki, pp. 95–110. Albany: State University of New York Press.

di Pellegrino, G., L. Fadiga, L. Fogassi, V. Gallese, and G. Rizzolatti. 1992. Understanding Motor Events: A Neurophysiological Study. *Experimental Brain Research* 91: 176–80.

Dimberg, U., M. Thunberg, and K. Elmehed. 2000. Unconscious Facial Reactions to Emotional Facial Expressions. *Psychological Science* 11: 86–89.

Dugatkin, L. A. 1997. *Cooperation among Animals: An Evolutionary Perspective.* New York: Oxford University Press.

Eisenberg, N. 2000. Empathy and Sympathy. In *Handbook of Emotion,* ed. M. Lewis and J. M. Haviland-Jones, pp. 677–91. 2nd ed. New York: Guilford Press.

Fehr, E., and K. M. Schmidt. 1999. A Theory of Fairness, Competition, and Cooperation. *Quarterly Journal of Economics* 114: 817–68.

Feistner, A. T. C., and W. C. McGrew. 1989. Food-Sharing in Primates: A Critical Review. In *Perspectives in Primate Biology,* ed. P. K. Seth and S. Seth, vol. 3, pp. 21–36. New Delhi: Today & Tomorrow's Printers and Publishers.

Flack, J. C., and F. B. M. de Waal. 2000. "Any Animal Whatever": Darwinian Building Blocks of Morality in Monkeys and Apes. *Journal of Consciousness Studies* 7: 1–29.

Frank, R. H. 1988. *Passions within Reason: The Strategic Role of the Emotions.* New York: Norton.

Freud, S. 1913. *Totem and Taboo.* New York: Norton.

Gallup, G. G. 1982. Self-Awareness and the Emergence of Mind in Primates. *American Journal of Primatology* 2: 237–48.

Ghiselin, M. 1974. *The Economy of Nature and the Evolution of Sex.* Berkeley: University of California Press.

Gould, S. J. 1980. So Cleverly Kind an Animal. In *Ever Since Darwin,* pp. 260–67. Harmondsworth, UK: Penguin.

Greene, J., and J. Haidt. 2002. How (and Where) Does Moral Judgement Work? *Trends in Cognitive Sciences* 16: 517–23.

Haidt, J. 2001. The Emotional Dog and Its Rational Tail: A Social Intuitionist Approach to Moral Judgment. *Psychological Review* 108: 814–34.

Harcourt, A. H., and F. B. M. de Waal. 1992 *Coalitions and Alliances in Humans and Other Animals.* Oxford: Oxford University Press.

Hatfield, E., J. T. Cacioppo, and R. L. Rapson. 1993. Emotional Contagion. *Current Directions in Psychological Science* 2: 96–99.

Hirschleifer, J. 1987. In *The Latest on the Best: Essays in Evolution and Optimality,* ed. J. Dupre, pp. 307–26. Cambridge, Mass.: MIT Press.

Hobbes, T. 1991 [1651]. *Leviathan.* Cambridge: Cambridge University Press.

Hoffman, M. L. 1981a. Is Altruism Part of Human Nature? *Journal of Personality and Social Psychology* 40: 121–37.

———. 1981b. Perspectives on the Difference between Understanding People and Understanding Things: The Role of Affect. In *Social Cognitive Development,* ed. J. H. Flavell and L. Ross, pp. 67–81. Cambridge: Cambridge University Press.

Hume, D. 1978 [1739]. *A Treatise of Human Nature.* Oxford: Oxford University Press.

Huxley, T. H. 1989 [1894]. *Evolution and Ethics.* Princeton: Princeton University Press.

Katz, L. D. 2000. *Evolutionary Origins of Morality: Cross-Disciplinary Perspectives.* Exeter, UK: Imprint Academic.

Killen, M., and L. P. Nucci. 1995. Morality, Autonomy and Social Conflict. In *Morality in Everyday Life: Developmental Perspectives,* ed. M. Killen and D. Hart, pp. 52–86. Cambridge: Cambridge University Press.

Kropotkin, P. 1972 [1902]. *Mutual Aid: A Factor of Evolution.* New York: New York University Press.

Ladygina-Kohts, N. N. 2001 [1935]. *Infant Chimpanzee and Human Child: A Classic 1935 Comparative Study of Ape Emotions and Intelligence.* Ed. F. B. M. de Waal. New York: Oxford University Press.

Lipps, T. 1903. Einfühlung, innere Nachahmung und Organempfindung. *Archiv für die gesamte Psychologie* 1: 465–519.

Lorenz, K. Z. 1954. *Man Meets Dog.* London: Methuen.

———. 1966 [1963]. *On Aggression.* London: Methuen.

Masserman, J., M. S. Wechkin, and W. Terris. 1964. Altruistic Behavior in Rhesus Monkeys. *American Journal of Psychiatry* 121: 584–85.

Mayr, E. 1997. *This Is Biology: The Science of the Living World.* Cambridge, Mass.: Harvard University Press.

Mencius. 372–289 BC. *The Works of Mencius.* English translation by Gu Lu. Shanghai: Shangwu.

Midgley, M. 1979. Gene-Juggling. *Philosophy* 54: 439–58.

O'Connell, S. M. 1995. Empathy in Chimpanzees: Evidence for Theory of Mind? *Primates* 36: 397–410.

Preston, S. D., and F. B. M. de Waal. 2002a. The Communication of Emotions and the Possibility of Empathy in Animals. In *Altruistic Love: Science, Philosophy, and Religion in Dialogue,* ed. S. G. Post, L. G. Underwood, J. P. Schloss, and W. B. Hurlbut, pp. 284–308. Oxford: Oxford University Press.

——— 2002b. Empathy: Its Ultimate and Proximate Bases. *Behavioral & Brain Sciences* 25: 1–72.

Pusey, A. E., and C. Packer. 1987. Dispersal and Philopatry. In *Primate Societies,* ed. B. B. Smuts et al., pp. 250–66. Chicago: University of Chicago Press.

Rawls, J. 1972. *A Theory of Justice.* Oxford: Oxford University Press.

Reiss, D., and L. Marino. 2001. Mirror Self-Recognition in the Bottlenose Dolphin: A Case of Cognitive Convergence. *Proceedings of the National Academy of Science* 98: 5937–42.

Ridley, M. 1996. *The Origins of Virtue.* New York: Viking.

Roes, F. 1997. An Interview of Richard Dawkins. *Human Ethology Bulletin* 12 (1): 1–3.

Rothstein, S. I., and R. R. Pierotti. 1988. Distinctions among Reciprocal Altruism, Kin Selection, and Cooperation and a Model for the Initial Evolution of Beneficent Behavior. *Ethology & Sociobiology* 9: 189–209.

Sanfey, A. G., J. K. Rilling, J. A. Aronson, L. E. Nystrom, and J. D. Cohen. 2003. The Neural Basis of Economic Decision-making in the Ultimatum Game. *Science* 300: 1755–58.

Schleidt, W. M., and M. D. Shalter. 2003. Co-evolution of Humans and Canids, an Alternative View of Dog Domestication: *Homo homini lupus?* *Evolution and Cognition* 9: 57–72.

Silk, J. B., S. C. Alberts, and J. Altmann. 2003. Social Bonds of Female Baboons Enhance Infant Survival. *Science* 302: 1231–34.

Singer, T., B. Seymour, J. O'Doherty, K. Holger, R. J. Dolan, and C. D. Frith. 2004. Empathy for Pain Involves the Affective But Not Sensory Components of Pain. *Science* 303: 1157–62.

Smith, A. 1937 [1759]. *A Theory of Moral Sentiments.* New York: Modern Library.

Sober, E., and D. S. Wilson. 1998. *Unto Others: The Evolution and Psychology of Unselfish Behavior.* Cambridge, Mass.: Harvard University Press.

Taylor, C. E., and M. T. McGuire. 1988. Reciprocal Altruism: Fifteen Years Later. *Ethology & Sociobiology* 9: 67–72.

Taylor, S. 2002. *The Tending Instinct.* New York: Times Books.

Todes, D. 1989. *Darwin without Malthus: The Struggle for Existence in Russian Evolutionary Thought.* New York: Oxford University Press.

Trivers, R. L. 1971. The Evolution of Reciprocal Altruism. *Quarterly Review of Biology* 46: 35–57.

van Schaik, C. P. 1983. Why Are Diurnal Primates Living in Groups? *Behaviour* 87: 120–44.

Watts, D. P., F. Colmenares, and K. Arnold. 2000. Redirection, Consolation, and Male Policing: How Targets of Aggression Interact with Bystanders. In *Natural Conflict Resolution,* ed. F. Aureli and F. B. M. de Waal, pp. 281–301. Berkeley: University of California Press.

Wechkin, S., J. H. Masserman, and W. Terris. 1964. Shock to a Conspecific as an Aversive Stimulus. *Psychonomic Science* 1: 47–48.

Westermarck, E. 1912 [1908]. *The Origin and Development of the Moral Ideas.* Vol. 1. 2nd ed. London: Macmillan.

———. 1917 [1908]. *The Origin and Development of the Moral Ideas.* Vol. 2. 2nd ed. London: Macmillan.

Wicker, B., C. Keysers, J. Plailly, J. P. Royet, V. Gallese, and G. Rizzolatti. 2003. Both of Us Disgusted in My Insula: The Common Neural Basis of Seeing and Feeling Disgust. *Neuron* 40: 655–64.

Williams, G. C. 1988. Reply to Comments on "Huxley's Evolution and Ethics in Sociobiological Perspective." *Zygon* 23: 437–38.

Wispé, L. 1991. *The Psychology of Sympathy.* New York: Plenum.

Wrangham, R. W. 1980. An Ecological Model of Female-Bonded Primate Groups. *Behaviour* 75: 262–300.

Wright, R. 1994. *The Moral Animal: The New Science of Evolutionary Psychology.* New York: Pantheon.

Yerkes, R. M. 1925. *Almost Human.* New York: Century.

Zahn-Waxler, C., B. Hollenbeck, and M. Radke-Yarrow. 1984. The Origins of Empathy and Altruism. In *Advances in Animal Welfare Science,* ed. M. W. Fox and L. D. Mickley, pp. 21–39. Washington, D.C.: Humane Society of the United States.

Zahn-Waxler, C., M. Radke-Yarrow, E. Wagner, and M. Chapman. 1992. Development of Concern for Others. *Developmental Psychology* 28: 126–36.

Zajonc, R. B. 1980. Feeling and Thinking: Preferences Need No Inferences. *American Psychologist* 35: 151–75.

———. 1984. On the Primacy of Affect. *American Psychologist* 39: 117–23.

I. The Science of Religion
II. The Religion of Science

RICHARD DAWKINS

THE TANNER LECTURES ON HUMAN VALUES

Delivered at

Harvard University
November 19 and 20, 2003

RICHARD DAWKINS is Charles Simonyi Professor of the Public Understanding of Science at the University of Oxford. He was born in Kenya, educated in England, and took his D.Phil under the Nobel Prize winner Niko Tinbergen at Oxford. He was an assistant professor at Berkeley before returning to Oxford. He is a fellow of the Royal Society and the recipient of the Michael Faraday Award, the Nakayama Prize, the International Cosmos Prize, the Kistler Prize, and the Bicentennial Kelvin Medal of the Royal Philosophical Society of Glasgow, among others. His numerous publications include *The Selfish Gene* (1976); *The Blind Watchmaker: Why the Evidence of Evolution Reveals a Universe without Design* (1982), which won both the Royal Society of Literature Award and the *Los Angeles Times* Literary Prize; *River Out of Eden: A Darwinian View of Life* (1995); *Climbing Mount Improbable* (1996); *Unweaving the Rainbow: Science, Delusion, and the Appetite for Wonder* (1997); *A Devil's Chaplain: Reflections on Hope, Lies, Science, and Love* (2003); and *The Ancestor's Tale: A Pilgrimage to the Dawn of Evolution* (2004).

I. THE SCIENCE OF RELIGION

It is with trepidation and humility that I come, from the oldest university in the English-speaking world to what must surely be the greatest. My trepidation is not lessened by the titles that, perhaps unwisely, I gave the organizers all those months ago. Anybody who publicly belittles religion, however gently, can expect hate mail of a uniquely unforgiving species. But the very fact that religion arouses such passions catches a scientist's attention.

As a Darwinian, the aspect of religion that catches *my* attention is its profligate wastefulness, its extravagant display of baroque uselessness. Nature is a miserly accountant, grudging the pennies, watching the clock, punishing the smallest waste.[1] If a wild animal habitually performs some useless activity, natural selection will favour rival individuals who devote the time, instead, to surviving and reproducing. Nature cannot afford frivolous *jeux d'esprits*. Ruthless utilitarianism trumps, even if it doesn't always seem that way.

I am a Darwinian student of animal behaviour—an ethologist and follower of Niko Tinbergen. You won't be surprised, therefore, if I talk about animals (nonhuman animals, I should add, for there is no sensible definition of an animal that excludes ourselves). The tail of a male bird of paradise, extravagant though it seems, would be penalised by females if it were less so. The same for the time and labour that a male bower bird puts into making his bower. Anting is the odd habit of birds, such as jays, of "bathing" in an ant's nest and apparently inciting the ants to invade the feathers. Nobody knows for sure what the benefit of anting is: perhaps some kind of hygiene, cleansing the feathers of parasites. My point is that uncertainty as to detail doesn't—nor should it—stop Darwinians from believing, with great confidence, that anting must be for something.

Such a confident stance is controversial—at Harvard if nowhere else—and you may be aware of the wholly unwarranted slur that functional

1. Natural selection, as Charles Darwin said, "is daily and hourly scrutinizing, throughout the world, every variation, even the slightest; rejecting that which is bad, preserving and adding up all that is good; silently and insensibly working, whenever and wherever opportunity offers, at the improvement of each organic being..." (*On the Origin of Species* [London: John Murray, 1859]).

hypotheses are untestable "Just So Stories." This is such a ridiculous claim that the only reason it has come to be widely accepted is a certain style of bullying advocacy originating, I reluctantly have to say, at Harvard. All you have to do to test a functional hypothesis of a piece of behaviour is to engineer an experimental situation in which the behaviour doesn't happen, or in which its consequences are negated. Let me give a simple example of how to test a functional hypothesis.

Next time a housefly lands on your hand, don't immediately brush it off; watch what it does. You won't wait long before it brings its hands together as if in prayer, then wrings them in what seems like ritual fastidiousness. This is one of the ways in which a fly grooms itself. Another is to wipe a hind leg over the same side wing. They also rub middle and hind feet together, or middle and front. Flies spend so much time self-grooming that any Darwinian would immediately guess that it is vital for survival.[2] And this is a testable hypothesis.

An appropriate experimental design is the "Yoked Control." Put a matched pair of flies in a small arena and watch them. Every time Fly A starts to groom itself, scare both into flight. After two hours of this regime, Fly A will have done no grooming at all. Fly B will have groomed itself a lot. It will have been scared off the ground as many times as A, but at random with respect to its grooming. Now put A and B through a battery of comparison tests. Is A's flying performance impaired by dirty wings? Measure it and compare it with B's. Flies taste with their feet, and it is a reasonable hypothesis that "foot washing" unclogs their sense organs. Well-tried methods for measuring the taste threshold of flies have been published. Compare the threshold sugar concentration that A and B can taste. Compare their tendency to disease. As a final test, compare the two flies' vulnerability to a chameleon.

Repeat the trial with lots of pairs of flies and do a statistical analysis comparing each A with its corresponding B. I would put my shirt on the A flies' being significantly impaired in at least one faculty vitally affecting survival. The reason for my confidence is purely the Darwinian conviction that natural selection would not have allowed them to spend so

---

2. The more so because—this is less paradoxical than it sounds—grooming is often instantly fatal. When a chameleon, for example, is around, grooming is very likely to be the last thing the fly does. Predatory eyes often lock onto movement. A motionless target goes unnoticed. A flying target is difficult to hit. A grooming fly's shuttling limbs stimulate the predator's movement-detectors, but the fly as a whole is a sitting target. The fact that flies spend so much time grooming, in spite of its being so dangerous, argues for a very strong survival value.

much time on an activity if it were not useful. This is not a "Just So Story"; the reasoning is thoroughly scientific, and it is fully testable.

Religious behaviour in bipedal apes occupies large quantities of time. It devours huge resources. A medieval cathedral would consume hundreds of man-centuries in the building. Sacred music and devotional paintings largely monopolised medieval and renaissance talent. Thousands, perhaps millions, of people have died, often accepting torture first, for loyalty to one religion rather than a scarcely distinguishable alternative. Devout people have died for their gods, killed for them, fasted for them, whipped blood from their backs, undertaken a lifetime of celibacy, sworn themselves to lonely silence for the sake of religion. Nobody does this kind of list better than Steven Pinker, and I'm going to quote *How the Mind Works* on the peculiar problems you face in the United States—whether in spite of or because of the constitutional separation of church and state I do not know:

> According to polls, more than a quarter of today's Americans believe in witches, almost half believe in ghosts, half believe in the devil, half believe that the book of Genesis is literally true, sixty-nine percent believe in angels, eighty-seven percent believe that Jesus was raised from the dead, and ninety-six percent believe in a God or universal spirit.

More generally, Pinker remarks,

> In culture after culture, people believe that the soul lives on after death, that rituals can change the physical world and divine the truth, and that illness and misfortune are caused and alleviated by spirits, ghosts, saints, fairies, angels, demons, cherubim, djinns, devils and gods.[3]

Though the details differ across cultures, no known culture lacks some version of the time-consuming, wealth-consuming, hostility-provoking, fecundity-forfeiting rituals of religion. All this presents a major puzzle to anyone who thinks in a Darwinian way. We guessed why jays ant; my old maestro Niko Tinbergen did an experimental test of why seagulls remove empty eggshells from the nest (eggshells are conspicuous and attract predators). Isn't religion a challenge, an *a priori* affront to Darwinism, demanding similar explanation? Why do we pray and

---

3. Steven Pinker, *How the Mind Works* (New York: Norton, 1997).

indulge in costly practices that, in many individual cases, more or less totally consume our lives?

Of course the caveats must now come tumbling in. Religious behaviour is Darwinian business only if it is widespread, not some weird anomaly. Apparently it *is* universal, and the problem won't go away just because the details differ across cultures. As with language, the underlying phenomenon is universal, though it plays out differently in different regions. Not all individuals are religious, as most of this educated audience will testify. But religion is a human universal: every culture, everywhere in the world, has a style of religion that even nonpractitioners recognize as the norm for that society, just as it has a style of clothing, a style of courting, and a style of meal-serving.

Could it be a recent phenomenon, sprung up since our genes underwent most of their natural selection? Its ubiquity argues against any simple version of this idea. Nevertheless there is a version of it that it will be my main purpose to advocate today. The propensity that was naturally selected in our ancestors was not religion per se. It had some other benefit, and it only incidentally manifests itself as religious behaviour. We'll understand religious behaviour only after we have renamed it. Once again, it is natural for an ethologist to use an example from non-human animals.

The "dominance hierarchy" was first discovered as the "pecking order" in hens. Each hen learns which individuals she can beat in a fight, and which beat her. In a well-established dominance hierarchy, little overt fighting is seen. Stable groupings of hens, who have time to sort themselves into a pecking order, lay more eggs than hens in coops whose membership is continually changed. This might suggest an "advantage" to the phenomenon of the dominance hierarchy. But that's not good Darwinism, because the dominance hierarchy is a group-level phenomenon. Farmers may care about group productivity, but natural selection doesn't.

For a Darwinian, the question "What is the survival value of the dominance hierarchy?" is an illegitimate question. The proper question is "What is the individual survival value of deferring to stronger hens? And of punishing lack of deference from weaker ones?" Darwinian questions have to direct attention toward the level at which genetic variations might exist. Tendencies to aggression or deference in individual hens are a proper target because they either do or easily might vary genetically. Group phenomena like dominance hierarchies don't in themselves vary genetically, because groups don't have genes. Or at least you'll have your work cut out arguing some peculiar sense in which a group phenomenon could be subject to genetic variation. You might contrive it via some version of what I have called the *Extended Phenotype,* but I am too sceptical to accompany you on that theoretical journey.

My point, of course, is that religion may be like the dominance hierarchy. "What is the survival value of religion?" may be the wrong question. The right question may have the form, "What is the survival value of some as yet unspecified individual behaviour, or psychological characteristic, which manifests itself, under appropriate circumstances, as religion?" We have to rewrite the question before we can sensibly answer it.

I must first acknowledge that other Darwinians have gone straight for the unrewritten question and proposed direct Darwinian advantages of religion itself—as opposed to psychological predispositions that accidentally manifest themselves as religion. There is a little evidence that religious belief protects people from stress-related diseases. The evidence is not good, but it would not be surprising. A non-negligible part of what a doctor can provide for a patient is consolation and reassurance. My doctor doesn't literally practise the laying on of hands. But many's the time I have been instantly cured of some minor ailment by a reassuringly calm voice from an intelligent face surmounting a stethoscope. The placebo effect is well documented. Dummy pills, with no pharmacological activity at all, demonstrably improve health. That is why drug trials have to use placebos as controls. It's why homeopathic remedies appear to work, even though they're so dilute that they have the same amount of the active ingredients as the placebo control—zero molecules.

Is religion a medical placebo, which prolongs life by reducing stress? Perhaps, although the theory is going to have to run the gauntlet of sceptics who point out the many circumstances in which religion increases stress rather than decreases it. In any case, I find the placebo theory too meagre to account for the massive and all-pervasive worldwide phenomenon of religion. I do not think we have religion because our religious ancestors reduced their stress levels and hence survived longer. I don't think that's a big enough theory for the job.

Other theories miss the point of Darwinian explanations altogether. I mean suggestions such as "Religion satisfies our curiosity about the universe and our place in it." Or "Religion is consoling. People fear death and are drawn to religions that promise we'll survive it." There may be some psychological truth here, but it's not in itself a Darwinian explanation. As Steven Pinker has said,

...it only raises the question of *why* a mind would evolve to find comfort in beliefs it can plainly see are false. A freezing person finds no comfort in believing he is warm; a person face-to-face with a lion is not put at ease by the conviction that it is a rabbit.[4]

A Darwinian version of the fear-of-death theory would have to be of the form, "Belief in survival after death tends to postpone the moment when it is put to the test." This could be true or it could be false—maybe it's another version of the stress and placebo theory—but I shall not pursue the matter. My only point is that this is the *kind* of way in which a Darwinian must rewrite the question. Psychological statements—that people find some belief agreeable or disagreeable—are proximate, not ultimate explanations.

Darwinians make much of this distinction between proximate and ultimate. Proximate questions lead us into physiology and neuroanatomy. There is nothing wrong with proximate explanations. They are important, and they are scientific. But my preoccupation today is with Darwinian ultimate explanations. If neuroscientists, such as the Canadian Michael Persinger, find a "god centre" in the brain, Darwinian scientists like me want to know why the god centre evolved. Why did those of our ancestors who had a genetic tendency to grow a god centre survive better than rivals who did not? The ultimate Darwinian question is not a better question, not a more profound question, not a more scientific question than the proximate neurological question. But it is the one I am talking about today.

Some alleged ultimate explanations turn out to be—or in some cases avowedly are—group selection theories. Group selection is the controversial idea that Darwinian selection chooses among groups of individuals, in the same kind of way as it chooses among individuals within groups. The Cambridge anthropologist Colin Renfrew, for example, suggests that Christianity survived by a form of group selection because it fostered the idea of in-group loyalty and brotherly love. The American evolutionist D. S. Wilson has made a similar suggestion in *Darwin's Cathedral.*

Here's a made-up example, to show what a group-selection theory of religion might look like. A tribe with a stirringly belligerent "god of battles" wins wars against a tribe whose god urges peace and harmony, or a tribe with no god at all. Warriors who believe that a martyr's death will send them straight to paradise fight bravely and willingly give up their

4. Pinker, *How the Mind Works*, p. 555.

lives. So tribes with certain kinds of religion are more likely to survive in intertribal selection, steal the conquered tribe's cattle, and seize their women as concubines. Such successful tribes spawn daughter tribes who go off and propagate more daughter tribes, all worshipping the same tribal god. Notice that this is different from saying that the *idea* of the warlike religion survives. Of course it will, but in this case the point is that the group of people who hold the idea survive.

There are formidable objections to group selection theories. A partisan in the controversy, I must beware of riding off on a hobby horse far from today's subject. There is also much confusion in the literature between true group selection, as in my hypothetical example of the God of Battles, and something else that is *called* group selection but turns out to be either kin selection or reciprocal altruism. Or there may be a confusion of "selection between groups" and "selection between individuals in the particular circumstances furnished by group living."[5]

Those of us who object to group selection have always admitted that in principle it can happen. The problem is that, when it is pitted against individual-level selection—as when group selection is advanced as an explanation for individual self-sacrifice—individual-level selection is likely to be stronger. In our hypothetical tribe of martyrs, a single self-interested warrior, who leaves martyrdom to his colleagues, will end up on the winning side because of their gallantry. Unlike them, however, he ends up alive, outnumbered by women and in a conspicuously better position to pass on his genes than his fallen comrades.

This is an oversimplified toy example, but it illustrates the perennial tension between group selection and individual selection. Group-selection theories of individual self-sacrifice are always vulnerable to subversion from within. If it comes to a tussle between the two levels of selection, individual selection will tend to win because it has a faster turnover. Mathematical models arguably come up with special conditions under which group selection might work. Arguably, religions in human tribes set up just such special conditions. This is an interesting line of theory to pursue, but I shall not do so here.

Instead, I shall return to the idea of rewriting the question. I previously cited the pecking order in hens, and the point is so central to my thesis that I hope you will forgive another animal example to ram it home. Moths fly into the candle flame, and it doesn't look like an

---

5. All these confusions are exemplified by D. S. Wilson's lifelong crusade in favour of what he calls group selection.

accident. They go out of their way to make a burnt offering of themselves. We could label it "self-immolation behaviour" and wonder how Darwinian natural selection could possibly favour it. My point, again, is that we need to rewrite the question before we can even attempt an intelligent answer. It isn't suicide. Apparent suicide emerges as an inadvertent side-effect.

Artificial light is a recent arrival on the night scene. Until recently, the only night lights were the moon and the stars. Because they are at optical infinity, their rays are parallel, which makes them ideal compasses. Insects are known to use celestial objects to steer accurately in a straight line. They can use the same compass, with reversed sign, for returning home after a foray. The insect nervous system is adept at setting up a temporary rule of thumb such as "Steer a course such that the light rays hit your eye at an angle of 30°." Since insects have compound eyes, this will amount to favouring a particular ommatidium.

But the light compass relies critically on the celestial object being at optical infinity. If it isn't, the rays are not parallel but diverge like the spokes of a wheel. A nervous system using a 30° rule of thumb to a candle, as though it were the moon, will steer its moth, in a neat logarithmic spiral, into the flame.

It is still, on average, a good rule of thumb. We don't notice the hundreds of moths who are silently and effectively steering by the moon or a bright star, or even the lights of a distant city. We see only moths hurling themselves at our lights, and we ask the wrong question. Why are all these moths committing suicide? Instead, we should ask why they have nervous systems that steer by maintaining an automatic fixed angle to light rays, a tactic that we notice only on the occasions when it goes wrong. When the question is rephrased, the mystery evaporates. It never was right to call it suicide.

Once again, apply the lesson to religious behaviour in humans. We observe large numbers of people—in many local areas it amounts to 100 percent—who hold beliefs that flatly contradict demonstrable scientific facts as well as rival religions. They not only *hold* these beliefs but devote time and resources to costly activities that flow from holding them. They die for them, or kill for them. We marvel at all this, just as we marvelled at the "self-immolation behaviour" of the moths. Baffled, we ask why. Yet again, the point I am making is that we may be asking the wrong question. The religious behaviour may be a misfiring, an unfortunate manifestation of an underlying psychological propensity that in other circumstances was once useful.

What might that psychological propensity have been? What is the equivalent of the parallel rays from the moon as a useful compass? I shall offer a suggestion, but I must stress that it is only an example of the kind of thing I am talking about. I am much more wedded to the general idea that the question should be properly put than I am to any particular answer.

My specific hypothesis is about children. More than any other species, we survive by the accumulated experience of previous generations. Theoretically, children might learn from experience not to swim in crocodile-infested waters. But, to say the least, there will be a selective advantage to child brains with a rule of thumb: Believe whatever your grown-ups tell you. Obey your parents, obey the tribal elders, especially when they adopt a solemn, minatory tone. Obey without question.

I have never forgotten a horrifying sermon, preached in my school chapel when I was little. Horrifying in retrospect: at the time, my child brain accepted it as intended by the preacher. He told the story of a squad of soldiers, drilling beside a railway line. At a critical moment the drill sergeant's attention was distracted, and he failed to give the order to halt. The soldiers were so well schooled to obey orders without question that they carried on marching, right into the path of an oncoming train. Now, of course, I don't believe the story, but I did when I was nine. The point is that the preacher wished us children to regard as a *virtue* the soldiers' slavish and unquestioning obedience to an order, however preposterous. And, speaking for myself, I think we *did* regard it as a virtue. I wondered whether I would have had the courage to do my duty by marching into the train.

To be fair, I don't think the preacher thought he was delivering a religious message. It was more military than religious, from what I remember: in the spirit of Tennyson's "Charge of the Light Brigade," which he may well have quoted:

"Forward the Light Brigade!"
Was there a man dismayed?
Not though the soldier knew
Some one had blundered:
Theirs not to make reply,
Theirs not to reason why,
Theirs but to do and die:
Into the valley of Death
Rode the six hundred.

From the high command's point of view it would be madness to allow every individual soldier discretion over whether or not to obey orders. Soldiers are drilled to become as much like computers as possible.

Computers do what they are told. They slavishly obey whatever instructions are properly delivered in their own programming language. This is how they do useful things like word-processing and spreadsheet calculations. But, as an inevitable by-product, they are equally automatic in obeying bad instructions. They have no way of telling whether an instruction will have a good effect or a bad. They simply obey, as soldiers are supposed to.

It is their unquestioning obedience that makes computers vulnerable to infection by viruses and worms. A maliciously designed program that says: "Copy me to every name in any address list that you find on this hard disk" will simply be obeyed, and then obeyed again by the other computers to which it is sent, in exponential expansion. It is impossible to design a computer that is usefully obedient and at the same time immune to infection.

If I have done my softening-up work well, you will already have completed the argument about child brains and religion. Natural selection builds child brains with a tendency to believe whatever their parents and tribal elders tell them. And this very quality automatically makes them vulnerable to infection by mind viruses. For excellent survival reasons, child brains need to trust parents, and trust elders whom their parents tell them to trust. An automatic consequence is that the truster has no way of distinguishing good advice from bad. The child cannot tell that "If you swim in the river you'll be eaten by crocodiles" is good advice but "If you don't sacrifice a goat at the time of the full moon, the crops will fail" is bad advice. They both sound equally trustworthy. They are both advice from a trusted source, both delivered with a solemn earnestness that commands respect and demands obedience.

The same goes for propositions about the world, about the cosmos, about morality, and about human nature. And, of course, when the child grows up and has children of her own, she will naturally pass the whole lot on to her own children—nonsense as well as sense—using the same impressive gravitas of manner.

On this model, we should expect that, in different geographical regions, different arbitrary beliefs having no factual basis will be handed down, to be believed with the same conviction as useful pieces of traditional wisdom, such as the belief that manure is good for the crops. We should also expect that these nonfactual beliefs will evolve over generations, either by random drift or by following some sort of analogue of Darwinian selection, eventually showing a pattern of significant divergence from common ancestry. Languages drift apart from a common parent, given sufficient time in geographical separation. The same is true of traditional beliefs and injunctions, handed down the generations, initially because of the programmability of the child brain. I shall mention this again in my second lecture.

And now, here's a charming story from my newspaper, the *Independent,* at Christmas one year. In a school Nativity Play, the Three Wise Men were played by Shadbreet Bains (a Sikh), Musharaff Khallil (a Muslim), and Adele Marlowe (a Christian), all aged four.

No, it is *not* charming, it is grotesque. How could any decent person think it right to label four-year-old children with the cosmic and theological opinions of their parents? To see this, imagine an identical photograph, with the caption *changed* as follows: "Shadbreet Bains (a Keynesian), Musharaff Khallil (a Monetarist), and Adele Marlowe (a Marxist), all aged four." Wouldn't this be a candidate for prosecution as child abuse? Yet, because of the weird privileged status of religion, not a squeak of protest was heard—nor is it ever heard on any similar occasion. In the *Independent,* the only complaint in the subsequent Letters to the Editor was from "The Campaign for Real Education," whose spokesman said multifaith religious education was extremely dangerous because: "Children these days are taught that all religions are of equal worth, which means that their own has no special value."

FIGURE 1. Shadbreet Bains (a Sikh), Musharaff Khallil (a Muslim), and Adele Marlowe (a Christian), all aged four.

FIGURE 2. Shadbreet Bains (a Keynesian), Musharaff Khallil (a Monetarist), and Adele Marlowe (a Marxist), all aged four.

Just imagine the outcry if the caption had read, "Shadbreet Bains (an Atheist), Musharaff Khallil (an Agnostic), and Adele Marlowe (a Secular Humanist), all aged four." In Britain, where we lack a constitutional separation between church and state, atheist parents usually go with the flow and let schools teach their children whatever religion prevails in the culture. The–Brights.net is scrupulous in setting out the rules for children to sign up: "The decision to be a Bright must be the child's. Any youngster who is told he or she must, or should, be a Bright can NOT be a Bright." Can you even begin to imagine the Roman Catholic church issuing such a self-denying ordinance?

Our society, including the nonreligious sector, has accepted the preposterous idea that it is normal and right to slap religious labels on tiny children, although no other comparable labels. Please, please raise your consciousness about this, and raise the roof whenever you hear it happening. A child is not a Christian child, not a Muslim child, not a Jewish child, but a child of Christian parents, a child of Muslim parents, or a child of Jewish parents. That terminology, by the way, would be an excellent piece of consciousness-raising for the children themselves. It would sow the seed of the idea that religion is something for them to choose—or not—when they become old enough to do so.

I must again stress that the hypothesis of the programmability of the child brain is only one example. The message of the moths and the candle flame is more general. As a Darwinian, I am proposing a family of hypotheses, all of which have in common that they do not ask what is the survival value of religion. Instead they ask, "What was the survival value, in the wild past, of having the kind of brain which, in the cultural present, manifests itself as religion?" And I should add that child brains are not the only ones that are vulnerable to infection of this kind. Adult brains are too, especially if primed in childhood. Charismatic preachers can spread the word far and wide among adults, as if they were diseased persons spreading an epidemic.

So far, the hypothesis suggests only that brains (especially child brains) are *vulnerable* to infection. It says nothing about which viruses will infect. In one sense it doesn't matter. Anything the child believes with sufficient conviction will get passed on to its children, and hence to future generations. This is a nongenetic analogue of heredity. Some people will say it is memes rather than genes. I don't want to sell memetic terminology to you today, but it is important to stress that we are not talking about genetic inheritance. What is genetically inherited, according to the theory, is the tendency of the child brain to believe what it is told. This is what makes the child brain a suitable vehicle for nongenetic heredity.

If there is nongenetic heredity, could there also be nongenetic Darwinism? Is it arbitrary which mind viruses end up exploiting the vulnerability of child brains? Or do some viruses survive better than others? This is where those theories that I earlier dismissed as proximate, not ultimate, come in. If fear of death is common, the idea of immortality might survive as a mind virus better than the competing idea that death snuffs us out like a light. Conversely, the idea of posthumous punishment for sins might survive, not because children like the idea but because adults find it a useful way to control them. One could devote a whole lecture to listing religious ideas and examining the possible "survival value" of each. I did a bit of this in my essay "Viruses of the Mind" (originally written for Dan Dennett and now reprinted in *A Devil's Chaplain*), but I have no time for that here. The important point is that survival value does not have its normal Darwinian meaning of genetic survival value. This is not the normal Darwinian conversation about why a gene survives in preference to its alleles in the gene pool. This is about why one idea survives in the pool of ideas in preference to rival ideas. It is this notion of rival ideas surviving, or failing to survive, in a pool of ideas that the word "meme" was intended to capture.

Let's go back to first principles and remind ourselves of exactly what is going on in natural selection. The necessary condition is that accurately self-replicating information exists in alternative, competing versions. Following George C. Williams in his *Natural Selection,* I shall call them "codices" (singular "codex"). The archetypal codex is a gene: not the physical molecule of DNA but the information it carries.

Biological codices, or genes, are carried around inside bodies whose qualities—phenotypes—they helped to influence. The death of the body entails the destruction of any codices that it contains, unless they have previously been passed on to another body, in reproduction. Automatically, therefore, those genes that positively affect the survival and reproduction of bodies in which they sit will come to predominate in the world, at the expense of rival genes.

A familiar example of a *nongenetic* codex is the so-called chain letter, although "chain" is not a good word. It is too linear, doesn't capture the idea of explosive, exponential spread. Equally ill-named, and for the same reason, is the so-called chain reaction in an atomic bomb. Let's change "chain letter" to "postal virus" and look at the phenomenon through Darwinian eyes.

Suppose you received through the mail a letter that simply said, "Make six copies of this letter and send them to six friends." If you slavishly obeyed the instruction, and if your friends and their friends did too, the letter would spread exponentially and we'd soon be wading knee deep in letters. Of course most people would not obey such a bald, unadorned instruction. But now, suppose the letter said, "If you do not copy this letter to six friends, you will be jinxed, a voodoo will be placed on you, and you will die young, in agony." Most people still wouldn't send it on, but a significant number probably would. Even quite a low percentage would be enough for it to take off.

The promise of reward may be more effective than the threat of punishment. We have probably all received examples of the slightly more sophisticated style of letter, which invites you to send money to people already on the list, with the promise that you will eventually receive millions of dollars when the exponential explosion has advanced further. Whatever our personal guesses as to who might fall for these things, the fact is that many do. It is an empirical fact that chain letters circulate.

Oliver Goodenough and I published in *Nature* a short article about a famous postal virus, the inane but widely travelled St. Jude Letter. In any gathering of people the likelihood is high that some will have received the St. Jude Letter; maybe more than once. The St. Jude doesn't ask you for money, so there isn't even a whiff of a plausible rationale to justify its bald assertion that if you send the letter on you will accrue fabulous riches, and if you do not you will perish in misery. Nevertheless, the U.S. Post Office reports that the St. Jude letter has been right round the world in great waves (at least nine times at the time of our paper).

Postal viruses also appeal to human sentiment. The most famous example is the Craig Shergold Letter, which gained a new lease of life when the Internet came along. In 1989, a nine-year-old British boy called Craig Shergold was diagnosed with a brain tumour. Somebody circulated a letter saying that Craig's ambition before he died was to get into the *Guinness Books of Records* for receiving the most "get well cards." It asked people to send the boy a card and forward the requesting letter on to others. It was this last clause that turned the letter into a virus. Within a year, Craig had broken the record; as a result of the publicity, his case came to the attention of a good surgeon, who operated on him, and he is still alive. But the cards kept on coming. The Internet kicked in, and, by 1999, a quarter of a billion cards had arrived. Craig, who was by then nineteen, asked that they should stop. King Canute had as much success with the tide. Cards continued to flood in at a rate of about 300,000 per week.

Various mutant versions of the letter are now in existence. At some point "get well card" mutated to "business card" or, in another strain of the virus, to "birthday card." Craig's age mutated to seven (perhaps more appealing than nine) and (perhaps via seven) to seventeen, but in any case he is now twenty-three. His name mutated many times. A partial list of *variants* now in circulation includes Craig Shergold (original wild type), Craig Sheford, Craig Shirgold, Craig Shelford, Craig Sherford, Craig Sheppard, Greg Sherold, and Greg Sherwood. The cards are still coming, in spite of repeated efforts by him and his family to stop them.

The point of the story is that no genes are involved, yet postal viruses display an entirely authentic epidemiology, including the successive waves of infection rolling around the world and including the evolution of new mutant strains of the original virus.

And the lesson for understanding religion, to repeat, is that when we ask the Darwinian question "What is the survival value of religion?" we don't have to mean genetic survival value. The conventional Darwinian question translates into "How does religion contribute to the survival and reproduction of individual religious people and hence the propagation of genetic propensities to religion?" But my point is that we don't need to being genes into the calculation at all. There is at least something

Darwinian going on here, something epidemiological going on, which has nothing to do with genes. It is the religious ideas themselves that survive, or fail to survive, in direct competition with rival religious ideas.

It is at this point that I have an argument with some of my Darwinian colleagues. Purist evolutionary psychologists will come back at me and say something like this. Cultural epidemiology is possible only because human brains have certain evolved tendencies, and by evolved we mean genetically evolved. You may document a worldwide epidemic of reverse baseball hats, or an epidemic of copycat martyrdoms, or an epidemic of total-immersion baptisms. But these nongenetic epidemics depend upon the human tendency to imitate. And we ultimately need a Darwinian—by which they mean genetic—explanation for the human tendency to imitate.

And this, of course, is where I return to my theory of childhood gullibility. I stressed that it was only an example of the kind of theory I want to propose. Ordinary genetic selection sets up childhood brains with a tendency to believe their elders. Ordinary, straight-down-the-line Darwinian selection of genes sets up brains with a tendency to imitate, hence indirectly to spread rumours, spread urban legends, and believe cock-and-bull stories in chain letters. But *given* that genetic selection has set up brains of this kind, they then provide the equivalent of a new kind of nongenetic heredity, which might form the basis for a new kind of epidemiology, and perhaps even a new kind of nongenetic Darwinian selection. I believe that religion, along with chain letters and urban legends, is one of a group of phenomena explained by this kind of nongenetic epidemiology, with the possible admixture of nongenetic Darwinian selection. If I am right, religion has no survival value for individual human beings, nor for the benefit of their genes. The benefit, if there is any, is to religion itself.

II. THE RELIGION OF SCIENCE

Carl Sagan, in his inspiring book *Pale Blue Dot,* wrote the following:

> How is it that hardly any major religion has looked at science and concluded, "This is better than we thought! The Universe is much bigger than our prophets said, grander, more subtle, more elegant"? Instead they say, "No, no, no! My god is a little god, and I want him to stay that way." A religion, old or new, that stressed the magnificence of the Universe as revealed by modern science might be able to

draw forth reserves of reverence and awe hardly tapped by the conventional faiths. Sooner or later, such a religion will emerge.[1]

Sagan was often accused of scientism, defined by the *Oxford Dictionary* as "a term applied (freq. in a derogatory manner) to a belief in the omnipotence of scientific knowledge and techniques...." Here are three of the usage specimens given by the dictionary:

Scientism, as a belief that science can furnish answers to all human problems, makes science a substitute for philosophy, religion, manners, and morals.

It really appeared to many educated people that at last all the secrets of the universe would be discovered and all the problems of human life solved. This superstition...we may call "Scientism."

...scientism represents the same superstitious attitude which, in previous times, ascribed such power to a supernatural agency.

"Scientism" is one of those words, like "reductionism," which is only ever uttered with a sneer. I am frequently accused of scientism myself; sometimes explicitly accused of elevating science to a religion—usually by the kind of person who thinks "elevate" is an appropriate verb to use.

In this lecture I shall vigorously forswear any suggestion that science is, or should be, a religion. But I'll recognize at least enough commonality between them to feed a worthwhile debate. Science is *not* a religion, but it does some of the things over which religion once felt a certain *droit de seigneur*. Not morality, I must add. I shall not talk about morality at all today, mostly for lack of time.

Religions used to feed on the sense of rapt wonder that we associate with scientific writers such as Loren Eiseley, Lewis Thomas, and Carl Sagan himself. An Anglican clergyman, one of my teachers of whom I was fond, told me of the never-forgotten instant that triggered his own calling. As a boy, he was lying prone in a field, his face buried in the grass. He suddenly became preternaturally aware of the tangled stems and roots, as a whole new world—the world of ants and beetles and, though he may not have been aware of them, soil bacteria and other micro-organisms by the billions. At that moment, the micro-world of the soil seemed to swell and become one with the universe, and with the

1. Carl Sagan, *Pale Blue Dot* (London: Headline, 1995), p. 52.

soul of the boy contemplating them. He interpreted the experience in religious terms, and it eventually led him to the priesthood. But much the same mystic feeling is common among scientists. I am only one of many who have experienced it.

In his boyhood at least, my clergyman was unlikely to have known the closing lines of *On the Origin of Species,* the famous "entangled bank" passage, "with birds singing on the bushes, with various insects flitting about, and with worms crawling through the damp earth." Had he read the passage, he would certainly have empathized with it and, instead of the priesthood, might have been led to Darwin's view that all was "produced by laws acting around us."[2]

> Thus, from the war of nature, from famine and death, the most exalted object which we are capable of conceiving, namely, the production of the higher animals, directly follows. There is grandeur in this view of life, with its several powers, having been originally breathed into a few forms or into one; and that, whilst this planet has gone cycling on according to the fixed law of gravity, from so simple a beginning endless forms most beautiful and most wonderful have been, and are being, evolved.[3]

All Carl Sagan's books and, I would like to hope, my own touch those nerve-endings of transcendent awe that religion, in past times, monopolised. For this reason, I often hear myself described as a deeply religious person. An American correspondent asked her professor whether he had a view about me. "Sure," he replied. "He's positive science is incompatible with religion, but he waxes ecstatic about nature and the universe. To me, that *is* religion!" But is "religion" the right word to use? I think not. Words are our servants, not our masters, but that's no excuse for actively misleading people.

Much unfortunate misunderstanding is caused by failure to distinguish what might be called Einsteinian religion from supernatural religion. The last words of Stephen Hawking's *A Brief History of Time,* "For then we should know the mind of God," have notoriously misled people toward the misconception that Hawking is religious.[4] Ursula Goodenough's *The Sacred Depths of Nature* clearly shows that she is a complete atheist. Yet she goes to church regularly, and there are numerous pas-

---

2. Charles Darwin, *On the Origin of Species* (London: John Murray, 1859), p. 489.

3. Ibid., p. 490.

4. Stephen Hawking, *A Brief History of Time* (New York: Bantam Books, 1988).

sages in her book, and especially in the publisher's blurbs, that seem to be almost begging to be taken out of context and used as ammunition for supernaturalist religion. She calls herself a "religious naturalist."

The present astronomer royal, Sir Martin Rees, goes to church as an "unbelieving Anglican," out of "loyalty to the tribe." He has no supernatural beliefs but shares exactly the sense of wonder that the universe provokes in many of us. Plenty of intellectual atheists proudly call themselves Jews, and observe Jewish rites, mostly out of loyalty to an ancient tradition but also because of a muddled (in my view) willingness to label as "religion" the Einsteinian sense of wonder that many of us share. A large number of scientists who give the impression they are religious turn out to be religious only in the Einsteinian sense. What, then, was Einstein's religion?

One of Einstein's most quoted remarks is: "Science without religion is lame, religion without science is blind." But listen to the context in which that most eagerly repeated sentence appears. He characterises "religion" as

> the faith in the possibility that the regulations valid for the world of existence are rational, that is, comprehensible to reason. I cannot conceive of a genuine scientist without that profound faith. The situation may be expressed by an image: science without religion is lame, religion without science is blind.... I must nevertheless qualify this assertion....5

And Einstein goes on to make it very clear that he is using the word "religion" in a special sense that leaves no room at all for a personal God.

Einstein was obviously quite annoyed at the way religious apologists continually misused his name in their support. He wrote in a letter:

> It was, of course, a lie what you read about my religious convictions, a lie which is being systematically repeated. I do not believe in a personal God and I have never denied this but have expressed it clearly. If something is in me which can be called religious then it is the unbounded admiration for the structure of the world so far as our science can reveal it.

5. Conference on Science, Philosophy and Religion in Their Relation to the Democratic Way of Life, *Science, Philosophy, and Religion: A Symposium* (New York, 1941).

Einstein said that his God was Spinoza's, and Spinoza believed that "neither intellect nor will appertain to God's nature."[6] "God's will" simply means the laws of nature. Here are some more quotations from Einstein, to give a flavour of Einsteinian religion.

> I am a deeply religious nonbeliever. This is a somewhat new kind of religion.

> I have never imputed to Nature a purpose or a goal, or anything that could be understood as anthropomorphic. What I see in Nature is a magnificent structure that we can comprehend only very imperfectly, and that must fill a thinking person with a feeling of humility. This is a genuinely religious feeling that has nothing to do with mysticism.

> The idea of a personal God is quite alien to me and seems even naive.

Einstein, then, was certainly not a theist. He was repeatedly indignant at the suggestion. Was he a deist? Or a pantheist?

Let's remind ourselves of the terminology. A theist believes in a supernatural intelligence who does some combination of the following: answers prayers; forgives (or punishes) sins; frets about right and wrong, and knows when we do them (or even *think* them); intervenes in the world by performing miracles. A deist is one who believes in a supernatural intelligence whose activities are confined to setting up the laws that govern the universe in the first place. The deist God never intervenes thereafter. A pantheist uses the word "God" as a nonsupernatural synonym for Nature, or for the Universe, or for the lawfulness that governs the workings of the universe.

Deists differ from theists in that their God does not answer prayers, is not interested in sins or confessions, does not read our thoughts, and above all does not intervene with capricious miracles. Deists differ from pantheists in that the deist God is some kind of cosmic intelligence who set up the laws of the universe, rather than the pantheist's metaphoric or poetic *synonym* for the laws of the universe. Pantheism is sexed-up atheism. Deism is watered-down theism. The evidence agrees that Einstein was not a deist but a pantheist, and this is what I mean by Einsteinian religion. It is summarised in yet another quotation:

---

6. Max Jammer, *Einstein and Religion* (Princeton University Press, 1999), p. 44.

To sense that behind anything that can be experienced there is a something that our mind cannot grasp and whose beauty and sublimity reaches us only indirectly and as a feeble reflection, this is religiousness. In this sense I am religious.

In this sense, I too am religious.

There is every reason to think that famous Einsteinisms like "God is subtle but he is not malicious" and "He does not play dice" and "Did God have a choice in creating the Universe?" are not deistic, and certainly not theistic. "God does not play dice" should be translated as "Randomness does not lie at the heart of all things." "Did God have a choice in creating the Universe?" means "Could the universe have begun in any other way than the way in which it did begin?" Einstein was using "God" here in a purely metaphorical, poetic sense. So is Stephen Hawking, and so are most of those physicists who occasionally slip into the language of religious metaphor. Paul Davies's *The Mind of God* seems to hover somewhere between Einsteinian pantheism and an obscure form of deism—for which he was rewarded with the million-dollar Templeton Prize. And talking of the Templeton Prize, Dan Dennett said to me, "Richard, if ever you fall on hard times..."

Dennett, as you know, coined the useful distinction between cranes and skyhooks. Cranes are explanatory devices that actually do some explanatory work. Natural selection is the champion crane of all time. It has lifted life from primeval simplicity to the dizzy heights of complexity, beauty, and apparent design that we marvel at today. Skyhooks do no explanatory work and usually demand more explanation than they provide. This is why I don't go along with those who find only a trivial difference between deism, which postulates a creative intelligence at the beginning of the universe, and pantheism, which doesn't.

Creative intelligence is something that needs explaining in its own right. Darwinian evolution provides an explanation—the only workable explanation so far suggested—for the existence of intelligence. Creative intelligence comes into the world *late,* as the derived product of a long process of gradual change: the slow evolution of nervous systems, or some other kind of computational machinery (which may be secondarily designed by evolved nervous systems). In this respect, deism is as bad as theism: creative intelligence had some sort of prior existence and is responsible for designing the universe, with the laws and constants that eventually, through evolution, brought into being our kind of creative intelligence. This wasteful and unparsimonious view is radically different from the Einsteinian use of God as a poetic synonym for the laws of the universe. A universe that begins with creative intelligence is a very different kind of universe from a universe in which creative intelligence is *explained* as emerging after millions of years of evolution.

In the Einsteinian sense I am religious. But I prefer not to call myself religious because I think it is misleading. It is misleading because, for the vast majority of people, "religion" implies supernaturalism. For the same reason, I would have preferred it if physicists such as Einstein, Hawking, and others would refrain from using the word "God" in their special physicists' metaphorical sense. The metaphorical God of the physicists is light-years away from the interventionist, miracle-wreaking, thought-reading, sin-punishing, prayer-answering God of the theists and of ordinary language. Deliberately to confuse the two is, in my opinion, an act of intellectual high treason.

From now on, unless otherwise stated, when I speak of religion in this lecture it will be theistic, supernaturalist religion, as understood and practised by the vast majority of people who call themselves religious.

Theistic religions have traditionally offered answers to questions that today we hand over to science: questions of cosmology and biology, which are nowadays answered by, for example, the Big Bang theory and the theory of evolution. What has happened today is that sophisticated theologians wisely abandon *explanation*—which religion does badly—to science, which does it well. Instead, theology concentrates on topics like morality and guidance for life. Science doesn't pretend to do morality, and it doesn't do it well. It is by no means clear that religion does it well either. Indeed, I think a powerful case for the opposite can be made, but that is not my topic here.

Today's theological sophists insist that religion and science do not compete because they are not directly comparable. They occupy non-communicating realms, nonoverlapping magisteria. Science explores the way the universe is, and how things work. Religion has nothing to say on this, but it has its own equally important domain: morals, values, and "ultimate" questions.

Others try to sum it up as: "Science is concerned with 'how questions,' religion with 'why questions.'" There is something maddening about the complacent silliness of assuming, without further discussion, that "why" questions have some sort of universal, ultimate legitimacy.

To begin with a relatively trivial point, there are unequivocally scientific questions in which everyone happily uses the *word* "why": Why is the sky blue? Why does hot air rise? Why are predators rarer than their prey? Even in the sense of "what is the purpose of...?" "why" can be translated into scientific terms. In my previous lecture I asked why birds ant and offered the answer: "To delouse their feathers." The respectable Darwinian translation is implicit: "Ancestral birds with a genetic tendency to ant had more offspring because they were less likely to suffer from louse-borne diseases."

"What is the purpose of a boomerang?" invites a very different kind of answer, in terms of the deliberate intentions of the designer or of the user. It is because deliberate purpose sits so prominently at the forefront of human consciousness that some find creationist explanations of the natural world appealing. I suspect that this may also supply the explanation for our having to wait till the nineteenth century for a Darwin to solve a problem that, with hindsight, seems easier than the hard problems solved two centuries earlier by Newton and Galileo, and two millennia earlier by Archimedes and Pythagoras.

"What is the purpose of a light bulb?"; "What is the purpose of a firefly's luminescent organ?"; and "What is the purpose of the sun?" sound superficially similar. They are utterly different. The first invites an answer in terms of human intention, the second in terms of Darwinian natural selection. The third deserves no answer at all in my opinion, but, within the framework of a religion, it can be treated as a special case of the light-bulb question, where the deliberate intention is that of a divine rather than a mortal person. In this case the answer might be: "The purpose of the sun is to give us warmth, to enable us to see, and to sustain plant life so we can eat."

Science would not so much deny the answer as deny the legitimacy of ever asking the question in the first place. The mere fact that it is possible to frame a question in the English language doesn't make it legitimate. "What is the purpose of the sun?" is no more legitimate than "What is the colour of jealousy?" In poetic vein, we might say green is the colour of jealousy and red the colour of anger, but poetry moves us into a different realm, the realm of neither religion nor science.

Setting aside questions that science ignores or rejects, like the colour of jealousy or the purpose of the sun, are there any deep and important questions that science cannot answer? Of course there are many that science cannot *yet* answer. But are there any that science in principle can never answer? Very possibly. We don't know. An example might be: "Where did the laws and fundamental constants of physics come from?" But if science cannot answer such questions, that emphatically doesn't mean that any other discipline—for example, religion—can.

I have previously quoted a conversation I had with the professor (i.e., chairman) of astrophysics at Oxford. I asked him to explain the Big Bang to me and he did so, rather well. I went on: "Then where did the fundamental laws and constants of physics come from in the first place?" "Ah," he said with a smile, "Now we move beyond the realm of science. This is where I have to hand over to our good friend the chaplain." But, I was tempted to reply, why the chaplain?...Why not the gardener or the chef?

There are some profoundly difficult questions about the origin of the universe, about the origin of physical law and fundamental constants, about the curvature of space-time, about the paradoxical behaviour of quanta, and about the nature of consciousness. It may be that humanity will never reach the quietus of complete understanding. But *if* we do, I venture the confident prediction that it will be science, not religion, that brings us there. And if that sounds like scientism, so much the better for scientism.

I am anxious not to be misunderstood, so let me stress again that I am *not* expressing confidence that humanity *will* succeed in answering the deep questions of existence. But in the (possibly unlikely) event that we *do* succeed, I am very confident that it is more likely to be through scientific than religious ways of thinking. However unlikely it may be that science will one day understand everything about the cosmos and the nature of life, it is even less likely that religion will.

The flip side of "two separate magisteria" is the claim that religion "keeps off science's patch." Religion is supposed to confine itself to its proper domain—whatever that might be—leaving to science questions of how the world works. That way, science and religion can coexist in a respectful, even "loving," to quote Steve Gould, concordat. In practice, however, religion seldom respects science's patch and is normally to be found trampling—if nowadays rather sheepishly—all over it.

Pope John Paul II recently gained kudos in the scientific community by coming down, firmly and unequivocally, in favour of evolution. This seems a clear case of respecting science's patch. Yet at the same time the pope's church, with his encouragement, promotes a whole range of doctrines that simply are scientific claims. Jesus lacked a human father. He walked three days after his death. God intervenes at crucial moments in evolution. God intervenes in human affairs to save particular individuals from disease. Mary's body went physically to heaven, with no trace of it remaining on earth. This last one is especially notable since it implies that heaven is a physical place, a scientific claim if ever there was one. It was promulgated by Pope Pius XII as recently as 1950.

All miracle stories are about alleged facts that fall clearly in the domain of science. Miracles are the subject of a double standard that is certainly patronising and arguably duplicitous. Sophisticated theologians dismiss miracles as of no importance, quaint stories, perhaps with symbolic or allegorical significance. To ask whether they are literally true is naïve, simplistic, missing the point. Who would be so insensitive, so reductionist, so *scientistic* even, as to ask whether the Miracle of Lourdes, or the Apparition of Fatima, or the stigmata of Padre Pio really happened?

That's what theologians say when they are talking to scientists, or to the sort of educated audience that would attend a Tanner Lecture. You would think there is no conflict with science, no wayward straying from magisterium to magisterium! But seek out the pilgrims who flock to Lourdes or St. Peter's Square, Fatima or Medjugorje, and ask them whether they believe miracles really happen, literally. We all know what their answer will be. Of *course* they believe it, not as some watered-down symbolic allegory—by which they'd feel short-changed—but as literal truth. And they are encouraged to do so by bishops and archbishops, whatever those prelates may say when talking to scientists or other educated audiences.

Far from religion keeping off science's turf, it is precisely the apparent scientific content of miracles that attracts people into churches and mosques. It is only when these stories are challenged on scientific grounds that apologists scuttle for cover behind the wall of "separate magisteria." But you cannot have it both ways. Priests should either come out fighting for their miracles, admitting the corollary that they are trampling on science's territory—and good luck to them—or they should take "separate magisteria" seriously and honestly admit that miracles don't literally happen—in which case, just watch those congregations melt away.

This is one reason—there aren't many—for respecting fundamentalist creationists. At least they are honest and consistent about what they believe: unlike sophisticated theologians who say one thing for the academy and something very different for the congregation.

Before leaving miracles, I need to make an important qualification. An alleged event that violates the expectations of *existing* science should not be treated as a miracle. Never forget (Arthur C.) Clarke's Third

Law: "Any sufficiently advanced technology is indistinguishable from magic."[7] Radio is not a miracle, but it would certainly have seemed so in the Middle Ages. Religious miracles, however, are not sold to congregations as exploiting as-yet-undiscovered scientific principles. Nobody is suggesting that Mother Teresa's medallion (the healing power of which was the "miracle" needed to justify her beatification) generated a force field hitherto unknown to physics, a field that, one day, science will make available to everybody. No, the church's claim is precisely that a miracle is a one-off violation of the laws of physics, which God, because he made those laws, can break when he chooses, for example, to signal that Mother Teresa should be a saint. Miracles are capricious, singular departures from normality. This is emphatically not keeping off science's turf; *not* separate magisteria.

Scientific journals like the *Quarterly Review of Biology* occasionally devote a whole issue to one particular question. One could imagine a symposium issue devoted to why the dinosaurs went extinct, with papers devoted to different theories or lines of evidence. Scientists often disagree, and they can even become acrimonious. But, though disagreements might figure in our symposium issue of the journal, the authors will at least agree on what it would take to make them change their minds: evidence. If they disagree today, it is because the evidence is so far incomplete.

But imagine that science worked in a very different way. Suppose the contents list of our Symposium Issue of the *Quarterly Review of Biology* looked like the one in Figure 3:

The first item on the list is a typical scientific paper. I don't think any reasonable person could deny that the rest of the list constitutes a fair satire on how religions typically support their beliefs.

How do we know what to *believe?* My *Quarterly Review* satire signals five partially overlapping types of answer to the question. Four of them come from religion, only one from science.

1. Evidence. The facts support X.
2. Tradition. Our people have always believed X.
3. Authority. My Holy Book (or priest) says X.
4. Faith. I just *know* X in my bones.
5. Revelation. An inner voice tells me X.

7. "Hazards of Prophecy: The Failure of Imagination," in *Profiles of the Future: An Inquiry into the Limits of the Possible* (New York: Harper and Row, 1973).

CONTENTS

FIGURE 3.

First, evidence. Scientists believe X because we have seen evidence for it. Philosophers may turn this around: the X hypothesis has withstood strenuous attempts to falsify it. But I am not concerned with such refinements. It still counts as evidence, even if technically all our beliefs are on probation. Nor shall I lose any time on fashionable claims that science is just the white, Western, patriarchal view of truth. Science works. That is why when you go to an international conference on cultural relativism you go by Boeing 747 rather than by magic carpet.

Let me list just a tiny sample of what we know, or have very strong reason to believe, through evidence-based science. Our universe began at a particular time, more than ten billion and less than twenty billion years ago, and has been expanding ever since. Much of the mass in the universe is agglomerated in stars, spherical nuclear furnaces in which the ninety-two naturally occurring elements are being formed. Earth is between four and five billion years old. Its surface is not static but composed of movable plates on which the visible continents sit. We know approximately the shape of the map of the world at any given date in the past, and it looks increasingly unfamiliar the farther back we go. Life has been a major feature of earth's surface layers for at least the last half of the planet's existence, probably more. All known life is descended from a common ancestor, which shared the same highly specific digital genetic code. We know the code precisely, know how it is translated word for word, and have an approximate idea of how bodily form emerges as a result. Ancestral forms change gradually and divergently into descendant life forms over millions of years, the process being guided in functional directions by the nonrandom survival of random variations in genetically coded information. We now have the means to know, if only we had the time and the money to grind it out, the entire family tree relating every living species to every other living species. And we have the means to estimate the date of each branch point in millions, or tens of millions, of years. The list of things we know as a result of scientific evidence is formidably large.

As for what we know as a result of religious evidence, the less said the better. Miracles, as we have seen, are a source of embarrassment to educated theologians, although they are helpful in recruiting congregations. The other kind of evidence adduced by religious apologists is that presented by "scientific creationists," nowadays euphemistically disguised as "intelligent design theorists." Obviously at Harvard there is no need to waste time on them, and I shall pass straight on to the second of my list of five grounds for belief: tradition.

One of the most striking features of religion is that it runs in families. This country, like my own, has many Christians and Jews. If we lived in Pakistan or India we'd be worshipping Allah or the Hindu pantheon of hundreds of gods. If we'd been brought up in ancient Greece, we'd be worshipping Zeus and Apollo. If Vikings, Wotan and Thor. Out of hundreds of possible religions, the vast majority of people just happen to end up in the same religion as their parents. And isn't it a remarkable coincidence: whichever religion you are brought up in, it always turns out to be the right religion.

We are all familiar with those maps of the world, colour-shaded to denote predominant language. Atlases use the same kind of colour-coding to designate predominant religion. Since religions hold contradictory beliefs about important truths, it is as if those truths depended upon the geographical location of the believer. We have become so accustomed to this that it doesn't seem strange. It is exactly what you would expect from the theory of religion that I tried to outline yesterday. To get an idea of how preposterous it is, imagine that the colours on the map are coded for areas where the local population favours different theories of how the dinosaurs went extinct. Imagine that science worked in such a way. But science, on the contrary, is international. Scientists in different countries look at the same evidence and, if the evidence is strong enough, will all eventually come to the same conclusion. It may not always quite work out like that, but that is the ideal to which all scientists aspire.[8]

Tradition is almost wholly absent from science. To a small extent, dynasties of scientists can be discerned: scientists occasionally appear to inherit the opinions, or the approach to science, of their professor, or even their grand-professor or great-grand-professor. But it is only a minor effect, given far less weight than evidence, which is available to all. Similarly, there is some slight tendency for scientists from different parts of the world to follow different national approaches. But such regionalism is again negligible compared to the universalism of science. And all scientists subscribe to the *ideal* of universal cross-culturalism of science. Confronted with the same strong evidence, an Indian scientist, an American scientist, and a Japanese scientist will come to the same conclusion.

I shall leave tradition there and switch to the next item on the list of reasons for believing things: authority. Authority in religion is of two kinds, scriptural and priestly authority, and both are only too familiar. But just imagine if science worked in the same way: "*On the Origin of Species* is the inspired word of the Prophet Darwin. No word of it can possibly be mistaken. All Darwinian children must learn to recite it by heart, nodding their little heads backward and forward as they do so." Just imagine if biologists, instead of going out into the field and doing research on seagulls or antelopes or dandelions, spent their time locked in argument about exactly what Darwin meant in chapter 6, line 32. Or, worse, exactly what some learned exegete meant in his *interpretation* of Darwin's inspired words. There is no need to continue. The point is made.

The doctrine of papal infallibility and the fatwa on Salman Rushdie are only extreme examples of the power of priestly authority. There is no doubt that Salman Rushdie was, and perhaps still is, in real physical

8. I cannot resist an anecdote at the expense of certain schools of social science. An undergraduate student close to me is studying at a British university (not my own). Her degree subject is Human Science, which is a mixture of science and social science. She loves the science but hates the social science because its teachers are avowedly antiscientific and anti-Darwinian. She told me that one lecturer in anthropology even went so far as to say that the beauty of anthropology, as opposed to science, is that when two anthropologists look at the same evidence they come to opposite conclusions. I hasten to add that this was his personal opinion, not necessarily typical of all anthropologists. But you can imagine how discouraging such nihilistic nonsense is to a young aspiring scholar.

danger because of priestly authority. In Iran, on July 21, 1998, Ruhollah Rowhani, a 52-year-old man with four children, was hanged for allegedly converting a Muslim woman to the Bahai faith. On August 18, 2001, Dr. Younus Shaikh, a Pakistani medical doctor, was sentenced to death for speculating, in front of students who subsequently reported him to the religious authorities, that the Prophet Muhammad might not have been a Muslim before he invented the religion at the age of forty.[9] Just imagine if science worked like *that*.

To be fair, scientists, too, sometimes argue by authority, but it is not something we are proud of. It happens in spite of scientific principles, not in pursuit of them. William Thomson, Lord Kelvin, was one of the fathers of thermodynamics and among the leading physicists of the nineteenth century. His authoritative thermodynamic calculation that the age of the earth did not allow enough time for evolution was a thorn in the side of Darwin, who, sadly, didn't live long enough to see his own vindication by the discovery of radioactivity. Kelvin wielded his authority not only as one of the most eminent physicists of the age but also on behalf of physics itself, which was, and still is, respected as senior to biology or geology. Kelvin, in effect, said that physics didn't allow enough time for evolution, so Darwin's biology must be wrong. Darwin could have retorted—but didn't—that biology demonstrates that evolution is a fact, so Kelvin's physics must be wrong. The following authoritative opinions are also attributed to Lord Kelvin. Radio has no future. Heavier-than-air flying machines are impossible. X-rays will prove to be a hoax.

There is a defensible version of the argument from authority. It is like betting on a horse on the recommendation of a reliable tipster: "John Maynard Smith has an excellent track record. He has been right so many times in the past that, if he supports a theory, you would be wise to take it seriously." There is nothing wrong with this kind of argument, so long as it is used only as a guide to which hypotheses are likely to be worth testing. Argument from authority is *never* used by scientists as evidence that something in the world of nature must be the case. It routinely is used in exactly this way in religion.

Let me move on from authority to faith. Faith means believing something in spite of lack of evidence. In religion, faith is a virtue. Religious people gain special kudos if they steadfastly believe, in the teeth of evi-

9. Happily, after an international outcry and strong representations to the Pakistan government, Dr. Shaikh has now been released.

dence to the contrary. Doubting Thomas, the patron saint of scientists, who wanted evidence of the resurrection of Jesus, is held up to us as less virtuous than the other disciples whose faith was strong enough to need none.

Tertullian said *Certum est quia impossibile est* (it is certain because it is impossible). In the seventeenth century, when dying for one's faith was as common in Christian circles as it is in Islam today, Sir Thomas Browne said: "I *desire* to exercise my faith in the difficultest point; for to credit ordinary and visible objects is not faith, but perswasion." And he lamented: "Methinks there be not impossibilities enough in religion for an active faith."[10] Faith in the teeth of evidence was satirised in Douglas Adams's Electric Monk, a labour-saving device that you could buy to do your believing for you. It was advertised as "capable of believing things they wouldn't believe in Salt Lake City."[11] When we first encounter the Electric Monk, on a horse, it believes, in the teeth of all the evidence, that the whole world is bright pink.

What about faith in science? Again, it happens. And again, it is treated with suspicion. The astronomer Sir Arthur Eddington used the solar eclipse of 1919 to test General Relativity's prediction that light from the stars would be bent as it passed close to the sun. Eddington's measurements brilliantly vindicated the prediction and turned Einstein into a worldwide celebrity. But Einstein himself was insouciant. Any other result and... "I would have felt sorry for the dear Lord. The theory is correct."[12] Scientific ears hear that with a *frisson* of naughtiness. Such faith, presumably based on aesthetic elegance, does smack of religion. Luckily, Einstein was right. The evidence did support him, and it continues to do so.

There are indeed physicists whose faith in the aesthetic beauty of their equations would lead them to mistrust contrary evidence from experiment. But if repeated experiments persistently told the same story they would, however reluctantly, climb down. Experimental evidence ultimately trumps mathematical beauty, in what T. H. Huxley lamented as: "The great tragedy of science—the slaying of a beautiful hypothesis by an ugly fact."[13] Einstein also, as we have seen, wrote of "faith in the

10. *Religio Medici,* section 9.

11. *Dirk Gently's Holistic Detective Agency* (New York: Simon and Schuster, 1987).

12. Max Jammer, *Einstein and Religion* (Princeton: Princeton University Press, 2002), p. 53.

13. *Oxford Dictionary of Quotations,* 4th ed., ed. Angela Partington (Oxford: Oxford University Press, 1992), p. 358.

possibility that the regulations valid for the world of existence are rational, that is, comprehensible to reason,"[14] and he added that he could not conceive of a genuine scientist without that profound faith. I can't either.

The same Sir Arthur Eddington sounded superficially as though he was expressing blind faith in the Second Law of Thermodynamics when he said:

> If someone points out to you that your pet theory of the universe is in disagreement with Maxwell's equations—then so much the worse for Maxwell's equations. If it is found to be contradicted by observation—well, these experimentalists do bungle things sometimes. But if your theory is found to be against the second law of thermodynamics I can give you no hope; there is nothing for it but to collapse in deepest humiliation.[15]

Eddington's advice could, in effect, be reworded in the form of an instruction to a patent inspector (such as, now that I think about it, Einstein himself). If an inventor tries to patent a perpetual motion machine, Eddington was in effect saying, don't even bother to look at his drawings. Don't waste your time working through his calculations. You know, without even looking, that his idea cannot work.

A more commonplace type of faith in science arises because no one individual has the time or the ability to check the evidence. I believe what physicists tell me about the speed of light, and I believe what geology textbooks tell me about plate tectonics, even though I haven't examined the evidence myself. I believe it because I know how the system of peer review works. I know that a result that is sufficiently earth-shaking (metaphorically or literally) will have been repeated by other groups of scientists, checked and rechecked by sceptical experts who could, if I sought them out, explain the details to me.

I know that bad science is sometimes done, and even fraudulent science. A scientist who is detected in fraud is drummed out of the profession. Unfortunately, because fiddling data is such a heinous offence in scientific eyes, scientists are extremely averse to suspecting it in colleagues, whistle-blowers are given a hard time, and the result is that some fraud gets through. But the procedure of science is such that it will

---

14. Conference on Science, Philosophy and Religion in Their Relation to the Democratic Way of Life, *Science, Philosophy, and Religion: A Symposium.*

15. *The Nature of the Physical World* (New York: Macmillan, 1948), p. 74.

eventually be detected, at least if the fraudulent finding is important enough to arouse attention. And if it is not important, well, perhaps we can regretfully live with it. The point is that a scientist caught falsifying data would be disgraced for life. The same cannot be said even of the *aspirations* of certain other professions, let alone the practice.[16]

To repeat, scientists have faith in secondhand evidence because nobody has the time or the ability to check it all personally. The culture of science relies heavily upon honesty. The honesty is proximally policed by the peer review system, and ultimately by the universally accepted knowledge that the entire enterprise of science would be pointless if scientists fiddled their data.

Scientists often use faith to guide them in deciding what theories are likely to be worth testing. But finally, those theories have to be tested. Scientists have faith of a kind, but it is not blind faith, it is faith shored up by evidence, and by a culture of scepticism and honesty.

Finally, revelation. In religion, private, internal revelation is treated as a reason for belief in something. I have already mentioned the doctrine of the Assumption of the body of Mary into heaven. A Dark-Age legend grew into a mediaeval tradition, but it was finally made into a doctrine of the Roman Catholic Church only when, as late as 1950, its truth was revealed to Pope Pius XII. "We pronounce, declare and define it to be a divinely revealed dogma: that the Immaculate Mother of God, the ever Virgin Mary having completed the course of her earthly life, was assumed body and soul to heavenly glory."[17]

This kind of revelation really doesn't happen in science. The nearest approach is the kind of aesthetic, poetic affirmations that scientists, especially physicists as we have seen, sometimes make. A lovely example is from the great American physicist John Archibald Wheeler: "...we will grasp the central idea of it all as so simple, so beautiful, so compelling

---

16. Scientists are not like trial lawyers, paid to advocate a particular point of view as strongly as possible, whether they believe it or not, confident in the knowledge that somebody else is paid to advocate the opposite. Here too, individual scientists sometimes lapse, but, yet again, this is reprehended by the scientific community. It is foreign to the culture of science, even if it sometimes happens. With lawyers, it is positively admired. John Mortimer, famous English lawyer and raconteur, tells humorous stories of adversarial tactics. One respected old advocate used to blow up an inflatable cushion to distract the jury, just when his opponent was reaching the climax of his eloquence. Even if this didn't happen in fact, it is close enough to legal culture to be regarded as funny. Lawyers laugh at Mortimer's old lawyer with affection, not horror at the possible injustice meted out by the distracted jury. Advocacy is foreign to the culture of science, and is reproved when it surfaces.

17. *Munificentissimus Deus: Apostolic Constitution of Pope Pius XII Defining Dogma of the Assumption,* November 1, 1950.

that we will say to each other, 'Oh, how could it have been otherwise! How could we all have been so blind for so long!'"[18]

Or listen to the great Indian astrophysicist Subrahmanyan Chandrasekhar (1910–95):

> This "shuddering before the beautiful," this incredible fact that a discovery motivated by a search after the beautiful in mathematics should find its exact replica in Nature, persuades me to say that beauty is that to which the human mind responds at its deepest and most profound.[19]

The relationship of beauty to truth constantly recurs in physics. Isaac Newton himself, in one of his occasional moments of modesty, referred to it:

> I don't know what I may seem to the world, but as to myself, I seem to have been only like a boy playing on the sea-shore and diverting myself in now and then finding a smoother pebble or a prettier shell, whilst the great ocean of truth lay all undiscovered before me.[20]

And of course we again can't leave out the greatest physicist since Newton: "The most beautiful thing we can experience is the mysterious. It is the source of all true art and science."[21] This brings us full circle.

And to my conclusion. Science is not a religion. It is much more than a religion. It has all the virtues that religion once had, with none of the vices that religion still has. And all this with no mention of its usefulness. Great as it undoubtedly is, the usefulness of science is trivial compared with its power to inspire and uplift the spirit.

18. "How Come the Quantum?" *Annals of the New York Academy of Sciences* 480 (1986): 304.

19. *Truth and Beauty: Aesthetics and Motivations in Science* (Chicago: University of Chicago Press, 1987), p. 54.

20. David Brewster, *Memoirs of the Life, Writings, and Discoveries of Sir Isaac Newton* (Johnson Reprint Corp., June 1955).

21. "The World As I See It," *Forum and Century* 84 (1929): 193–94.

Fellow Creatures: Kantian Ethics and Our Duties to Animals

CHRISTINE M. KORSGAARD

THE TANNER LECTURES ON HUMAN VALUES

Delivered at

University of Michigan
February 6, 2004

CHRISTINE M. KORSGAARD is Arthur Kingsley Porter Professor of Philosophy at Harvard University. She was educated at the University of Illinois and received a Ph.D. from Harvard. She has held positions at Yale, the University of California at Santa Barbara, and the University of Chicago, and visiting positions at Berkeley and UCLA. She is a member of the American Philosophical Association and a fellow of the American Academy of Arts and Sciences. She has published extensively on Kant, and about moral philosophy and its history, the theory of practical reason, the philosophy of action, and personal identity. Her two published books are *The Sources of Normativity* (1992) and *Creating the Kingdom of Ends* (1996).

When {man} first said to the sheep, "the pelt which you wear was given to you by nature not for your own use, but for mine" and took it from the sheep to wear it himself, he became aware of a prerogative which . . . he enjoyed over all the animals; and he now no longer regarded them as fellow creatures, but as means and instruments to be used at will for the attainment of whatever ends he pleased.

IMMANUEL KANT [1]

Any action whereby we may torment animals, or let them suffer distress, or otherwise treat them without love, is demeaning to ourselves.

IMMANUEL KANT [2]

1. HUMAN BEINGS AS ENDS-IN-THEMSELVES

Perhaps no theme of Kant's ethics resonates more clearly with our ordinary moral ideas than his dictum that a human being should never be used as a mere means to an end. "You are just using me!" is one of the most familiar forms of moral protest. Nearly any modern person, asked

---

1. CBHH 8:114, p. 225. Kant's ethical works are cited in the traditional way, by the volume and page number of the standard German edition, *Kants Gesammelte Schriften*, edited by the Royal Prussian (later German) Academy of Sciences (Berlin: George Reimer, later Walter de Gruyter & Co., 1900–), which are found in the margins of most translations. I have also supplied the page numbers of the translations. The translations I have used are as follows:

C2 = *The Critique of Practical Reason,* translated and edited by Mary Gregor, in the Cambridge Texts in the History of Philosophy series. Cambridge: Cambridge University Press, 1997.

CBHH = "Conjectures on the Beginning of Human History," in *Kant: Political Writings,* trans. H. B. Nisbet, ed. Hans Reiss. 2nd ed. Cambridge: Cambridge University Press, 1991.

G = *Groundwork of the Metaphysics of Morals,* translated and edited by Mary Gregor, in the Cambridge Texts in the History of Philosophy series. Cambridge: Cambridge University Press, 1997.

LE = *Lectures on Ethics,* trans. Peter Heath, ed. Peter Heath and J. B. Schneewind. New York: Cambridge University Press, 1997. These are actually students' notes from Kant's ethics courses.

MM = *The Metaphysics of Morals,* translated and edited by Mary Gregor, in the Cambridge Texts in the History of Philosophy series. Cambridge: Cambridge University Press, 1996.

2. *LE* 27:710, p. 434.

to make a list of practices that are obviously wrong, would put slavery on the list, and Aristotle never seems so alien to us as when he complacently remarks that "the slave is a living tool."[3] A person, we now feel strongly, is not just a tool to be used for the achievement of other people's ends. Of course we do use each other as means to our ends all the time: the cab driver or friend who drives you to the airport, the doctor who treats your illnesses, the relative who lends you money, all do things that help you to promote your own ends. But to treat someone as a *mere* means, as Kant understands it, is to use her to promote your own ends in a way to which she herself could not possibly consent.[4] In philosophical ethics, for the past couple of centuries, the primary philosophical rival to Kantianism has been utilitarianism, the theory that we ought to promote the greatest good or happiness of the greatest number. And in the ongoing debate between these two theories, Kantians have had no greater weapon in our arsenal than the reminder that, in principle, utilitarianism permits a person to be sacrificed against his will if the interests of the many are sufficiently served by the sacrifice. Utilitarians have offered many arguments to show that such a sacrifice could not possibly, all things considered, be what does the most good. But the fact remains that, *in principle,* utilitarianism allows you to use a human being as a mere means to an end.

Kant argued that treating a person as a mere means violates the dignity every human being possesses as "an end-in-itself."[5] And he enshrined this idea in one of his formulations of the Categorical Imperative, the Formula of Humanity, which runs: "So act that you always treat humanity, whether in your own person or in the person of any other, always at the same time as an end, never merely as a means."[6] Kant identifies our humanity with our rational nature, a capacity he thinks of as

---

3. *The Nicomachean Ethics* VIII.11 1161b4, p. 1835. I have quoted from the translation by W. D. Ross, revised by J. O. Urmson, in *The Complete Works of Aristotle: The Revised Oxford Translation,* ed. Jonathan Barnes, vol. 2, using the usual marginal column and line numbers from the standard Bekker edition of the Greek text (Princeton: Princeton University Press, 1984).

4. The sense of "could not possibly" here is literal. The victims of forceful, coercive, and deceptive actions cannot consent because these actions by their nature give their victims no opportunity to consent. For a defense of this interpretation, see Korsgaard, "The Right to Lie: Kant on Dealing with Evil," in Korsgaard, *Creating the Kingdom of Ends,* pp. 133–58, especially pp. 138–39; and Onora O'Neill, "Between Consenting Adults," chapter 6 in her *Constructions of Reason: Explorations of Kant's Practical Philosophy.*

5. The idea of an "end-in-itself" is introduced at *G* 4:428, p. 36; "dignity" is explained at *G* 4:434–35, pp. 42–43.

6. *G* 4:429, p. 38.

distinctive of human beings, and he identifies our *practically* rational nature with our capacity to govern ourselves by autonomous rational choice. Respect for humanity, Kant believes, demands that we avoid all use of force, coercion, and deception, that is, all devices that are intended to override or redirect the autonomous choices of others.[7] At the same time, it demands that we help to promote the ends of others, other things being equal, when they need our help.[8] This is because an essential aspect of respecting your own humanity is regarding your own chosen ends as good and worthy of pursuit. When that same respect is accorded to others, it demands that we also regard their chosen ends as good and worthy of pursuit.

Kant describes rational beings who respect one another's humanity as forming what he calls the "Kingdom of Ends." Like the Kingdom of God on earth, the Kingdom of Ends is a spiritual or notional community, constituted by the relations among human beings with a shared commitment to a certain conception of themselves. But with a characteristic Enlightenment twist, Kant reconceives this spiritual kingdom as a kind of constitutional democracy, in which each citizen has a legislative voice. In the Kingdom of Ends, the autonomy of every person is respected and, within the limits imposed by that respect, the goods chosen by each are pursued. Moral laws may be viewed as the laws, legislated by all rational beings in congress, of the Kingdom of Ends.[9]

When people are confronted with this account of morality, the question almost immediately arises: but what about non-rational beings? If the value of humanity springs from our capacity to be governed by autonomous rational choice, what are we to say about those who, we presume, have no such capacity? What about infants who are not yet rational or the very old and demented who are rational no longer? What about the severely retarded and the incurably insane? And what about the non-human animals? Are none of these to be regarded as ends-in-themselves? And if not, does that mean that we are allowed to use them as mere means to our ends?

---

7. These restrictions follow from the conception of what others can "possibly consent to" that I described in note 4.

8. *G* 4:430, p. 39. "Other things being equal" because the duty to help others is an "imperfect" duty: we have a certain discretion about whom we help and how and how much.

9. Kant defines the Kingdom of Ends as "a systematic union of various rational beings through common laws" and also as "a whole both of rational beings as ends in themselves and of the ends of his own that each may set himself." *G* 4:433, p. 41.

In my view, most of these questions are misguided. On Kant's conception of rationality, most of the beings I just mentioned *are* rational beings. Some of them are, for various reasons, unable to reason *well;* some of them are at stages of their lives when reason is undeveloped, inert, or non-functional. These conditions, I believe, do not affect their standing as rational beings under the Kantian conception. Those claims require defense, but I won't be giving that defense in this essay. My concern here is with the one group mentioned who, I believe, really are *not* rational beings: the non-human animals.[10] I am going to argue that despite appearances, and despite what he himself thought, Kant's arguments reveal the ground of our obligations to the other animals.

2. ANIMALS AND RATIONAL ANIMALS

I am going to begin by laying out a conception of what an animal is, and how a rational animal is different from a non-rational one.

An animal is a certain kind of living entity. According to an ancient theory first advanced by Aristotle, an *entity* (or substance) is matter arranged in a way that enables it to do something, matter arranged functionally.[11] A car, for example, is matter arranged so as to travel at high speeds under human guidance. A living thing, Aristotle claimed, is a special kind of entity. It is matter arranged in such a way as to maintain and reproduce that very arrangement. Aristotle claimed that the most characteristic activities of living things are therefore nutrition and reproduction. Though for the most part made of fragile materials that are always being damaged and used up, living things are arranged in a way that enables them to constantly replace those fragile materials through the process of nutrition. And they also impose their arrange-

---

10. In the section that follows I present a conceptual account of the difference between rational and non-rational animals. It is of course an empirical question which things in nature, if anything, fit the categories I lay out there. I believe that in fact the distinction I make marks the boundary between human beings and the other animals. This is partly because I believe that convincing accounts can be given of how "rationality" in the sense I define it may be linked to certain other attributes that have been thought of as distinctively human. Kant offers some of these accounts himself in CBHH, as I discuss below. But it is possible that there are rational beings other than human beings, including some of the other species of animals that we find on this planet. And it is of course possible that the conceptual distinctions I draw are not fine enough to capture the phenomena. These questions cannot be settled *a priori.*

11. These ideas are found primarily in Aristotle's *Metaphysics* and especially in his book *On the Soul.* Kant's discussion of purposiveness in nature in the *Critique of Teleological Judgment* suggests that he is in a general way sympathetic to them.

ment on other bits of matter through reproduction. So living things carry on as if they had a purpose, but as if that purpose was simply to be, and to keep on being, what they are. They are self-maintaining entities.

An animal, in turn, is a living thing of a special kind—one capable of perception and voluntary motion. Animals maintain themselves in part by forming representations or conceptions of their environment and guiding themselves around in the environment in accordance with those representations. These two tasks—forming a conception of your environment (that is, belief), and guiding yourself around in the environment (that is, action)—may be carried out in either of two ways, which I will call the instinctive and the rational.

Our main concern is with action, and to locate the difference I need to explain Kant's conception of action.[12] Kant believes that an action always involves the interaction of two factors, an incentive and a principle. Don't be thrown by that word "incentive"; it does not mean an economic reward.[13] The incentive is the thing that makes it occur to an agent to act. It is a kind of motivationally loaded representation of an object, produced by perception or thought. When you are under the influence of an incentive, you perceive or think of a certain object as desirable or aversive in some specific way—as edible, erotically appealing, dangerous, a rival, interesting, or whatever it might be. The principle determines what the agent does, or tries to do, when he is confronted with that kind of incentive: the agent sees things of that kind as *to-be-eaten*, *to-be-mated-with*, *to-be-fled*, *to-be-fought*, *to-be-inspected*, or whatever. Incentives and principles exist in natural pairs, for an agent's principles determine which incentives he is subject to as well as what he does about them. For instance, if you are a human being whose principle is to help those in need, then the perceived neediness of another presents you with an incentive to help. If you are a cat whose principle is to chase small scurrying creatures, then the movements of a mouse or a bug are an incentive to give chase.

As that example is meant to suggest, a non-human animal's principles are its instincts. To say that an animal acts on instinct is to say that

---

12. This account of action is suggested by the account at MM 6:211–14, together with an account of the workings of instinct suggested by the discussion in CBHH.

13. The German is *Triebfeder*, alternatively translated as "incentive" (Gregor, James W. Ellington); "impulsion" (H. J. Paton); "spring" (Thomas K. Abbot); and "drive" (Lewis White Beck). None of these exactly captures the idea, which is explained in the text.

it acts on the basis of an established connection between a certain kind of representation (the incentive) and a primitively normative response, an automatic sense that a certain action is *called for* or made *appropriate* by the representation. I say that the animal responds "normatively" to the incentive, rather than merely that the incentive causes the animal's movements, because the concept of action is not adequately captured by the idea of a movement caused by a mental representation. The smell of baking pie can cause you to salivate, or to go to the kitchen, but the first of those responses is not an action, and the second is. And the difference between them cannot rest merely in the particular appropriateness or efficiency of the second response itself; it has to rest in the agent's grasp of the second response as somehow appropriate. In the case of human beings we can say that the agent goes to the kitchen because he takes his interest in the pie to be a reason for doing so, while he does not salivate because he thinks he has a reason for doing so. How exactly this difference between action and reaction is to be captured in an account of non-rational action is a difficult question, but it is clear that there is such a difference. The difference between mere reaction and genuine action may be less well-marked in the case of non-rational animals than in the case of human beings—although for that matter it is not always very well marked with us—but it is certainly there.[14]

Every animal is born equipped to make some of these instinctive normative connections, but the idea of instinctual action that I am advancing here does not depend on that fact. To that extent I am using the term "instinct" more broadly than usual. It is quite common to contrast the idea of an "instinctive response" with a "learned response." Because of this usage, the idea of instinct has fallen into some disfavor with scientists, who have come to realize how much more depends on learning than they once believed. But the term "instinct" as I am using it is not limited to inborn principles. What I will call an "intelligent" animal is one who is characterized by its ability to learn from its experiences. It is able to extend its repertoire of practically significant representations beyond those with which nature originally supplied it. So intelligence is

14. I should also note here that the slippery word "instinct" is sometimes used for mere reactions like salivating. I am not using it that way here: I am using it for forms of belief and action, both of which involve a certain "taking one thing to count in favor of another" on the part of the animal.

a capacity to forge new connections or principles, to increase your stock of appropriate responses. After the puppy's encounter with the porcupine and the beehive, the porcupine and the beehive get added to the category of the *to-be-avoided* and are now perceived in that way.

Rationality and intelligence are often confused.[15] But at least as Kant understands rationality, they are not the same thing. Kant believed that human beings have developed a specific form of self-consciousness, namely, the ability to perceive, and therefore to think about, the grounds of our beliefs and actions *as grounds.* Here's what I mean: an animal who acts from instinct is conscious of the object of its fear or desire, and conscious of it as *fearful* or *desirable,* and so as *to-be-avoided* or *to-be-sought.* That is the ground of its action. But a rational animal is, in addition, conscious *that* she fears or desires the object, and *that* she is inclined to act in a certain way as a result.[16] That's what I mean by being conscious of the ground *as a ground.* So as rational beings we are conscious of the principles on which we are inclined to act. Because of this, we have the ability to ask ourselves whether we *should* act in the way that we are instinctively inclined to. We can say to ourselves: "I am inclined to do act-A for the sake of end-E. But should I?" We have the ability to question whether the responses our incentives present to us as appropriate really are so, and therefore whether we have reason for acting in the ways that they suggest.[17]

The same contrast exists in the theoretical realm, the realm of belief. An intelligent but non-rational animal may be moved to believe or expect one thing when it perceives another, having learned to make a certain causal connection or association between the two things in the

15. Just to take one example, Mary Midgley, in her discussion of Kant in her essay "Persons and Non-Persons," in *In Defense of Animals,* ed. Peter Singer, uses them as synonyms, and therefore wonders how intelligent an animal has to be in order to have moral standing on Kant's account. See especially p. 56.

16. Being conscious of the ground of your beliefs and actions as grounds is a form of *self*-consciousness because it involves identifying *yourself* as the *subject* of certain of your own mental representations.

17. See Korsgaard, *The Sources of Normativity,* lecture III, for a more detailed account of this way of understanding the human condition. I should note here that formulating the question as "whether we really have a reason" to act as the incentive suggests a realist conception of reasons—as if they were already out there and we are checking whether our maxim corresponds to them. As I will make clear later in this essay, that is not the conception I have in mind: I believe that Kant is best understood as a "constructivist" about reasons and values: his view is that we create values and reasons through moral legislation.

past.[18] But as rational animals we are *aware* that we are inclined to take one thing as evidence for another, and therefore we can ask whether we should. For instance we can ask whether we should take a certain perception as a reason for a belief. Although a non-rational animal may be described as following certain principles in its beliefs and actions, those principles are not the objects of its attention. Rational animals, by contrast, think about and therefore *assess* the principles that govern our beliefs and actions.[19]

Kant also believed that the formal principles of reason express this capacity for self-conscious assessment. Suppose you desire a certain end-E, and you are inclined to perform a certain act-A as a result. You want to know whether you have a good reason to do this act for the sake of this end.[20] I won't try to fill in all the steps here, but Kant believed that the test of whether you have such a reason is whether the principle of "Doing act-A for the sake of end-E" can function as a normative principle. And he believed that we can answer that question by asking whether we can

18. I use the term "association" advisedly here, for I think that David Hume, in his *Treatise of Human Nature,* ed. L. A. Selby-Bigge, gives an excellent description of the workings of what I am here calling intelligence, although he mistook it for a description of the workings of reason. See especially book I, part III.

19. In the text I emphasize the differences between rationality and intelligence, but of course in fact they work together. Once our principles are in our own mental view, we can think about them intelligently as well as rationally. In particular, I believe that it is the combination of the two powers that enables us to form *hypotheses.* An intelligent animal that has often encountered bees may learn that they sting, and avoid them accordingly. It may also, from association, avoid other things that look like bees. An animal that can think about, rather than merely follow, the connection between bees and stinging can wonder whether all striped insects, or all buzzing insects, sting, form an hypothesis, and investigate accordingly. I am tempted to believe that this is one of the reasons why human beings appear to be exponentially more intelligent than the other animals.

20. As Kant sees it, the question here isn't just whether the act is an effective and efficient means to the end; it is a question about the whole package, about whether there is a reason for doing-the-act-for-the-sake-of-the-end. Effectiveness of the act is one aspect of the question, but, as I am about to explain in the text, so is the universalizability of the whole. Relatedly, Kant of course thinks it is within our capacity to reject the whole package, and so give up the pursuit of the end, if we judge the action to be wrong. This ability to set aside our inclinations when the actions motivated by them would be wrong is an essential aspect of our freedom. Non-rational animals do not have this kind of freedom. There is a subtle but important difference between two kinds of inhibition at work in the claim I have just made. A non-rational animal can inhibit an instinctive response if another instinctive response is stronger; but a rational animal can inhibit instinctive response altogether in the face of normative judgment. Failure to distinguish between these two kinds of inhibition has led to great confusion not only about freedom of the will but also in the social-scientific theory of rationality. See Korsgaard, "The Myth of Egoism," especially pp. 17–19.

will that our principles, or maxims as he calls them, should be universal laws. That's how he arrives at his famous categorical imperative, in its Universal Law Formulation: "Act only on a maxim that you can will as a universal law."21 Because we regulate our conduct in this way—in accordance with our own conception of laws—Kant describes us as having "legislative wills," and it is this fact that he identifies with both autonomy and practical rationality.22 We legislate, morally, to ourselves and each other, through our wills.

What all of this means is that rationality, for Kant, is the capacity for normative self-government. Rationality makes us capable of assessing and judging the principles that govern our beliefs and actions, and of regulating our beliefs and actions in accordance with those judgments. Rationality also makes it *necessary* for us to exercise this capacity, for as long as we are conscious of our principles, to some extent we cannot help but assess them. Once they are before our minds, we must decide whether to endorse or reject them, and act accordingly. According to Kant, the fact that human beings live under this kind of normative self-government is the distinctive difference between human beings and the other animals. And it is clear from this account why Kant thinks that we are the only moral animals, in the sense that we are the only animals whose conduct is subject to moral guidance and moral evaluation.23 We cannot expect the other animals to regulate their conduct in accordance with an assessment of their principles, because they are not conscious of their principles. They therefore have no moral obligations. But it is not obvious why Kant should think that it follows that we have no obligations to them. That is the question to which I now turn.

21. First stated at *G* 4:402, p. 15. The argument I am discussing here is roughly that of *G* 4:446–47, pp. 52–53.

22. The actual phrase Kant most often uses is "a will giving universal law." The idea is introduced at *G* 4:432.

23. There are people who are inclined to blame non-human animals for cruel or disorderly behavior, or to praise them for sympathy and cooperativeness and displays of maternal love. And there are moral theories, such as Hume's, that can make sense of this kind of praise and blame. On Hume's theory it appears that non-human animals may have what are called "natural virtues," admirable qualities that do not depend on the capacity of those who have them for moral thought. But no one—not even this sort of moral philosopher—would blame a non-human animal for being *unprincipled* or *thoughtless*. So everyone should agree that at least some moral qualities are essentially tied to the capacity for rational reflection. For Hume's account of the natural virtues, see the *Treatise of Human Nature,* book III, part III.

3. KANT'S ATTITUDE TO NON-HUMAN ANIMALS

Kant's own attitude about the moral status of non-human animals is puzzling. In the argument leading up to the Formula of Humanity, Kant frankly categorizes non-human animals as mere means. He says:

> Beings...without reason, have only a relative worth, as means, and are therefore called *things*, whereas rational beings are called *persons* because their nature...marks them out as an end in itself....[24]

The contrast comes up again in the essay "Conjectures on the Beginnings of Human History," in which Kant speculates about the emergence of humanity from our animal past. Using the story of the Garden of Eden as his model, Kant describes a process leading from the origins of self-consciousness to the development of morality that comes in four steps. First, as human beings become self-conscious in the sense I described earlier, the ability to compare the objects to which we are instinctively drawn with other objects that resemble them prompts us to try those other objects. Self-consciousness enables Eve to reflect on the fact that she is instinctively drawn to, let's say, eating pears, and then, having noticed that *apples* are similar to pears, she gets the idea that she might try one of those too.[25] The fateful result is the first free choice—that is, the first choice not governed by instinct—ever made in human history. Self-consciousness also brings with it the ability to inhibit our impulses, which in turn brings sexual sublimation and with it romantic love and the sense of beauty. That is the second step. Next we begin to anticipate the future, acquiring both the capacity to be motivated by concern for the future and the terrifying knowledge of our own mortality.[26] And then, Kant says:

---

24. *G* 4:428, p. 37. Interestingly, Kant does not in general divide the world into ends-in-themselves and mere means. As we will see later, his theory of value allows for, and even requires, a category of things that have a relative worth as ends: things that we value for their own sakes although they are not ends-in-themselves, and that get their value from our own needs and interests. This is the status Kant reserves for the ends we pursue in our actions. In general, something's having the status of a relatively valuable end depends on someone's happening to care about it, so this status could not be used to ground a general duty to animals. But it is rather striking that it does not seem to occur to Kant here that we might value natural objects for their own sakes in this way.

25. This is the practical analogue to the activity of forming hypotheses discussed in note 19.

26. These remarks summarize CBHH 8:111–14, pp. 223–25.

The fourth and last step which reason took, thereby raising man completely above animal society, was his...realisation that he is the true end of nature.... When he first said to the sheep, "the pelt which you wear was given to you by nature not for your own use, but for mine" and took it from the sheep to wear it himself, he became aware of a prerogative which, by his nature, he enjoyed over all the animals; and he now no longer regarded them as fellow creatures, but as means and instruments to be used at will for the attainment of whatever ends he pleased. This...implies...an awareness of the following distinction: man should not address other *human beings* in the same way as animals, but should regard them as having an equal share in the gifts of nature.... Thus man had attained a position of *equality with all rational beings,* because he could claim to be an end in himself....[27]

Our realization that we are ends-in-ourselves is here firmly linked with the moment when we ceased to regard the other animals as fellow creatures and began to consider them as mere means instead. It is particularly haunting that Kant imagines Adam *addressing* these remarks *to* the sheep, as if that one last vestige of the peaceable kingdom, the ability to communicate with the other animals, was still in place at the moment when we turned our backs on them.

So when we look at what Kant thinks about how we should treat non-human animals, his views come as something of a surprise.[28] Kant does think we have the right to kill the other animals, but it must be quickly and without pain, and cannot be for the sake of mere sport. He does not say why we should kill them, and the subject of eating them does not come up directly, but presumably that is one of the reasons he has in mind.[29] He does not think we should perform painful experiments on non-human animals "for the sake of mere speculation, when the end could also be achieved without these."[30] He thinks we may

27. CBHH 8:114, p. 225. I have changed Nisbet's rendering of the German *Pelz* from "fleece" to "pelt," although the German can go either way, because I think that the rendering "fleece" softens Kant's harsh point; a sheep, after all, may easily share its fleece.

28. The main discussions are at *MM* 6:442–44, pp. 192–93; *LE* 27:458–60, pp. 212–13; and *LE* 27:710, pp. 434–35.

29. The question of eating animals comes up only indirectly when Kant mentions the fact that in England butchers are not allowed to serve on juries because their profession is thought to habituate them to death. *LE* 27:459–60, p. 213.

30. *MM* 6:443, p. 193. It is not clear whether these two requirements are meant to function together or separately, so it is a little hard to know how much of a limitation Kant intends this to be.

make the other animals work, but not in a way that strains their capacities. The limitation he mentions sounds vaguely as if it were drawn from the golden rule: we should only force them to do such work as we must do ourselves.[31] And if they do work for us, he thinks that we should be grateful. In his course lectures, Kant at this point sometimes told his students a story about G. W. Leibniz carefully returning a worm he had been studying to its leaf when he was done.[32] And both in his lectures and in the *Metaphysics of Morals,* Kant has hard words for people who shoot their horses or dogs when they are no longer useful.[33] Such animals should be treated, Kant says, "just as if they were members of the household."[34] He remarks with some approval that "in Athens it was punishable to let an aged work-horse starve." He tells us that "any action whereby we may torment animals, or let them suffer distress, or otherwise treat them without love, is demeaning to ourselves."[35]

But these moral duties, it turns out, are not owed *to* the other animals, but rather to ourselves. Kant thinks we are misled by what he calls an "amphiboly"—in this case, a natural tendency to mistake an internal relation for an external one—to suppose that we owe these duties to the other animals.[36] The "amphiboly" is possible not only with respect to non-human animals, but also with respect to plants and other naturally beautiful objects. In all of these cases, the duty to ourselves in question is the duty to cultivate feelings that are conducive to morality. In the case of plants and beautiful natural objects, the feeling to be cultivated is the love of the beautiful. The love of the beautiful, Kant says, is a disposition to love something even apart from any intention to use it; perhaps this disposes us to love people for their own sakes. In the case of what Kant calls "the animate but nonrational part of creation," he says:

> ...violent and cruel treatment of animals is...intimately opposed to a human being's duty to himself...; for it dulls his shared feeling of their suffering and so weakens and gradually uproots a natural dispo-

31. *MM* 6:443, p. 196.

32. *LE* 27:459, pp. 212–13.

33. *MM* 6:443, p. 193; *LE* 27:459, p. 212.

34. *MM* 6:443, p. 193. But why only "as if"?

35. *LE* 27:710, p. 434.

36. For Kant's account of "amphiboly," see the *Critique of Pure Reason,* trans. Norman Kemp Smith, pp. 276–81; A260/B316–A268/B324 in the Prussian Academy edition pagination.

sition that is very serviceable to morality in one's relations with other people.[37]

In his course lectures, Kant made the same point by saying that non-human animals are "analogues" of humanity and that we therefore "cultivate our duties to humanity" when we practice duties to animals as analogues to human beings.[38]

But why don't we owe these duties directly to the other animals? In the *Metaphysics of Morals,* Kant argues explicitly that human beings can have duties only to human beings. He says:

> ...a human being has duties only to human beings (himself and others), since his duty to any subject is moral constraint by that subject's will.[39]

Kant thinks that we can have duties only to someone who is in a position to morally constrain or obligate us *by his will,* and that only someone with a legislative will can do that. The non-human animals cannot obligate us because they do not have legislative wills.

It is important to notice what this argument actually says, and what it does not say. What it actually says is that non-human animals cannot obligate us because without legislative wills they cannot legislate for us or participate in the moral legislation to which as rational beings we are subject. Kant does not say that a human being, as an end-in-itself, is a

---

37. *MM* 6:443, pp. 192–93.

38. *LE* 27:459, p. 212. The idea that we can "cultivate" virtue by doing something that is not itself virtuous (or anyway, not virtuous except insofar as it counts as cultivation) sounds nearly incoherent. But the expression used in this passage is careless. In the *Metaphysics of Morals* Kant makes it clear that he does not have in mind anything like Aristotelian habituation; all that he means is that we can cultivate emotions that are *useful,* in a somewhat external way, to morality. I believe that the view of the emotions behind this conception of their role in moral life and also the view of pleasure and pain that is behind Kant's conception of the emotions are both mistaken. Kant thinks of pleasure and pain, and therefore of the emotions, as something like brute tastes, rather than as having a perceptual aspect. I follow Aristotle in thinking of pleasure and pain as something like the perception of reasons, or at least of the natural good and evils in which reasons are grounded. On Kant's view, an emotion such as sympathy can give you a kind of taste for helping that accidentally coincides with your duty, while on the Aristotelian view sympathy may serve as a perception of the grounds of moral legislation. I have discussed these ideas in *The Sources of Normativity,* §§4.3.1–4.3.12, pp. 145–56 (my only previously published discussion of our duties to non-human animals), and in "From Duty and For the Sake of the Noble: Kant and Aristotle on Morally Good Action," in *Aristotle, Kant, and the Stoics: Rethinking Happiness and Duty,* ed. Stephen Engstrom and Jennifer Whiting, especially pp. 223–27.

39. *MM* 6:442, p. 192; see also *MM* 6:241, pp. 32–33.

precious commodity like a Ming Dynasty vase, while a non-human animal is an expendable commodity like a grocery-store wine glass. In a
sense, it is not an argument *from* the value of rational beings, or of the
lives of rational beings, *to* our obligations to rational beings at all.
Instead, it is an argument *from* the capacity to obligate, or the lack of
that capacity, to the assignment of a certain kind of value. Or, perhaps
more properly speaking, it is an argument that identifies a certain kind
of value—being an end-in-oneself—with the capacity to obligate. So
Kant isn't arguing that we have no obligations to non-human animals
because they or their lives lack a certain kind of value. He is arguing that
they lack this value because they cannot place us under obligations. The
question, of course, is whether he is right.

4. THE END-IN-ITSELF AND THE LEGISLATIVE WILL

This identification between being an end-in-itself and having a legislative will is reflected in the argument of Kant's *Groundwork of the Metaphysics of Morals.* Kant's argument for the Formula of Humanity proceeds
in two steps. He says:

> The ground of this principle [the Formula of Humanity] is: rational
> nature exists as an end in itself. The human being necessarily repre-
> sents his own existence in this way: so far it is...a subjective princi-
> ple of human actions. But every other rational being...represents
> his existence in this way...on...the same rational ground that
> also holds...for me; thus it is at the same time an objective prin-
> ciple....[40]

So Kant argues first that the conception of ourselves as ends-in-ourselves
is a "subjective principle of human actions." He then adds that this "subjective principle" has an objective ground. In a footnote attached to that
last remark, Kant refers us to the section where he argues that all rational
beings are autonomous. So his claim is that autonomy provides the
objective ground for our view of ourselves as ends-in-ourselves. What
does Kant mean by all this?

I believe that when Kant claims that the conception of ourselves as
ends-in-ourselves is a "subjective principle of human action," he means
that we human beings regard ourselves as capable of conferring value on

40. *G* 4:428–29, p. 37.

the objects of our choices.[41] That is, we take our choices to be the source of legitimate normative claims, claims we make on all rational beings. As he makes clear in the text leading up to this argument, Kant does not believe that the ends that human beings pursue have, in and of themselves, some sort of objective value that is prior to our interest in them. He says, "The ends that a rational being proposes at his discretion as effects of his actions (material ends) are all only relative; for only their mere relation to a specially constituted faculty of desire on the part of the subject gives them their worth."[42] More generally, Kant rejects a certain form of value realism, which holds that certain states of affairs or objects *just are* intrinsically valuable, and that it is rational to desire or promote them because they have that value. According to Kant, we do not desire things because they are valuable; rather, we take them to be valuable because we desire them. We desire things because they satisfy our appetites, please our senses, stimulate our curiosity, arouse our faculties, make us feel interested and empowered and alive. We desire things because, given our psychology, they are suited to satisfy, arouse, or please us.[43] Yet as rational beings, who are conscious of our choices and the grounds of those choices, we can pursue our ends only if we are satisfied that doing so is good—that is, that our ends are worthy of pursuit. Since our ends are not good in themselves, but only relative to our own interests, it must be that we take our own interest in something to confer a kind of value upon it, sufficient to make it worthy of rational choice. And that means that we accord a kind of value to ourselves. "What matters to me," the human being in effect says to himself, "really matters, and is worth pursuing, because *I* matter." And he embodies this conception of himself in his actions, both by pursuing the things he cares about as genuine goods, and by demanding that others help him to pursue them when he is in need.[44] That is the sense in which the conception of ourselves as ends-in-ourselves is a subjective principle of human action. We regard ourselves as *sources* of value—that is to say, as sources of normative claims that are binding on ourselves and others.

---

41. See also Korsgaard, "Kant's Formula of Humanity," in *Creating the Kingdom of Ends*, pp. 106–32.

42. *G* 4:428, p. 36.

43. I don't mean that psychological suitability or the satisfaction of need is the reason for our desiring things; I mean that it is the cause or ground of our desire.

44. As Kant puts in *The Metaphysics of Morals*, we "make ourselves an end for others" by this sort of demand. *MM* 6:393, p. 156.

The crucial move in Kant's argument, for our purposes, comes later in the *Groundwork,* when he connects this conception of ourselves with the idea that we have legislative wills. Let me now say a word more about what Kant means when he characterizes our wills as legislative. Earlier, I said that because we are self-conscious, we are able to assess our instinctive impulses to act. When you experience, say, a desire to do act-A for the sake of end-E, you can ask yourself whether you should do that, whether you have a reason. According to Kant that amounts to asking the question of the categorical imperative—whether the maxim "I will do act-A for the sake of end-E" can function as a universal law. Now suppose that the maxim in question fails the universal law test—you cannot will your maxim as a law. (Below I will say more about how exactly you determine this.) You are now "willing a law," for you now lay it down as a universal law that one must not do act-A for the sake of end-E, and you act autonomously when you conform yourself to that law by refraining from the action. Since the maxim fails the universal law test, all rational beings must also acknowledge the force of this law, and that means that you can also obligate others in its name.

Now suppose instead that your maxim passes the categorical imperative test: you can will to do act-A for the sake of end-E, and, accordingly, you endorse the principle of doing so and act on it. Even in this case, you exhibit a legislative will, for you have now adopted E as your end. And assuming that Kant's other arguments go through, this means that people have an obligation, many other things being equal, to help you in your pursuit of this end. In effect you have laid it down that it is a good thing, worthy of anyone's pursuit, that you should have this end, or be able to do it, or whatever it might be, depending on the nature of the end.

It is essential to see that, in Kant's system, all genuine value comes from legislative acts of the sorts I've just described. Kant says that "nothing can have a worth other than that which the law determines for it."[45] Importantly, there is a way in which even the special value of humanity as an end-in-itself comes from our own legislative acts. This is because in the very act of treating our own ends as good and worthy of pursuit, in spite of their lack of any inherent value, we in effect *confer* the

45. *G* 4:436, p. 43.

status of end-in-itself on ourselves.[46] In other words, value, as Kant sees it, is a human creation, made both possible and necessary by rationality. Because we are rational, we cannot act without at least implicitly endorsing the principles upon which we act, and in that sense willing them as laws. These acts of endorsement or legislation are what transform mere desiring into acts of valuing. And for Kant acts of valuing are the source of all value—all legitimate normative claims—not the other way around. Obligation does not arise from value: rather, obligation and value arise together from acts of the legislative will.

Because he believes that all value and obligation arise in this way from moral legislation, Kant concludes that only human beings can obligate us, and that therefore only human beings are ends-in-themselves. He says:

> ...morality is the condition under which alone a rational being can be an end in itself, since only through this is it possible to be a law-giving member in the Kingdom of Ends.[47]

But actually he is conflating two slightly different conceptions of the end-in-itself here. In one sense, an end-in-itself is the source of legitimate normative claims—claims that must be recognized by all rational agents. In another sense, an end-in-itself is someone who can *give* the force of law to his claims, by participation in moral legislation. Kant's metaphysics of value does make it logical to connect these two ideas, because of the way in which he traces all value—all legitimate normative claims—to acts of the legislative will. If we have obligations concerning animals, they can only follow from laws that we legislate ourselves. The only possible source of law and obligation is a rational will, and, *in this sense,* a non-rational animal cannot be the source of obligation. But it

---

46. In other words, our assigning ourselves the status of end-in-itself is not an exception to the view that the status of end-in-itself depends on the capacity to obligate. I regard myself as an end-in-myself because the dictate of my own mind can obligate me. (See also note 61.) One might suppose—indeed I think Kant may have supposed—that my capacity to obligate myself shows up only in my capacity to limit my conduct in accordance with *moral* laws. That is, he might have supposed that I do not obligate myself when I decide to pursue an otherwise optional end that I have deemed worthy of my choice. He held that we are not obligated to pursue our own happiness, on the (false) ground that we always inevitably pursue it. I think this is inconsistent with his view that we obligate others when we choose an end: if others are obligated to pursue my own happiness as a good, then so am I. Later, I will explain why I think that choosing optional ends manifests the conception of oneself as an end-in-itself.

47. *G* 4:435, p. 42.

does not follow that the other animals cannot be ends-in-themselves in the first sense—the sources of legitimate normative claims—because it does not follow that there is no sense in which they can obligate us.

Laws are by their very nature universal, according to Kant, and a universal law can extend its protection to someone who did not participate, and could not have participated, in its legislation. In his political philosophy, Kant explicitly recognized this by introducing a category of what he called "passive citizens"—including, as he supposed, women, children, apprentices, and house servants—whose rights are protected by the laws of the state even though they may not vote.[48] We are not now likely to have much patience with this category as applied to human beings, but the concept is clear enough.[49] Or indeed, even without it, we can make sense of the idea of a law protecting one who did not and could not have made it, since our most basic laws—against theft and murder, say—protect even foreigners from these violations. Suppose only men can vote, and they make a law asserting that everyone is guaranteed a right of free speech. Can a woman then obligate a man to desist from trying to silence her? In the sense of making a law, or participating in making a law, compelling him to desist, she cannot. In the sense of having a claim on him in the name of a law whose authority he acknowledges, she can. The fact that non-human animals cannot participate in moral legislation is insufficient to establish that they cannot obligate us in this later sense. The question, then, is whether we human beings ever find it necessary, on rational reflection, to will laws whose protection extends to the other animals.

5. Universal Laws for the Treatment of Animals

Now it would be nice if I could, at this point, formulate a maxim, run Kant's universal law test, show you that it leads to a certain duty, and that the duty in question is owed to the other animals as well as to people. But the argument is not going to be so easy, for there are notorious problems making Kant's universal law test work in any algorithmic

---

48. *MM* 6:314–15, pp. 91–92.

49. Some people would say that children do belong in this category. I don't agree with that, because I think "child" does not name a type of person or citizen, but rather a stage in a person or citizen's life. I realize that sounds like a mere redescription, but I believe that it actually has moral force. This is not the place to make the case, but in general I think it is important not to confuse life-stages with types of beings.

way. And, interestingly, these problems come to the fore when we try to test maxims involving the treatment of animals, for several reasons. Elsewhere I have argued that on the best reading of the universal law test, to ask whether you can will a maxim as a universal law is to ask whether you can will the universal practice of pursuing a certain end by means of a certain action without undercutting the effectiveness of that action.[50] For instance, to take one of Kant's own examples: Suppose you are in need of money, and you consider promising a potential lender that, if he lets you have the money, you will pay him back next week, although you know that in fact you will not be able to repay. You propose to make a false promise. According to Kant, you should ask whether you could at the same time will that everyone who needed money attempted to get it in this way. Kant claims that, under these conditions, people would just laugh at promises to repay money as "vain pretenses," rather than lending money on the strength of them.[51] Since making a false promise would then not *be* a means of getting the money that you need, you could not rationally will to get money by that means. So you cannot will your maxim as a universal law.[52]

But how well this test works depends on which of two types of act are involved in the maxim. Some act-types are purely natural, in the sense that they depend only on the laws of nature for their possibility. Walking and running, slugging and stabbing, tying up and killing—these are act-types that are made possible by the laws of nature. Other act-types depend for their possibility not merely on natural laws, but also on the existence of certain social practices or conventions. Writing a check, taking a course, and running for office are act-types of this kind: you can perform such acts only in societies with the sorts of practices and conventions that make them possible. Now where a maxim involves an act-type that must be sustained by practices and conventions, and at the same time violates the rules of those practices and conventions, it is

50. See Korsgaard, "Kant's Formula of Universal Law," in *Creating the Kingdom of Ends,* pp. 77–105, for further discussion.

51. *G* 4:422, p. 32.

52. It is important to remember that this is a thought experiment, designed to determine whether your maxim can serve as a universal law and so can be a normative principle. The argument in the text is not supposed to provide your motive for avoiding the false promise. Your motive springs from the fact that your autonomy commits you to willing only maxims that can serve as laws; the thought experiment shows you whether your maxim can serve as a law.

relatively easy to find the kind of problem that Kant supposed the universal law test would reveal.[53] This is because practices and conventions are unlikely to remain effective in the face of their universal abuse. That's what happens in the false promising case: if everyone abuses the convention of promising, promising ceases to work as a way of getting things done. But maxims involving purely natural actions are hard to rule out by means of the test. This is why another of Kant's examples, that of committing suicide in order to escape your own misery—he thinks that is wrong—cannot be made to work in the same way as the false promising example.[54] Suicide is a method of escaping your own misery that depends only on the laws of nature for its effectiveness, not on any convention. No matter how universally practiced it is, it will work.

I think it is obvious that most of the things that human beings do to non-human animals that come up for moral scrutiny are natural acts in this sense. The relationships between human beings and the other animals are not generally governed by shared practices and conventions. Most of the things we do to non-human animals that raise moral questions are natural actions like eating them for pleasure, or experimenting on them for information, or hunting them for sport, methods that will produce the desired results no matter how universally practiced they are.[55] So the test is not going to rule them out. But since the test would fail to rule out the same sorts of actions when practiced on human beings, we should not take this as evidence that such actions are not wrong. We should only take it as signifying the inadequacy of the test.

This is not to say that an action involving the abuse of a convention between human beings and non-human animals is not conceivable. Imagine a vivisectionist who calls out to a former pet, "Here kitty kitty kitty...Daddy's going to give you a treat," as a way of luring the animal to the laboratory table. No matter what you think about animal experimentation, you must be a very hard character indeed if you don't find

53. What kind of problem does the test reveal? The universal law test is best equipped to expose maxims whose wrongness rests in a failure of reciprocity, a willingness to perform actions whose effectiveness is parasitic on the fact that others do not act in this way. So another way to put the point I am about to make in the text is to say that reciprocity is not the moral issue involved in our dealings with the other animals.

54. *G* 4:421–22, pp. 31–32.

55. Hunting or fishing a species into extinction might be an exception to this, but a universal law test that proved that would not demonstrate a duty to the animals in question; it would only demonstrate a duty to other human beings who might wish to hunt and fish.

that scenario disturbing. Yet even in this kind of case we are not likely to construct a successful universal law test. Kant's argument against the universalizability of false promising depends on the thought that in a world where people in need of money regularly offered false promises, lenders would eventually *get the idea*. They would know that these promises were insincere.[56] That's why Kant thinks making such promises would cease to be a way of getting money if it were made universal law. Whether he is right or not, non-human animals are likely to be gullible even to the most universally practiced of human tricks. But again, this appears to be an inadequacy in Kant's test, not a vindication of playing tricks on non-human animals, lest we license playing tricks on gullible human animals.

Maxims involving the treatment of non-human animals, then, have precisely the features that put Kant's universal law test under the most strain. Usually, when confronted with such problems, Kantians turn for help to the Formula of Humanity, which seems to work far better as a casuistical tool. In many cases where it seems difficult to work out whether a maxim could serve as a universal law without undercutting its own effectiveness, it seems clear and obvious that the maxim describes an action that treats someone as a mere means.[57] But it may seem impossible to get help from the Formula of Humanity in this case, since after all it is this very formula that translates the moral law into a law about how we are to treat human beings. Nevertheless, I believe that reflection on the argument for the Formula of Humanity can show us why we have obligations to the other animals.

6. The Natural Good and the Grounds of Legislation

The argument for the Formula of Humanity appeals to the fact that we take our choices to confer value on their objects. In that sense, I have suggested, we take ourselves, and our own interests and concerns, to matter, that is, to be the source of normative claims on ourselves and other rational beings. But we do not take our interests and concerns to matter only *because* they are the interests and concerns of an autonomous

---

56. More properly speaking, potential lenders would *always already* have got the idea. Strictly speaking, Kant's test involves imagining your maxim as a law of nature (*G* 4:421, p. 31), and the laws of nature are eternal.

57. See note 4; it is often easy to tell whether an action involves coercion and deception.

rational being.[58] The fact that I am autonomous enables me, many other things being equal, to legislate (to myself and other people) against what I take to be bad for me. But it does not follow that I legislate against it only because it is bad *for an autonomous being.* Think again of the case of passive citizenship. Only an active citizen can help to vote for a law against murder. But he need not vote for it merely because he considers the unwilling death of *an active citizen* to be a bad thing. If the citizens of a state can vote certain protections for all human beings, why couldn't citizens of the human moral community, the Kingdom of Ends, vote certain protections for all animal beings?[59] For instance, one might suggest, we demand that we not be tortured, injured, hunted, or eaten, not just because of the assault on our autonomous nature, but because of the assault on our animal nature; therefore we should not treat our fellow

58. Suppose someone says: I take my interests and concerns to matter simply because they are *mine*, not because they are the interests and concerns of an autonomous being *or* of an animate being. There are several things to say in response to this. First, this would of course block any form of universalization: "mine" functions as an indexical here, and indexicals in general block universalization. So if this move were correct, it would not get us duties to people but not non-human animals—rather, it would block duties in general. Second, it is at least odd to suppose that this thought could be the basis of my making a normative claim on other people—why should they take my concerns to matter simply because they are mine? Third, we need to be more specific about what the "mine" refers to here. If it refers to "me right now" I have no ground for thinking anyone's concerns will matter tomorrow. But if it is intended to refer to me tomorrow, we have to say what makes me "me" tomorrow. Is "me" tomorrow, for instance, the occupant of this spatio-temporally continuous human body tomorrow, whoever she may be? Then I at least must universalize over all occupants of this body. At this point a range of more substantive arguments, familiar from the personal identity literature, must be used to sort out what the actual object of your concern is. I give reasons for thinking that we identify with our humanity in *The Sources of Normativity,* especially §§3.4.1–3.4.10, pp. 113–25; I am now arguing that our humanity necessarily includes our animality.

59. In one place, Kant seems at first to be granting this point. In the *Metaphysics of Morals* we find a section devoted to "A human being's duty to himself as an animal being" (*MM* 6:421–28). This category appears to call into question Kant's claim that we cannot owe duties to non-human animals: if we can owe duties to *ourselves as* animal beings, why can't we owe parallel duties to other animal beings? Unfortunately, however, it turns out that the section is misnamed, for its content is all too consistent with Kant's earlier position. Our duties to ourselves as animal beings turn out to be merely duties *with respect to* our animal nature, not duties *to* our animal nature. The category covers the duties not to commit suicide, not to maim or disfigure oneself, not to masturbate, and not to stupefy oneself through the excessive use of food or drink or the use of narcotics. The common thread of Kant's arguments—I won't review them here—seems to be that we are not to use the capacities we share with the other animals in ways that are inconsistent with, or in some vaguer way inappropriate to, our moral nature. Suicide, for example, is supposedly forbidden because "to annihilate the subject of morality in one's own person is to root out the existence of morality itself from the world, so far as one can, even though morality is an end in itself" (*MM* 6:422–23, p. 177). Kant seems in fact to be urging us to treat *our own* animal being as a mere means, a sort of place to house moral nature.

animals in those ways.[60] Autonomy puts us in a position to make the demand, but it is not the reason *for* the demand.

That is a tempting thing to say, and I think something very close to that is the truth. But in the Kantian system, saying that we legislate against something *because* it is bad for our animal nature is not quite the right way to put it. For in the Kantian system, normative reasons and values are all *products* of the legislative will. As I said earlier, Kant sees the world of value as a human construction—values result from acts of valuing, rather than the reverse. Valuing is not a response to reasons and values that are already "out there." It is response to the need, created by self-consciousness, to endorse the grounds of our actions, and so to treat them as reasons.

This means that I can't quite make my point by saying that we object to pain and torture or injury *because* they are bad for us as animal beings. There are no normative reasons and values, and so no such normative "because," until we start valuing and disvaluing things. Although it sounds odd to put it this way, there is a sense in which, in Kant's system, we have *no general reason,* antecedent to all rational legislation, to pursue the things we take to be good for ourselves. Rather, when we do decide to pursue them, and so take ourselves to be the sources of value, we create these reasons. The decision to regard ourselves as the source of legitimate normative claims is the original act that brings the world of normative reasons and values into existence.[61]

60. One may be tempted—I think that Kant may have been tempted—to suppose that the only morally important thing here *is* the assault on our autonomous being. We *choose* not to be treated in these ways, and someone who treats us in those ways therefore violates our autonomous choice. And that is the morally important thing. For if we deny that pain and injury are intrinsically bad, then we must grant that a rational being may, for his own reasons, choose to undergo them, and that is a choice we should respect. That is certainly a conclusion Kant wants, and I think rightly so. But nevertheless, saying that respect for the other's choice is the only thing that matters ignores the question of the rational being's relation to himself, and the attitude toward himself expressed by the content of his choices, which I am about to discuss in the text.

61. In *The Sources of Normativity*, §4.4.2, pp. 161–64, I argue that the cost of refusing to take ourselves to be of value is having no reasons to act at all. This is why, even though we confer value on ourselves, we are not merely relatively valuable ends. The alternative view would be that human beings simply have intrinsic value, but there are several problems with this view. First of all, since the notion of intrinsic value is a metaphysical one, postulating that human beings just have it is inconsistent with Kant's general anti-metaphysical stance. Second, it is inconsistent with his view, mentioned earlier, that all value comes from legislation. Third, and relatedly, Kant would then be making an argument from value to obligation. I believe, and think that Kant believes, that no such argument is possible, although this raises complicated issues.

But *what* we decide to treat as the source of legitimate normative claims is not just our autonomous nature. For Kant clearly supposes that unless we find that we cannot will our maxims as universal laws, we will act on the natural incentives that prompt us to formulate those maxims. To take yourself to be an end-in-itself is to be inclined to treat your natural incentives as reasons. In fact, following a Stoic tradition, Kant characterizes our tendency to do that as a form of "self-love." The value we set on *ourselves,* as ends-in-ourselves, is not expressed merely in respecting our own autonomous choices, but also in the content of those choices—in particular, in choosing to pursue what I will call our "natural good."

To explain what I mean by this, I must return for a moment to the picture with which I began. An entity, I said, is matter organized so as to do something, to serve some purpose or function. In one familiar sense of the term "good," any entity in this sense has a good: its natural good is whatever enables it to function at all and to function well. It is in this sense that we say that rust, or riding the brakes, or bad gasoline is bad for a car: they impede its functioning. In another sense, of course, it is not really the car that these things are bad for, since the car exists not to serve itself but to serve us. Its function rests outside of itself.

So when we say that something is good or bad for a living thing, say a plant, we mean something slightly different. Since the function of a plant, in the sense I mentioned earlier, is to maintain itself, it is the plant's own needs, not our needs, that are affected by things that enable or interfere with its functioning. A plant therefore "has a good" in a slightly deeper sense than a car does, since what is "good for it" is more authentically good for *itself*.[62]

Even if you don't accept that, you can agree that an animal has a good in a deeper sense still. For an animal has the capacity to experience and pursue what is naturally good or bad for it. Of course I don't mean that non-human

---

62. Kant of course denies this when he suggests that plants and non-human animals are really made for us, not for themselves. But despite what he says in CBHH, his view that the world is made for human beings follows from, rather than supports, his view that only human beings are ends in themselves. In "Aristotle and Kant on the Source of Value," I argue that Kant supposes human beings must be the end of nature because the world can be justified only if the unconditional value of morality and other values conditional upon their consistency with morality are realized (*Creating the Kingdom of Ends,* pp. 225–48, especially pp. 239–43). If the argument of this paper is correct, the world would also be justified by being good for non-human animals, although only human beings could judge that it is so. And if the argument of this paper is correct, it is also true that the world is *not* justified in that way.

animals say to themselves that their ends are good; only rational animals do that. But in general, although not infallibly, an animal experiences the satisfaction of its needs and the things that will satisfy them as desirable or pleasant, and assaults on its being as undesirable or unpleasant. These experiences are the basis of its incentives, making its own good the end of its actions. In that sense, an animal is an organic system to whom its own good matters, an organic system that welcomes, desires, enjoys, and pursues its good. We could even say that an animal is an organic system that matters to itself, for it pursues its own good for its own sake.[63]

Of course some people will be tempted to say that only an animal with a self-conception can be said to "matter to itself." The difficulty with using that idea to draw any hard moral lines is that the idea of self-conception is not univocal. I have identified, as the form of self-consciousness characteristic of rational beings, a conception of one's inner states and activities *as* one's inner states and activities, an ability to say "this is how I am now disposed to act, or to think." That is a form of self-consciousness because one can situate oneself within one's inner world, identify oneself as the subject of one's own representations. Mirror recognition might be said to be the external analogue to that: a conception of one's outer states and activities as such, an ability to think something like "this is how I look." An animal who can recognize itself in the mirror can situate itself in the outer, public world, in the gaze of others. But some animals who lack the capacity for mirror recognition may be successfully named and called, and that might be thought to imply a certain sense of self. Animals who know their place in a social order or hierarchy also seem to have a certain sense of self, in the sense that they can situate themselves in that social hierarchy. Even animals who seem to know when a threat or offer is directed at or to them must have some

63. When I say that an animal "matters to itself," or, as I sometimes put it, exhibits "self-concern," I do not mean that an animal is self-interested in the familiar sense that is related to the idea of selfishness. Despite its familiarity, I don't believe that *that* conception of self-interest can even be coherently formulated. (On this see my "The Myth of Egoism," especially pp. 2–29.) Roughly speaking, I don't mean that it wants things for itself as opposed to caring for the good of its offspring or community, say. I mean rather that it experiences and pursues its own good, it takes its own good as its end, and that these facts change the nature of its good, or of what we mean when we say it has a good. Just as we show concern for another person by promoting that person's ends (whether they are self-oriented ends or not), so we show concern for ourselves by promoting our own. To put it another way, I am trying to describe what is special about the form of an animal's good, not something about its content. I thank Seana Shiffrin, Steve Darwall, and Peter Railton for prompting me to try to be clearer about this point.

sort of primitive self-conception. The description may be *more* appropriate to animals with a more highly developed consciousness and sense of self.64 But any animal who experiences its own good and pursues it as the end of its actions to that extent matters to itself. This is a still deeper sense of "good for" than we can apply to the plant. When we say that something is naturally good for an animal, we mean that it is good from its point of view.65

Because we are animals, we have a natural good in this sense, and it is to this that our incentives are directed. Our natural good, like the other forms of natural good that I have just described, is not, in and of itself, normative. But it is on our natural good, in this sense, that we *confer* normative value when we value ourselves as ends-in-ourselves. It is therefore our animal nature, not just our autonomous nature, that we take to be an end-in-itself.66

---

64. If the details could be worked out, the idea that a more profound form of self-conception makes a moral difference might be used to support the common intuition that in general it is worse to mistreat "higher" animals, and worst of all to mistreat human beings.

65. Strictly speaking, of course, we mean that an animal's good must be connected in the right way to things that are good from its point of view. No animal enjoys or welcomes medical treatment, but the results are appreciable from the animal's point of view.

Utilitarians would agree that animals have a good in virtue of their capacity for experience, especially the experience of pleasure and pain, but they understand the matter differently. They think pleasant and painful experiences are intrinsically good and bad respectively. On their view, this sense of "having a good" is completely distinct from the functional sense explained in the text, and is the one that matters morally. I think this view is based on a false conception of what pleasure and pain are, and have so argued in *The Sources of Normativity*. See note 38. What I say in the text is based on what I take to be the correct conception—that pleasures and pains are perceptions of the good. But for my purposes in making this particular step in the argument, the utilitarian conception will do nearly as well.

66. A member of the audience at the University of Michigan asked how I might block the claim that this only shows we must value the animal nature *of rational beings.* I think that the correct reply is a fairly familiar one—that anyone who made such a claim would be lying or engaged in self-deception. For comparison, imagine a white male who claims that in valuing his own freedom he is only valuing the freedom of white males: if, unknown to himself, he turned out to be a black woman (imagine a genetic test with somewhat startling results) then he would agree that his freedom doesn't matter. Our response would be that he's either insincere or deceiving himself, that he's suffering from a failure of reflective imagination. This kind of response is harder to articulate in talking about human beings and the other animals. We have to say your legislation against being tortured or hunted or eaten would stand even if you were not a rational being. And that claim is ambiguous: in one sense it would not, since you would then lack the power to legislate. But that sense is irrelevant. I want to say: the content of the legislation would stand, even though its form would fall. Allan Gibbard helpfully proposed to me that I should make the point R. M. Hare's way: ask the challenger to imagine that he is about to be deprived of his rational nature, but may now settle the question whether he will afterward be tortured or not. Can he really say: "In that case it won't matter"? See Hare, *Freedom and Reason,* pp. 222–24.

By saying this, I do not mean to imply that human incentives are simply the same as those of the other animals. Many of them are, of course: our love of eating and drinking and sex and playing; curiosity; our capacity for simply physical pleasure; our objection to injury and our terror of physical mutilation, pain, and loss of control. To the extent that we value and disvalue these things, we are valuing our animal nature; and when we legislate for and against these things, we are legislating on behalf of our animal nature. That is part of my point, and might be enough for my argument, but there is a somewhat deeper point that I also want to make.

Obviously there are other incentives, specifically human incentives, born of the complex interactions between our animal incentives and our rational and intellectual powers—say, the desire to experience beauty or to do science or philosophy.[67] But even in conferring value on the satisfaction of these specifically human desires, we are in a sense valuing our animal nature, for we are still conferring normative value on the kind of natural good characteristic of creatures who experience and pursue their own good.[68] We are affirming that good of a creature who has this kind of good, who matters to himself, is the source of normative claims, and building a system of values up from that fact. And that is the point here: Human beings, for Kant, are not distinguished from the other animals by being in connection with some sort of transcendental, rational order beyond nature with which the other animals have nothing to do. Instead we are distinguished by our ability to *construct* a transcendental, rational order out of the essential love of life and the goods of life that we share with the other animals.

So let me put the point this way. The strange fate of being an organic system that matters to itself is one that we share with the other animals.

---

67. There are also moral incentives, of course, that only rational beings experience. When you find that you cannot will a maxim as a universal law and therefore must will to refrain from an action or do some other action instead, the law itself presents the refraining or acting to you as something *necessary-to-be-done*. In that case you are motivated by what Kant calls "respect for law."

68. The general structure here—that moral value arises when the natural good is made the object of legislation—is one that we find in early modern voluntarists such as Samuel von Pufendorf and Thomas Hobbes. According to these thinkers, God or a sovereign creates moral obligation by making laws requiring what is in any case reasonable or good. A similar structure may also be found in early moral sense theorists, such as the Earl of Shaftesbury and Francis Hutcheson, who believed that the natural good is rendered moral or normative when the moral sense approves of it. For further discussion, see Korsgaard, *The Sources of Normativity*, especially §§1.3.1–1.3.4, pp. 21–27; and §§4.5.1–4.5.5, pp. 164–66.

In taking ourselves to be ends-in-ourselves we *legislate* that the natural good of a creature who matters to itself is the source of normative claims. Animal nature is an end-in-itself, because our own legislation makes it so. And that is why we have duties to the other animals.[69]

7. Epilogue: Does Ought Imply Can?

Many people are struck with the idea that if we are obligated to treat all animals as ends-in-themselves then it is nearly impossible to lead a morally decent life. This is one source of a certain kind of urgent questioning that vegetarians are often subjected to. Do you kill the spiders in your bedroom? Do you feed your cat meat? What would you do if you found out that plants are conscious? How far down the scale of life is moral concern supposed to go? Animals matter to themselves in the sense that they perceive and pursue their own natural good. We do not think of plants as perceiving and pursuing their good, and yet like animals they are essentially self-maintaining beings and in that sense are oriented toward their own good. And they exhibit a certain responsiveness to the environment, to light and moisture. Probably there is no distinct line in nature between such responsiveness, primitive patterns of

---

69. Why shouldn't the argument of this essay extend even further down the line of the different senses of "natural good" or "good for"? Our moral values spring from reflective endorsement of the natural good we are inclined to pursue as animals, but that natural good in turn depends on the sort of good to which plants are oriented, and that in turn to the general, functional capacity for having a good. Why shouldn't we think that implicit in our endorsement of our own self-concern is a concern for the good of anything that has a good? At the risk of being thought a complete lunatic, let me admit that I am tempted by this thought. There is no reason to believe that "moral standing" is an on-off notion: perhaps it comes in degrees or kinds. We respond normatively to plants; a drooping plant in need of a drink seems to present us with a reason to water it; a sapling growing from what seems to be almost sheer rock makes us want to cheer it on. Is this because we cannot help animistically imagining that the plant experiences its good? Is it because, as I say in the text, the line between plants and animals is unclear? Or is it perhaps because the shared condition of *life itself* elicits these responses? Or could it even be that we have duties, not only to our fellow creatures, but to our fellow entities? Granted, it sounds absurd to suggest that we might have duties to machines, yet still there is something in the far outer reaches of our normative thought and feeling that corresponds even to this. A general discomfort in the face of wanton destructiveness, a tendency to wince when objects are broken, an objection to the neglect or abuse of precision tools that isn't rooted completely in the idea of economic waste... Again it might be suggested that such feelings result from a kind of animistic imagination, that we imagine that the tool feels the badness of being broken. But what is it that calls forth that animistic imagination, unless it is a distant form of respect for functional identity itself, a condition we share with all entities? I do not mention these possible consequences of my argument in order to insist on them, but only to affirm that if someone thinks this follows I wouldn't regard that as a reduction to absurdity. Perhaps we *should* treat every kind of thing in accordance with its nature, that is, in accordance with the kinds of good and bads to which it is subject.

perception and response, and full-blown patterns of consciousness and action. Certainly there is no distinct line in nature between plants and animals. Nature is a realm of gradual shade-offs, not of hard lines. Why shouldn't we have obligations to all living things? But if we do, how can we possibly meet our obligations? For it is the nature of things that life preys on life, and we cannot help that.

Many philosophers believe in the principle that "Ought implies can": if you are obligated to do something, it must be possible for you to do it. When Kant himself advanced this principle, he meant that it is possible for us to be *motivated* to do what we know we ought to do.[70] Some philosophers have taken the principle in another sense, to mean that if you find that it is physically impossible for you to do something, you cannot be obligated to do it. There are, I think, two possible reasons for taking this view, but neither applies in a Kantian framework. Many philosophers in the empiricist tradition believe that there is a conceptual connection between being blameworthy and being obligated. They believe that the standards of praise and blame are defined first, and to say that you are obligated to do something means that others would rightly blame you if you omitted it.[71] Since we cannot be blamed for failing to meet impossible standards, we cannot be obligated to meet them. But for Kant to say that you are obligated to do something means that the laws you yourself endorse say that you should do it, not that you are rightly subject to blame. Blame is a different issue.[72]

The other reason why people think we could not be saddled with impossible obligations is that, if we were, we would have to conclude that the world is in a certain way morally objectionable, a way that forces us into wrongdoing. Life does prey on life; nature is a scene of suffering; if those things are repugnant to human moral standards, then the world is set up in a way we must deplore, but in which we must nevertheless participate. But on a Kantian conception of morality, this objection is

---

70. This is how I understand the "Fact of Reason" argument at *C2* 5:29–31, pp. 26–29.

71. This is true, although in somewhat different ways, of both sentimentalism and utilitarianism. In sentimentalist theories, obligation results from the internalization of the disapproving gaze of others. In at least some utilitarian theories, we say someone is obligated to do something, in the strict sense, only if it would be worth punishing or blaming him for omitting it, all things considered.

72. See Korsgaard, "Creating the Kingdom of Ends: Reciprocity and Responsibility in Personal Relations," in Korsgaard, *Creating the Kingdom of Ends*, pp. 188–221, especially pp. 197–200.

not to the purpose. For Kant believed that moral standards, like all rational standards, are essentially human standards, and there is no guarantee that the world will meet them, or make it possible for us to do so.[73]

But these difficulties do not give us a reason not to do our best: to treat all animals, as far as we possibly can, as fellow creatures, whose good matters for its own sake. There are hard questions about how to do this, but some conclusions are easy. We certainly don't need to hunt. A twenty-first-century citizen of a developed nation certainly doesn't need to eat animals. And the supposed necessity of performing cruel experiments on non-human animals certainly isn't established merely by citing the benefits that human animals might gain from those experiments.[74] For the dignity of rationality does not rest in a supposed right it gives us to ravish our fellow creatures for our own benefit. It rests in the ability it gives us to govern ourselves, as far as it is in our power, with the principles and standards that we ourselves endorse.

So I will end by putting my point another way. When Kant isolated the idea of an end-in-itself as the only possible source of value in the world of facts, I believe that he was exactly right. The reason there is such a thing as value in the world is that there are in the world beings who matter to themselves: who experience and pursue their own good. Were there no such beings, there would be no such thing as value. Were there no such beings, nothing would matter. But we are not the only such beings. We are the beings who create the order of moral values, the beings who choose to ratify and endorse the natural concern that all ani-

---

73. Kant did think that we had reason to *hope* that the world, in ways we cannot quite see, does cooperate with our moral endeavors. It is on this thought that his religious philosophy is based.

74. One sometimes hears that certain forms of experimentation for medical purposes stand a chance of "saving many human lives." I find this way of talking worrying, because I believe that the idea of "saving a life" has an irreducibly contextual aspect that is lost or obscured when we think in statistical terms. Since everyone does die eventually, the claim that someone or something has saved a life must refer to some specific occasion on which death was possible or likely. One cannot save lives without any reference to any such occasions, although one can in this general way extend the human life span. If I am about to die on the operating table, and a certain injection revives me, it has saved my life. A medication always used in such contexts could be said to save many lives. But there is a tendency to transpose this picture onto our thinking about forms of medical treatment that instead tend to prevent certain kinds of emergency situations from arising at all, or simply to extend the life span. I certainly do not mean to denigrate the value of such treatments, which generally speaking probably do a greater service to humanity than ones that more literally save lives. Nevertheless, the question whether it is worth torturing non-human animals to extend the human life span has a somewhat different edge to it than the question whether it is worth torturing non-human animals in order to "save human lives," and we need to be aware of the difference.

mals have for themselves. But what we ratify and endorse is a condition shared by the other animals. So we are not the only beings who matter. We are the only beings who on behalf of all animals can shake our fists at the uncaring universe, and declare that in spite of everything we *matter.*[75]

BIBLIOGRAPHY

Aristotle. *Metaphysics*. Translated by W. D. Ross. In *The Complete Works of Aristotle: The Revised Oxford Translation*, ed. Jonathan Barnes, vol. 2. Princeton: Princeton University Press, 1984.

—————. *The Nicomachean Ethics*. Translated by W. D. Ross, revised by J. O. Urmson. In *The Complete Works of Aristotle: The Revised Oxford Translation*, ed. Jonathan Barnes, vol. 2. Princeton: Princeton University Press, 1984.

—————. *On the Soul*. Translated by W. D. Ross. In *The Complete Works of Aristotle: The Revised Oxford Translation*, ed. Jonathan Barnes, vol. 1. Princeton: Princeton University Press, 1984.

Hare, R. M. *Freedom and Reason*. Oxford: Oxford University Press, 1963.

Hume, David. *Treatise of Human Nature*. Ed. L. A. Selby-Bigge. 2nd ed. revised by P. H. Nidditch. Oxford: Clarendon Press, 1978.

Kant, Immanuel. "Conjectures on the Beginning of Human History." In *Kant: Political Writings,* trans. H. B. Nisbet, ed. Hans Reiss. 2nd ed. Cambridge: Cambridge University Press, 1991.

—————. *The Critique of Judgment*. Trans. Werner Pluhar. Indianapolis: Hackett Publishing Co., 1987.

—————. *The Critique of Practical Reason*. Trans. and ed. Mary Gregor. Cambridge Texts in the History of Philosophy. Cambridge: Cambridge University Press, 1997.

—————. *Critique of Pure Reason*. Trans. Norman Kemp Smith. London: Macmillan/New York: St. Martin's Press, 1929.

—————. *Groundwork of the Metaphysics of Morals*. Trans. and ed. Mary Gregor. Cambridge Texts in the History of Philosophy. Cambridge: Cambridge University Press, 1997.

—————. *Lectures on Ethics*. Trans. Peter Heath, ed. Peter Heath and J. B. Schneewind. New York: Cambridge University Press, 1997.

—————. *The Metaphysics of Morals*. Trans. and ed. Mary Gregor. Cambridge Texts in the History of Philosophy. Cambridge: Cambridge University Press, 1996.

75. I would like to thank Allen Wood, Seana Shiffrin, and Marc Hauser, who served as my commentators at the University of Michigan, for their helpful comments on that occasion, as well as the audience at the University of Michigan, for many interesting and challenging questions and remarks. I'd also like to thank Arthur Kuflik for reading and commenting on an early draft of the lecture; and Charlotte Brown and Patricia Herzog for discussion of the issues treated here.

Korsgaard, Christine M. *Creating the Kingdom of Ends.* New York: Cambridge
    University Press, 1996.

————. "From Duty and For the Sake of the Noble: Kant and Aristotle on
    Morally Good Action." In *Aristotle, Kant, and the Stoics: Rethinking Happiness
    and Duty*, ed. Stephen Engstrom and Jennifer Whiting. New York: Cam-
    bridge University Press, 1996.

————. "The Myth of Egoism." Published by the Department of Philosophy at
    the University of Kansas as the Lindley Lecture for 1999.

————. *The Sources of Normativity.* Cambridge: Cambridge University Press,
    1996.

Midgley, Mary. "Persons and Non-Persons." In *In Defense of Animals,* ed. Peter
    Singer. Oxford: Basil Blackwell, 1985.

O'Neill, Onora. "Between Consenting Adults." Chapter 6 in her *Constructions of
    Reason: Explorations of Kant's Practical Philosophy*. Cambridge: Cambridge Uni-
    versity Press, 1989.

Reclaiming Universalism:
Negotiating Republican Self-Determination
and Cosmopolitan Norms

SEYLA BENHABIB

THE TANNER LECTURES ON HUMAN VALUES

Delivered at

University of California at Berkeley
March 15–19, 2004

SEYLA BENHABIB is the Eugene Meyer Professor of Political Science and Philosophy at Yale University and director of the Program in Ethics, Politics, and Economics. She was educated at the American College for Girls in Istanbul, Brandeis University, and received her Ph.D. from Yale University in 1977. She has taught at Boston University, The New School for Social Research, and Harvard, where she chaired the Program in Social Studies. In addition to her many scholarly articles and edited volumes, she is the author of *Critique, Norm and Utopia: A Study in the Foundations of Critical Theory* (1986); *Situating the Self: Gender, Community and Post-Modernism in Contemporary Ethics* (1992), which won the 1993 American Educational Studies Association Critics' Choice Award; *The Reluctant Modernism of Hannah Arendt* (1996, 2003); *The Claims of Culture: Equality and Diversity in the Global Era* (2002); and *The Rights of Others: Aliens, Residents and Citizens* (2004), which won the 2004 American Society for Social Philosophy Award.

I. THE PHILOSOPHICAL FOUNDATIONS OF COSMOPOLITAN NORMS

1. THE EICHMANN TRIAL

It is December 12, 1960. Israeli secret agents have captured Adolf Eich-mann, and the Israeli government has declared its intention to put Eich-mann on trial. Karl Jaspers writes to Hannah Arendt: "The Eichmann trial is unsettling...because I am afraid Israel may come away from it looking bad no matter how objective the conduct of the trial.... Its sig-nificance is not in its being a legal trial but in its establishing of histori-cal facts and serving as a reminder of those facts for humanity."[1] For the next several months and eventually years an exchange ensues between Hannah Arendt and her teacher and mentor, Karl Jaspers, about the legality or illegality of the Eichmann trial, about institutional jurisdic-tion, and about the philosophical foundations of international law and in particular of "crimes against humanity."

Arendt replies that she is not as pessimistic as Jaspers is about "the legal basis of the trial" (*Correspondence,* 414). Israel can argue that Eich-mann had been indicted in the first trial in Nuremberg and escaped arrest. In capturing Eichmann, Israel was capturing an outlaw—*hostis humani generis* (an enemy of the human race)—who had been condemned for "crimes against humanity." He should have appeared before the Nuremberg Court, but since there was no successor court to carry out its mission, Arendt thinks that Israeli courts have a plausible basis for assuming jurisdiction.[2]

---

1. *Hannah Arendt–Karl Jaspers Correspondence: 1926–1969,* ed. Lotte Kohler and Hans Saner, trans. Robert and Rita Kimber, pp. 409–10. All future references to *Correspondence* in the text are to this edition

2. In the epilogue to *Eichmann in Jerusalem,* written several years later, Arendt no longer considers the analogy of Eichmann's crime to "piracy" useful and points out that "[the] pirate's exception to the territorial principle—which, in the absence of an international penal code, remains the only valid principle—is made not because he is the enemy of all, and hence can be judged by all, but because his crime is committed in the high seas, and the high seas are no man's land." Hannah Arendt, *Eichmann in Jerusalem: A Report on the Banalit of Evil,* p. 261. All references in the text to "Arendt 1963" are to this edition.

According to Hannah Arendt, *genocide* is the one crime that truly deserves the title "crime against humanity."[3] "Had the court in Jerusalem," she writes, "understood that there were distinctions between discrimination, expulsion and genocide, it would have become clear that the supreme crime it was confronted with, the physical extermination of the Jewish people, was a crime against humanity, perpetrated upon the body of the Jewish people ..." (Arendt 1963: 269).

If, however, there are crimes that can be perpetrated against humanity itself, then the individual human being is considered not only as a being worthy of moral respect but as having a legal status as well that ought to be protected by international law. This legal status would take precedence over all existing legal orders and be binding on them (*Correspondence,* 419). In this sense, *crimes against humanity* are different from other crimes, which can only exist when there is a known and promulgated law that has been violated. But which are the laws that crimes against humanity violate, particularly if, as in the case of Eichmann and the Nazi genocide of the Jews, a state and its established legal system sanctify genocide and even order it to be committed? A crime, as distinct from a moral injury, cannot be defined independently of posited law and a positive legal order.

Arendt is aware that on account of philosophical perplexities there will be a tendency to think of crimes against humanity as "crimes against humanness" or "humaneness," as if what was intended was a moral injury that violated some kind of shared moral code. The Nuremberg Charter's definition of "crimes against humanity" (*Verbrechen gegen die Menschheit*) was translated into German as *Verbrechen gegen die Menschlichkeit* (crimes against humaneness), "as if," she observes, "the Nazis had simply been lacking in human kindness, certainly the understatement of the century" (Arendt 1963: 275; *Correspondence,* 423, 431).

Although Jaspers is willing to accept Arendt's distinction of *crimes against humanity* versus *humaneness,* he points out that, since international law and natural law are not "law in the same sense that underlies normal court proceedings" (*Correspondence,* 424), it would be most appropriate for Israel to transfer the competency to judge Eichmann to the

---

3. Although technically the Charter of the International Military Tribunal (the Nuremberg tribunal) defined "crimes against humanity" only with reference to crimes committed during international armed conflicts, after the Genocide Convention was adopted by the UN General Assembly on December 9, 1948, genocide was also included as a crime against humanity but left distinct due to its own jurisdictional status.

UN, to the International Court at the Hague, or to courts provided for by the UN Charter.

Neither Arendt nor Jaspers harbors any illusions, however, that the UN General Assembly would rise up to this task (Arendt 1963: 270). The postscript to *Eichmann in Jerusalem* ends on an unexpected and surprising note: "It is quite conceivable that certain political responsibilities among nations might someday be adjudicated in an international court; what is inconceivable is that such a court would be a criminal tribunal which pronounces on the guilt or innocence of individuals" (Arendt 1963: 298).

Why does Arendt deny that an International Criminal Court is conceivable? Does she mean that it is unlikely to come into existence, or rather that, even if it were to come into existence, it would be without authority? Her position is all the more baffling since her very insistence upon the juridical as opposed to the merely moral dimension of crimes against humanity suggests the need for a standing international body that would possess the jurisdiction to try such crimes committed by individuals.

We encounter here a perplexity whose significance goes well beyond the consistency or lack thereof in Arendt's views on international law. Although both Jaspers and Arendt are Kantians and are deeply indebted to the cosmopolitan legacy of Kantian thought, Arendt is more of a civic republican, or maybe even a political existentialist, than Jaspers is. Arendt, while a Kantian in moral theory, remains committed to a civic republican vision of political self-determination. She is therefore more skeptical that an international body with criminal jurisdiction can come into existence, although, as we will see below, this is by no means her last word on the matter.

* * *

I begin my reflections on "Reclaiming Universalism: Negotiating Republican Self-Determination and Cosmopolitan Norms" by recalling this exchange between Jaspers and Arendt on the fate of Eichmann. The Eichmann trial, much like the Nuremberg trials before it, captured some of the perplexities of the emerging norms of international and, eventually, cosmopolitan justice. It will be my thesis that since the UN Declaration of Human Rights in 1948 we have entered a phase in the evolution of global civil society that is characterized by a transition from *international* to *cosmopolitan* norms of justice. While norms of international justice frequently, though not always, emerge through treaty obligations to which states and their representatives are signatories, cosmopolitan norms of justice accrue to individuals as moral and legal persons in a worldwide civil society. Even if cosmopolitan norms also originate through treaty-like obligations, such as the UN Charter, their peculiarity is that they bind states and their representatives, sometimes against the will of the signatories themselves, because they create protections for individuals as human beings. This is the uniqueness of the many human rights agreements concluded since World War II. They signal an eventual transition from international law based on treaties to cosmopolitan law understood as public law that binds and bends the will of sovereign nations.

In contemporary thought, terms such as "globalization" and "empire" are often used to capture these transformations. Yet these terms are misleading, in that they fail to address the distinctiveness of cosmopolitan norms. Defenders of globalization reduce cosmopolitan norms to a thin version of the human rights to life, liberty, equality, and property, which are supposed to accompany the spread of free markets and trading practices. Theorists of "empire," most notably Tony Negri and Michael Hardt, distinguish between *imperialism* and *empire* in order to capture the novel logic of the international order.[4] While "imperialism" refers to a predatory, extractive, and exploitative order through which one (or more) sovereign power imposes its will on others, "empire" refers to an anonymous network of rules, regulations, and structures that entrap one in the system of global capitalism. Empire is a hegemon without a center. Thus it seems that global capitalism and cosmopolitan norms are imbricated in one another. Hardt and Negri's residual skepticism toward human rights and the rule of law is so intense, however, that in the final analysis they hollow out the real challenge of cosmopolitanism, which is the reconciliation of universalistic norms with democratic politics, in favor of an undifferentiated concept of the masses or of the multitude.

I argue that while the evolution of cosmopolitan norms of justice is a tremendous development, the relationship between democratic self-determination and cosmopolitan norms is fraught, both theoretically and politically. How can the will of democratic majorities be reconciled with norms of cosmopolitan justice? How can legal norms and standards, which originate outside the will of democratic legislatures, become

---

4. Michael Hardt and Antonio Negri, *Empire*.

binding upon them? To examine this fraught relationship will be my task in these lectures. In the first lecture, I clarify what I mean by cosmopolitanism by engaging in a complex dialogue with Arendt, Jaspers, and Kant (sections 2 and 3). The distinguishing feature of the period we are in cannot be captured through the *bon mots* of "globalization" and "empire"; rather, we are facing the rise of an international human rights regime and the spread of cosmopolitan norms, while the relationship between state sovereignty and such norms is becoming more contentious and conflictual (4). I conclude the first lecture by elucidating the "paradox of democratic legitimacy," namely, the necessary and inevitable limitation of democratic forms of representation and accountability in terms of the formal distinction between members and non-members (5). This is the core tension, even if not a contradiction, between democratic self-determination and the norms of cosmopolitan justice.

2. Cosmopolitanism and Discursive Scope

The term "cosmopolitanism," along with "empire" and "globalization," has become one of the key words of our times. For some, cosmopolitanism signifies an attitude of enlightened morality that does not place "love of country" ahead of "love of mankind" (Martha Nussbaum); for others, cosmopolitanism signifies hybridity, fluidity, and recognizing the internally differentiated and conflictual character of human selves and citizens, whose complex aspirations cannot be circumscribed by national fantasies and primordial communities (Jeremy Waldron). For a third group of thinkers, whose lineages are those of Critical Theory, cosmopolitanism is a normative philosophy for carrying the universalistic norms of discourse ethics beyond the confines of the nation-state (Jürgen Habermas, David Held, and James Bohman).[5]

My argument in these lectures is closely aligned with the aspirations of this latter group. In extending the norms of discourse ethics beyond

---

5. See Martha Nussbaum, "Patriotism and Cosmopolitanism," in *For Love of Country: Debating the Limits of Patriotism,* ed. Joshua Cohen, pp. 3–17; Jeremy Waldron, "Minority Cultures and the Cosmopolitical Alternative," in *The Rights of Minority Cultures,* ed. Will Kymlicka, pp. 93–119; Jürgen Habermas, "Kant's Idea of Perpetual Peace, with the Benefit of Two Hundred Years' Hindsight," in *Perpetual Peace: Essays on Kant's Cosmopolitan Ideal,* ed. James Bohman and Matthias Lutz-Bachmann, pp. 113–55; James Bohman, "The Public Spheres of the World Citizen," ibid., pp. 179–201; David Held, "Cosmopolitan Democracy and the Global Order: A New Agenda," ibid., pp. 235–53; David Held, *Democracy and the Global Order: From the Modern State to Cosmopolitan Governance.*

the confines of the nation-state, however, Held and Bohman in particular have not addressed the paradox of bounded communities. The question of "discursive scope" has not been given serious consideration. Here I part company from my Critical Theory colleagues and join in the anxiety expressed by Arendt's puzzling observations about an International Criminal Court. I do so, not because I agree with Arendt, but because I believe that this anxiety must be indulged in by any serious deliberative democrat. In my second lecture, I turn to the challenge formulated by Arendt and argue that the relationship between cosmopolitan norms and democratic will-formation can be conceptualized as a process of democratic iterations, often resulting in jurisgenerative politics.

What is meant by "discursive scope"? Since the discourse theory of ethics articulates a universalist moral standpoint, it cannot limit the scope of the *moral conversation* only to those who reside within nationally recognized boundaries; it views the moral conversation as potentially including all of *humanity.* Put sharply, every person, and every moral agent who has interests and whom my actions and the consequences of my actions can impact and affect in some manner or another, is potentially a moral conversation partner with me: I have a moral obligation to *justify my actions with reasons* to this individual or to the representatives of this being. I respect the moral worth of others by recognizing that I must provide them with a justification for my actions. We are all potential participants in such conversations of justification.

Due to the open-endedness of discourses of moral justification there will be an inevitable and necessary tension between those moral obligations and duties resulting from our membership in bounded communities and the moral perspective that we must adopt as human beings *simpliciter.* From a universalist and cosmopolitan point of view, however, boundaries, including state borders and frontiers, require moral justification. The stipulations of discourse ethics cannot be applied to the domain of political membership without the aid of further premises; nor is it necessary to do so. A discursive approach should place *significant limitations* on what can count as *morally permissible* practices of inclusion and exclusion, engaged in by sovereign polities.

This confronts the discourse theorist with a dilemma: a shared feature of all norms of membership including, but not only, norms of citizenship is that those who are affected by the consequences of these norms and, in the first place, by criteria of exclusion *per definitionem* cannot be party to their articulation. Membership norms impact those who are not members precisely by distinguishing insiders from outsiders, citizens from noncitizens. This then gives rise to a dilemma: either a discourse theory is simply *irrelevant* to membership practices in bounded communities in that it cannot articulate *any* justifiable criteria of exclusion, or it simply *accepts* existing practices of exclusion as *morally neutral* historical contingencies that require no further validation. This would suggest that a discourse theory of democracy is itself chimerical insofar as democracy requires a morally justifiable closure that discourse ethics cannot deliver.

Unlike communitarians who reduce the demands of morality to the claims of specific ethical, cultural, and political communities, and unlike realists and postmodernists who are skeptical that political norms can ever be subordinated to moral ones, I insist *upon the necessary disjunction as well as the necessary mediation between the moral and the ethical, the moral and the political.* The task is one of mediations, not reductions. How can one mediate moral universalism with ethical particularism? How can one mediate legal and political norms with moral ones? Such a strategy of mediation is crucial to reclaiming dialogic universalism.

My understanding of cosmopolitanism situates the philosophical project as one of mediations, not of reductions or of totalizations. I do not view cosmopolitanism as a global ethic as such; nor is it adequate to characterize cosmopolitanism through cultural attitudes and choices alone. I follow the Kantian tradition in thinking of cosmopolitanism as the emergence of norms that ought to govern relations among individuals in a global civil society. These norms are neither merely moral nor just legal. They may best be characterized as framing the "morality of the law," but in a global rather than a domestic context. They signal the eventual legalization and juridification of the rights claims of human beings everywhere, regardless of their membership in bounded communities. Membership in bounded communities, which may be smaller or larger than territorially defined nation-states, is nevertheless crucial. My task in these lectures is to offer a solution to the problems of discursive scope in ethical theory by thinking through cosmopolitan norms and bounded membership.

3. KANT'S COSMOPOLITAN LEGACY

The Eichmann trial and the Arendt-Jaspers exchange surrounding it are interesting precisely because they stand at the beginning of the evolution of cosmopolitan norms, the full implications of which have only become clear in our time. To appreciate Arendt's and Jaspers's positions, as well as the differences between them, it is necessary to examine briefly Kant's doctrine of cosmopolitan right. Arendt and Jaspers are grappling with a Kantian legacy: neither accepts legal positivism or natural law. Legal positivism, best captured by Thomas Hobbes's phrase "And Covenants, without the sword, are but Words,"[6] makes an immanent moral critique of legality impossible.[7] That is, from within the logic of the legal system itself, norms refer to other higher norms, in a system of conceptual and juridical hierarchy. Any criticism voiced against this system relies upon norms that transcend the logic of legality. The moral critique of legality presents an "extra-legal" moment, alien to the logic of the law. By contrast, after the experiences of the Third Reich and Nazi dictatorship, Arendt and Jaspers consider legal positivism a vacuous doctrine and reject as illusory that the legal system can serve as its own moral foundation; yet philosophically as well as historically, for them, natural law doctrines are also obsolete. For reasons that I cannot develop further here, they accept that to postulate a fixed human nature, as natural law doctrines do, is to fall into a metaphysics of substance and to view the human being as an entity. Following Martin Heidegger's insight that *Dasein* is the only being for whom the question of its existence is meaningful, they prefer the language of "human *Existenz*" or of the "human condition" to that of human nature.[8] The human condition refers to those circumstances under which life is given to human beings. These circumstances constrain our choices, but nevertheless we are free to choose our fate. Yet if natural law is not defensible, and legal positivism is morally suspect, how can one give meaning to concepts such as "crimes against humanity"?[9] Kant's doctrine of cosmopolitan right shows the way here.

---

6. Thomas Hobbes, *Leviathan,* ed. and with an introduction by C. B. McPherson, chap. 17, p. 223.

7. Legal positivism is a complicated and rich tradition, with distinct legacies in Anglo-Saxon and Continental jurisprudence. Not all legal positivists would subscribe to the "command view of the law," defended by Hobbes and further developed by John Austin (1788–1859). For a comprehensive account of the status of international law, and of the underlying philosophical puzzles associated with it, see Marti Koskenniemi, *The Gentle Civilizer of Nations: The Rise and Fall of International Law, 1870–1960,* pp. 39–54.

8. See Hannah Arendt: "the human condition is not the same as human nature," in *The Human Condition,* p. 10.

9. See, for example, the objections that American representatives made to the category of "laws of humanity" during international negotiations after World War I: "As pointed out by the American Representatives on more than one occasion, war was and is by its very nature

The conceptual innovation of Kant's doctrine of cosmopolitanism is that Kant recognized three interrelated but distinct levels of "right," in the juridical senses of the term.[10] First is domestic law, the sphere of posited relations of right, which Kant claims should be in accordance with a republican constitution; second is the sphere of rightful relations among nations (*Völkerrecht*), resulting from treaty obligations among states; third is cosmopolitan right, which concerns relations between persons and organized political entities in a global civil society.[11]

Kant introduces the term *Weltbürgerrecht* (cosmopolitan right) in the Third Article of "Perpetual Peace," with reference to the duty of hospitality.[12] The duty of hospitality is of interest because it touches upon the quintessential case of an individual coming into contact with an organized and bounded political entity. The German reads: "Das Weltbürgerrecht soll auf Bedingungen der allgemeinen Hospitalität eingeschränkt sein" ("Cosmopolitan right should be restricted to conditions of universal

---

inhuman, but acts consistent with the laws and customs of war, although these acts are inhuman, are nevertheless not the object of punishment of this court. A judicial tribunal only deals with existing law and only administers existing law, leaving to another forum infractions of the moral law and contrary to the laws and principles of humanity." U.S. Representatives on the Commission of Responsibilities, *Memorandum of Reservations to the Majority Report*, April 4, 1919, excerpted in Michael Marrus, *The Nuremberg War Crimes Trial 1945–46: A Documentary History*, p. 10.

10. I have dealt more extensively with Kant's doctrine of cosmopolitanism in *The Rights of Others: Aliens, Citizens and Residents*, chap. 1.

11. I disagree with Jeremy Waldron's reading of Kant's theory in terms of anthropological assumptions such as the fact that the earth is round, that therefore human beings must inevitably come into contact with one another, etc. These anthropological observations correspond to what we might call, borrowing a term from John Rawls, "the circumstances of cosmopolitan justice"; they neither serve as a philosophical foundation to it nor are the most important innovation in it. See Jeremy Waldron, "What Is Cosmopolitan?" *Journal of Political Philosophy* 8, no. 2 (2000): 227–43, here p. 238. A more detailed exchange with Jeremy Waldron's reading of cosmopolitanism is in preparation. See Seyla Benhabib, *Reclaiming Universalism: Democracy and Cosmopolitanism*, with comments by Jeremy Waldron, Bonnie Honig, and Will Kymlicka and a reply (Oxford University Press: forthcoming).

12. The Articles are titled "The Civil Constitution of Every State should be Republican"; "The Law of Nations shall be founded on a Federation of Free States"; and "The Law of World Citizenship shall be Limited to Conditions of Universal Hospitality." Much scholarship on this essay has focused on the precise legal and political form that these articles could or would take, and on whether Kant meant to propose the establishment of a world federation of republics (*eine föderative Vereinigung*) or a league of sovereign nation-states (*Völkerbund*). I have used the following Kant editions: Immanuel Kant, "Zum Ewigen Frieden: Ein philosophischer Entwurf" [1795], in *Immanuel Kants Werke (Schriften von 1790–1796)*, ed. A. Buchenau, E. Cassirer, and B. Kellermann, pp. 425–74 (referred to in the text as "Kant [1795] 1923"); Immanuel Kant, "Perpetual Peace: A Philosophical Sketch" [1795], trans. H. B. Nisbet, in *Kant: Political Writings*, ed. Hans Reiss, pp. 93–131 (referred to in the text as "Kant [1795] 1994").

hospitality." Kant [1795] 1923: 443). Kant himself notes the oddity of the locution "hospitality" in this context and therefore remarks that "it is not a question of philanthropy but of right." In other words, *hospitality* is not to be understood as a virtue of sociability, as the kindness and generosity one may show to strangers who come to one's land or who become dependent upon one's act of kindness through circumstances of nature or history; hospitality is a right that belongs to all human beings insofar as we view them as potential participants in a world republic. Likewise, following Kant, Arendt argues that "crimes against humanity" are not violations of moral norms alone, but violations of the rights of humanity in our person. Are these moral or juridical rights?

According to Kant, the right of hospitality entails a claim to temporary residency on the part of the stranger who comes upon us. This cannot be refused, if such refusal would involve the destruction—Kant's word here is *Untergang*—of the other. To refuse sanctuary to victims of religious wars, to victims of piracy or shipwreck, when such refusal would lead to their demise, is untenable. What remains unclear in Kant's discussion is whether such relations among peoples and nations involve acts of supererogation, which go beyond the reasonable demands of morality into the realm of altruism, or whether they entail a moral claim pertaining to the rights of humanity in the person of the other.

The right of hospitality is situated at the boundaries of the polity; it delimits civic space by regulating relations among members and strangers. It occupies that space between human rights and civil and political rights, between the rights of humanity in our person and the rights that accrue to us insofar as we are citizens of specific republics.

We may identify here the juridical and moral ambivalence that affects discussions of the right of asylum and refuge to this day. Are the rights of asylum and refuge rights in the sense of being *reciprocal moral obligations* that, in some sense or another, are grounded upon our mutual humanity? Or are these right claims in the legal sense of being *enforceable norms* of behavior that individuals and groups can hold each other to and, in particular, force sovereign nation-states to comply with? Kant's discussion provides no clear answer. The right of hospitality entails a moral claim with potential legal consequences, in that the obligation of the receiving states to grant temporary residency to foreigners is anchored in a republican cosmopolitical order. Such an order does not have a supreme executive law governing it. In this sense the obligation to show hospitality to foreigners and strangers cannot be enforced; it remains a voluntarily incurred obligation on the part of the political sovereign. The right of hospitality expresses all the dilemmas of a republican cosmopolitical order in a nutshell: how to create quasi-legally binding obligations through voluntary commitments and in the absence of an overwhelming sovereign power with the ultimate right of enforcement.

By delineating a conceptual space between universal norms of morality and positive law with respect to the actions and interactions of individuals in the world community—he uses the locution *der Erdkugel* to characterize this space—Kant laid the foundational stones for a post-Westphalian legal order. His "Perpetual Peace" essay signaled a watershed between two conceptions of sovereignty and paved the way for the transition from the first to the second. We can name these "Westphalian sovereignty" and "liberal international sovereignty."[13] In the classical Westphalian regime of sovereignty states are free and equal; they enjoy ultimate authority over all objects and subjects within a circumscribed territory; relations with other sovereigns are voluntary and contingent; these relations are limited in kind and scope to transitory military and economic alliances as well as cultural and religious affinities; above all, states "regard cross-border processes as a 'private matter' concerning only those immediately affected."[14]

By contrast, according to conceptions of liberal international sovereignty the formal equality of states is increasingly dependent upon their subscribing to common values and principles, such as the observance of human rights, the rule of law, and respect for democratic self-determination. Sovereignty no longer means ultimate and arbitrary authority over a circumscribed territory; states that treat their citizens in violation of certain norms, close their borders, prevent freedoms of market, speech, and association, and the like are thought not to belong within a specific society of states or alliances; the anchoring of domestic principles in institutions shared with others is crucial. In Michael Ignatieff's words, this mode of sovereignty is subject to the "naming and shaming" processes of civil and cultural sanctions, which, while not forcing states to comply militarily, nonetheless can influence their behavior.[15]

13. David Held, "Law of States, Law of Peoples: Three Models of Sovereignty," *Legal Theory* 8 (2002): 1–44; here pp. 4ff.

14. Ibid., p. 4.

15. Michael Ignatieff, *Human Rights as Politics and Idolatry,* with commentary by K. Anthony Appiah, David Hollinger, Thomas W. Laquer, and Diane F. Orentlicher, p. 12.

Cosmopolitan norms go beyond liberal international sovereignty in that, while historically the subjects of international law were states and organized political entities, "cosmopolitan right" envisages a conceptual and juridical space for a domain of rights-relations that would be binding upon nonstate actors as well as upon state actors when they come into contact with individuals who are not members of their own polities. Kant envisaged a world in which all members of the human race eventually would became participants in a civil order and enter into a condition of lawful association with one another. Yet this civil condition of lawful coexistence was not equivalent to membership in a republican polity. In an extremely important move, Kant argued that cosmopolitan citizens still needed their individual republics to be citizens at all. This is why he so carefully distinguished a "world government" from a "world federation." A "world government" would result only in a "universal monarchy," he argued, and would be a "soulless despotism," whereas a federative union (*eine föderative Vereinigung*) would still permit the exercise of citizenship within bounded communities (Kant [1795] 1923: 453).

Concepts such as "the right to universal hospitality," "crimes against humanity," and "the right to have rights" (Arendt) are the legacy of Kantian cosmopolitanism. In each instance, they articulate a shared philosophical perplexity: Kant, Arendt, and Jaspers want to give these concepts a binding power over and beyond the moral obligation that they impose on individual agents. These concepts should not be treated as mere "oughts"; they must generate binding norms not only for individuals but for collective actors as well, and, in the first place, for states and governments. The right to universal hospitality, for example, if it means anything at all, imposes an obligation on the political sovereign, by interdicting states to deny refuge and asylum to those whose intentions are peaceful and if refusing them sojourn would result in their demise. The right to have rights, in Arendt's memorable formulation,[16] prohibits states from *denaturalizing* individuals by denying them citizenship rights and state protection.

The concept of "crimes against humanity" expressly prohibits government officials, state bureaucrats, and others in positions of power from acting in such a way as to engage in "murder, extermination, enslavement, deportation, and other inhumane acts committed against any

---

16. See Hannah Arendt, *The Origins of Totalitarianism*, pp. 296–99.

civilian population, before or during war; or persecution on political, racial or religious grounds...whether or not in violation of domestic law of the country where perpetrated."[17] The "right to have rights" and "crimes against humanity" are intended not only to provide precepts of individual conduct but to articulate principles of public morality and institutional justice as well. They transcend the specific positive laws of any existing legal order by stipulating norms that no promulgated legislation ought to violate. What then is the philosophical puzzle concerning cosmopolitan norms? I distinguish among three different issues here:

- First are questions concerning the philosophical foundations of cosmopolitan right claims. Certainly, prior to Kant the Western legal tradition also recognized a sphere of international law that went beyond specific treaty obligations entered into by various sovereigns. Stoic conceptions of natural law, Roman conceptions of *jus gentium* (the law of nations), and Christian conceptions of the law of the Christian commonwealth established guidelines for nations in their dealings with one another. Kant relied upon the work of other natural law thinkers prior to him, such as Samuel von Pufendorf, Hugo Grotius, and Emmerich von Vattel.[18] But how could one justify *cosmopolitan right* without falling back upon some conception of a fixed human nature or a shared system of religious belief? What, if any, are the ontological foundations of cosmopolitan right after Kantian critical philosophy?

- Second, cosmopolitan right, if it is to deserve its name at all, must bind the actions and the will of sovereign legal and political entities. Cosmopolitan right "trumps" positive law, although there is no higher instance besides sovereign states, with the authority to enforce it. What is the authority of norms that themselves are not backed by a higher authority, either in the conceptual sense or in the sense of enforcement?

17. Article 6 (c), Charter of the International Military Tribunal, as cited in James Friedman, "Arendt in Jerusalem, Jackson at Nuremberg: Presuppositions of the Nazi War Crimes Trials," *Israel Law Review* 28, no. 4 (1994): 601–25; here p. 614.

18. Richard Tuck, *The Rights of War and Peace: Political Thought and International Order from Grotius to Kant.*

- Third, Kant, Arendt, and Jaspers, although anticipating a world society governed by cosmopolitan norms of justice, also proceed from the premise of a "divided" humankind that is organized into discrete, self-determining, and sovereign political entities. At times this is a concession to political realism on their part; more often though, and particularly for Kant and Arendt, the division of humankind into self-governing polities is not a *factum brutum*, but has a value in itself. Whereas Jaspers is ultimately willing to abdicate republican self-governance and entertain the possibility of world government,[19] neither Kant nor Arendt can reconcile world government with the values of private and public autonomy. Therefore, the tension between the demands of cosmopolitan justice and the values of republican self-governance is greatest in their work.

I address these philosophical puzzles in my lectures by discussing them in reverse order. I will proceed from an analysis of the tension between cosmopolitan norms and republican self-governance to discuss the authority of cosmopolitan norms and finally arrive at the ontological puzzle. My concern is less with the kind of ontological universe in which cosmopolitan norms can be said to "exist," but more with how these norms, whatever their ontological status, can shape, guide, and constrain our political life, by creating new spaces for evaluative articulation and by extending our political imagination.

4. The Rise of an International Human Rights Regime

Kant, Arendt, and Jaspers anticipated and intimated the evolution of cosmopolitan norms of justice. In the intervening years, institutional developments have led us to frame certain questions differently, while others can very much be understood in terms of puzzles they had identified. What are these institutional developments? Since the 1948 Universal Declaration of Human Rights an international human rights regime has emerged. By an "international human rights regime," I understand a set of interrelated and overlapping global and regional regimes that encompass human rights treaties as well as customary international law or international soft law.[20]

---

19. See Karl Jaspers, *The Origin and Goal of History,* trans. Michael Bullock, pp. 193–213.

20. Such examples would include the UN treaty bodies under the International Covenant on Civil and Political Rights, the International Covenant on Economic, Social and Cultural Rights, the International Convention on the Elimination of All Forms of Racial

The rise of multiple human rights regimes causes both collusion and confluence between international and domestic law. The consequence is a complex system of interdependence that gives the lie to Carl Schmitt's dictum that "there is no sovereign to force the sovereign."[21] As Gerald Neuman observes, "National constitutions vary greatly in their provisions regarding the relationship between international and domestic law. Some are more or less dualist, treating international norms as part of a distinct legal system.... Others are more or less monist, treating international law and domestic law as a single legal system, often giving some category of international norms legal supremacy over domestic legislation."[22] This transformation of human rights codes into generalizable norms that ought to govern the behavior of sovereign states is one of the most promising aspects of contemporary political globalization processes.

We are witnessing this development in at least three related areas:

i. *Crimes against Humanity, Genocide, and War Crimes.* The concept of *crimes against humanity*, first articulated by the Allied powers in the Nuremberg trials of Nazi war criminals, stipulates that there are certain norms in accordance with which state officials as well as private individuals are to treat one another, even, and precisely, under conditions of extreme hostility and war. Ethnic cleansing, mass executions, rape, and cruel and unusual punishment of the enemy, such as dismemberment, that occur under conditions of a "widespread or systematic attack" are proscribed and can all constitute sufficient grounds for the indictment and prosecution of individuals who are responsible for these actions,

---

Discrimination, the Convention on the Elimination of All Forms of Discrimination against Women, the Convention against Torture and Other Cruel, Inhuman or Degrading Treatment or Punishment, and the Convention on the Rights of the Child. The establishment of the European Union has been accompanied by a Charter of Fundamental Rights and by the formation of a European Court of Justice. The European Convention for the Protection of Human Rights and Fundamental Freedoms, which encompasses states that are not EU members as well, permits the claims of citizens of adhering states to be heard by a European Court of Human Rights. Parallel developments can be seen on the American continent through the establishment of the Inter-American System for the Protection of Human Rights and the Inter-American Court of Human Rights. See Gerald Neuman, "Human Rights and Constitutional Rights: Harmony and Dissonance," *Stanford Law Review* 55, no. 5 (May 2003): 1863–1901. By "soft law" is meant an international agreement that is not concluded as a treaty and therefore not covered by the Vienna Convention on the Law of Treaties. Such an agreement is adopted by states that do not want to have a treaty-based relationship and thus be governed by treaty or customary law in the event of a breach of their obligations.

21. Carl Schmitt, *The Concept of the Political*, trans., introduction, and notes by George Schwab.

22. Neuman, "Human Rights and Constitutional Rights," p. 1875.

even if they are or were state officials or subordinates who acted under orders. The refrain of the soldier and the bureaucrat—"I was only doing my duty"—is no longer an acceptable ground for abrogating the rights of humanity in the person of the other, even when, and especially when, the other is your enemy.

During the Nuremberg trials, the term "crimes against humanity" was used to refer to crimes committed during international armed conflicts.[23] Immediately after the Nuremberg trials, *genocide* was also included as a crime against humanity but was left distinct due to its own jurisdictional status, which was codified in Article II of the Convention on the Prevention and Punishment of the Crime of Genocide (1948). Genocide is the knowing and willful destruction of the way of life and existence of a collectivity whether through acts of total war, racial extinction, or ethnic cleansing. It is the supreme crime against humanity, in that it aims at the destruction of human variety, of the many and diverse ways of being human. Genocide does not only eliminate individuals who may belong to this or another group; it aims at the extinction of their way of life.[24]

War crimes, by contrast, as defined in the Statute of the International Criminal Tribunal for the Former Yugoslavia (1993), initially applied only to *international conflicts*. With the Statute of the International Criminal Tribunal for Rwanda (1994), recognition was extended to *internal armed conflict* as well. "War crimes" now refers to international as well as internal conflicts that involve the mistreatment or abuse of civilians and noncombatants as well as one's enemy in combat.[25]

Thus, in a significant development since World War II, crimes against humanity, genocide, and war crimes have all been extended to apply not only to atrocities that take place in international conflict situations but also to events *within* the borders of a sovereign country that may be perpetrated by officials of that country and/or by citizens during peacetime.

---

23. Charter of the International Military Tribunal, 1945, Art. 6 (c) as cited in Steven R. Ratner and Jason S. Abrams, *Accountability for Human Rights Atrocities in International Law: Beyond the Nuremberg Legacy*, pp. 26–45; William A. Schabas, *An Introduction to the International Criminal Court*, pp. 6–7.

24. Ratner and Abrams, *Accountability for Human Rights Atrocities*, pp. 35–36.

25. Ibid., pp. 80–110; Schabas, *Introduction to the International Criminal Court*, pp. 40–53.

The continuing rearticulation of these three categories in international law, and in particular their extension from situations of international armed conflict to civil wars within a country and to the actions of governments against their own people, has in turn encouraged the emergence of the concept of "humanitarian interventions."

ii. *Humanitarian Interventions.* The theory and practice of humanitarian interventions, which the United States and its North Atlantic Treaty Organization (NATO) allies appealed to in order to justify their actions against the ethnic cleansing of the civilian population in Bosnia and Kosovo, suggest that when a sovereign nation-state egregiously violates the basic human rights of a segment of its population on account of religion, race, ethnicity, language, or culture there is a *generalized moral obligation* to end actions such as genocide and crimes against humanity.[26] In such cases human rights norms trump state sovereignty claims. No matter how controversial in interpretation and application they may be, humanitarian interventions are based on the growing consensus that the sovereignty of the state over the life, liberty, and property of its citizens or residents is not unconditional or unlimited.[27] State sovereignty is no longer the ultimate arbiter of the fate of citizens or residents. The exercise of state sovereignty even within domestic borders is increasingly subject to internationally recognized norms that prohibit genocide, ethnocide, mass expulsions, enslavement, rape, and forced labor.

iii. *Transnational Migration.* The third area in which international human rights norms are creating binding guidelines upon the will of sovereign nation-states is that of international migration. *Humanitarian interventions* deal with the treatment by nation-states of their citizens or residents; *crimes against humanity* and *war crimes* concern relations among enemies or opponents in nationally bounded as well as extraterritorial settings. *Transnational migrations*, by contrast, pertain to the rights of individuals, not insofar as they are considered members of concrete bounded communities but insofar as they are human beings *simpliciter*, when they come into contact with, seek entry into, or want to become members of territorially bounded communities.

---

26. Allen Buchanan, "From Nuremberg to Kosovo: The Morality of Illegal International Legal Reform," *Ethics* 111 (July 2001): 673–705.

27. Michael Doyle, "The New Interventionism," in *Global Justice*, ed. Thomas W. Pogge, pp. 219–42.

The Universal Declaration of Human Rights recognizes the right to freedom of movement across boundaries—a right to emigrate (that is, to leave a country), but not a right to immigrate, a right to enter a country (Article 13). Article 14 anchors the right to enjoy asylum under certain circumstances, while Article 15 of the Declaration proclaims that everyone has "the right to a nationality." The second part of Article 15 stipulates: "No one shall be arbitrarily deprived of his nationality nor denied the right to change his nationality."[28]

Yet the Universal Declaration is silent on states' *obligations* to grant entry to immigrants, to uphold the right of asylum, and to permit citizenship to alien residents and denizens. These rights have no specific addressees, and they do not anchor *specific* obligations on the part of second and third parties to comply with them. Despite the cross-border character of these rights, the Universal Declaration upholds the sovereignty of individual states. Thus a series of internal contradictions between universal human rights and territorial sovereignty is built right into the logic of the most comprehensive international law document in our world.

The Geneva Convention of 1951 Relating to the Status of Refugees (and its Protocol added in 1967) is the second most important international legal document after the Universal Declaration. Nevertheless, neither the existence of this document nor the creation of the United Nations High Commissioner on Refugees has altered the fact that the Geneva Convention and its Protocol are binding on signatory states alone and can be brazenly disregarded by nonsignatories and, at times, even by signatory states themselves.

Some lament the fact that as international human rights norms are increasingly invoked in immigration, refugee, and asylum disputes, territorially delimited nations are challenged not only in their claims to control their borders but also in their prerogative to define the "boundaries of the national community." Others criticize the Universal Declaration for not endorsing "institutional cosmopolitanism," and for upholding an "interstatal" rather than a truly cosmopolitan international order.[29] Yet one thing is clear: the treatment by states of citizens and residents within their boundaries is no longer an unchecked prerogative.

---

28. Text available at http://www.unhchr.ch/udhr/lang/eng.htm.

29. For the first position, see David Jacobson, *Rights across Borders: Immigration and the Decline of Citizenship,* p. 5; for the second, Onora O'Neill, *Bounds of Justice,* p. 180.

One of the cornerstones of Westphalian sovereignty, namely, that states enjoy ultimate authority over all objects and subjects within their circumscribed territory, has been delegitimized through international law. I concur with David Held that cosmopolitan justice "conceives of international law as a system of public law. . . .Cosmopolitan sovereignty is the law of peoples because it places at its center the primacy of individual human beings as political agents, and the accountability of power."[30]

The evolution of cosmopolitan norms is rife with a central contradiction: while territorially bounded states are increasingly subject to international norms, states themselves are the principal signatories as well as enforcers of the multiple and varied human rights treaties and conventions through which international norms spread. In this process, the state is both sublated and reinforced in its authority. Throughout the international system, as long as territorially bounded states are recognized as the sole legitimate units of negotiation and representation, a tension, and at times even a fatal contradiction, is palpable: the modern state system is caught between *sovereignty* and *hospitality,* between the prerogative to choose to be a party to cosmopolitan norms and human rights treaties and the obligation to extend recognition of these human rights to all.

In a Kantian vein, by "hospitality" I mean all human rights claims that are cross-border in scope. The tension between sovereignty and hospitality is all the more real for liberal democracies since they are based on the fragile but necessary negotiation of constitutional universalism and territorial sovereignty.

30. Held, "Law of States, Law of Peoples," p. 1. In this article Held develops cosmopolitanism into a "moral and political outlook," characterized by adherence to seven principles: equal worth and dignity; active agency; personal responsibility and accountability; consent; reflexive deliberation; inclusiveness and subsidiarity; and avoidance of serious harm and the amelioration of urgent need (p. 24). I am puzzled by this list and fear that, with this move, cosmopolitanism is understood by Held as a "comprehensive doctrine" in Rawls's sense. A comprehensive doctrine entails not only a vision of justice but one of the good as well. I think that this is unnecessary; from the standpoint of a Kantian cosmopolitan federalist understanding it is also incoherent to make this move. What the elements of an "overlapping cosmopolitan consensus" are is an open question, but I disagree that to spell them out one must subscribe to a comprehensive account such as Held provides. Furthermore, many of these principles are aspects of a wide variety of moral theories, so it is unclear to me what is gained by this added stipulation.

5. THE PARADOX OF DEMOCRATIC LEGITIMACY

Ideally, democratic rule means that all members of a sovereign body are to be respected as bearers of human rights, and that the consociates of this sovereign freely associate with one another to establish a regime of self-governance under which each is to be considered both author of the laws and subject to them. This ideal of the original contract, as formulated by Jean-Jacques Rousseau and adopted by Kant, is a heuristically useful device for capturing the logic of modern democracies. Modern democracies, unlike their ancient counterparts, conceive of their citizens as rights-bearing consociates. The rights of the citizens rest upon the "rights of man." *Les droits de l'homme et de citoyen* do not contradict one another; quite to the contrary, they are coimplicated. This is the idealized logic of the modern democratic revolutions following the American and French examples.

The democratic sovereign draws its legitimacy not merely from its act of constitution, but, equally significantly, from the conformity of this act to universal principles of human rights that are in some sense said to precede and antedate the will of the sovereign and in accordance with which the sovereign undertakes to bind itself. "We, the people" refers to a particular human community, circumscribed in space and time, sharing a particular culture, history, and legacy; yet this people establishes itself as a democratic body by acting in the name of the "universal." The tension between universal human rights claims and particularistic cultural and national identities is constitutive of democratic legitimacy. Modern democracies act in the name of universal principles that are then circumscribed within a particular civic community. This is the "Janus face of the modern nation," in the words of Jürgen Habermas.[31]

Since Rousseau, however, we also know that the will of the democratic people may be legitimate but unjust, unanimous but unwise. "The general will" and "the will of all" may not overlap either in theory or in practice. Democratic rule and the claims of justice may contradict one another. The democratic precommitments expressed in the idealized allegiance to universal human rights—life, liberty, and property—need to be reactualized and renegotiated within actual polities as democratic intentions. Potentially, there is always a conflict between an interpreta-

---

31. Jürgen Habermas, "The European Nation-State: On the Past and Future of Sovereignty and Citizenship," in *The Inclusion of the Other: Studies in Political Theory*, ed. Ciaran Cronin and Pablo De Greiff, pp. 105–29; here p. 115.

tion of these rights claims that precede the declared formulations of the sovereign and the actual enactments of the democratic people that could potentially violate such interpretations. We encounter this conflict in the history of political thought as the conflict between liberalism and democracy, and even as the conflict between constitutionalism and popular sovereignty. In each case the logic of the conflict is the same: to assure that the democratic sovereign will uphold certain constraints upon its will in virtue of its precommitment to certain formal and substantive interpretations of rights. Liberal and democratic theorists disagree with one another as to the proper balance of this mix: while strong liberals want to bind the sovereign will through precommitments to a list of human rights, strong democrats reject such a prepolitical understanding of rights and argue that they must be open to renegotiation and reinterpretation by the sovereign people—admittedly within certain limits.

Yet this paradox of democratic legitimacy has a corollary that has been little noted: every act of self-legislation is also an act of self-constitution. "We, the people," who agree to bind ourselves by these laws, are also defining ourselves as a "we" in the very act of self-legislation. It is not only the general laws of self-government that are articulated in this process; the community that binds itself by these laws defines itself by drawing boundaries as well, and these boundaries are territorial as well as civic. The will of the democratic sovereign can extend only over the territory that is under its jurisdiction; democracies require borders. Empires have frontiers, while democracies have borders. Democratic rule, unlike imperial dominion, is exercised in the name of some specific constituency and binds that constituency alone. Therefore, at the same time that the sovereign defines itself *territorially,* it also defines itself in *civic* terms. Those who are full members of the sovereign body are distinguished from those who "fall under its protection," but who do not enjoy "full membership rights." Women and slaves, servants, propertyless white males, non-Christians, and nonwhite races were historically excluded from membership in the sovereign body and from the project of citizenship. They were, in Kant's famous words, "mere auxiliaries to the commonwealth."[32]

---

32. Immanuel Kant, "Die Metaphysik der Sitten in zwei Teilen" [1797], in *Immanuel Kants Werke,* p. 121; *The Metaphysics of Morals,* trans. and ed. Mary Gregor, p. 140.

The boundaries of the civil community are of two kinds then: first, these boundaries define the status of those who enjoy second-class citizenship status within the polity but who can be considered members of the sovereign people in virtue of cultural, familial, and religious attachments. Women, as well as nonpropertied males before the extension of universal suffrage, fell under this category; the status of these groups is distinct from that of other residents who not only have second-class status but who also do not belong to the sovereign people in virtue of relevant identity-based criteria. Such was the case with African-American slaves until after the Civil War and the declaration in 1865 of the 14th Amendment to the U.S. Constitution, which conferred U.S. citizenship upon African-American peoples; such was also the status of American Indians who were granted tribal sovereignty. The status of those of Jewish faith in the original thirteen colonies of the United States can be described as one of transition from being "a mere auxiliary to the commonwealth" to being a full-fledged citizen.

Second, in addition to these groups are those residents of the commonwealth who do not enjoy full citizenship rights because they do not possess the requisite identity criteria through which the people defines itself, or because they belong to some other commonwealth, or because they choose to remain as outsiders. These are the "aliens" and "foreigners" amidst the democratic people. They are different from second-class citizens like women and workers, as well as from slaves and tribal peoples. Their status is governed by mutual treaties among sovereign entities—as would be the case with official representatives of a state-power upon the territory of the other; and if they are civilians, and live among citizens for economic, religious, or other cultural reasons, their rights and claims exist in that murky space defined by respect for human rights on the one hand and by international customary law on the other. They are refugees from religious persecution, merchants and missionaries, migrants and adventurers, explorers and fortune-seekers.

I have circumscribed in general theoretical terms the paradox of democratic legitimacy. The paradox is that the republican sovereign should undertake to bind its will by a series of precommitments to a set of formal and substantive norms, usually referred to as "human rights."

While this paradox can never be fully resolved in democracies, its impact can be mitigated through the renegotiation and reiteration of the dual commitments to human rights and sovereign self-determination.

Popular sovereignty is not identical with territorial sovereignty, although the two are closely linked, both historically and normatively. Popular sovereignty means that all full members of the demos are entitled to have a voice in the articulation of the laws by which the demos governs itself. Democratic rule extends its jurisdiction to those who can view themselves as the authors of such rule. But there has never been a perfect overlap between the circle of those who stand under the law's authority and those recognized as full members of the demos. Every democratic demos has disenfranchised some, while recognizing only certain individuals as full citizens. Territorial sovereignty and democratic voice have never matched completely. Yet presence within a circumscribed territory, and in particular continuing residence within it, brings one under the authority of the sovereign—whether democratic or not. The new politics of cosmopolitan membership is about negotiating this complex relationship between rights of full membership, democratic voice, and territorial residence. While the demos, as the popular sovereign, must assert control over a specific territorial domain, it can also engage in reflexive acts of self-constitution, whereby the boundaries of the demos can be readjusted.

The evolution of cosmopolitan norms, from crimes against humanity to norms extending to refuge, asylum, and immigration, has caught most liberal democracies within a network of obligations to recognize certain rights claims. Although the asymmetry between the "demos" and the "populus," the democratic people and the population as such, has not been overcome, norms of hospitality have gone far beyond what they were in Kant's understanding: the status of alienage is now protected by civil as well as international laws; the guest is no longer a guest but a resident alien, as we say in American parlance, or a "foreign co-citizen," as Europeans say. In a remarkable evolution of the norms of hospitality, within the European Union in particular, the rights of third-country nationals are increasingly protected by the European Convention on Fundamental Rights and Freedoms, with the consequence that citizenship, which was once the privileged status entitling one to rights, has now been disaggregated into its constituent elements. Liberal democracies must learn to negotiate these paradoxes between the spread of cosmopolitan norms and the boundedness of democratic communities; that they can do so successfully is the topic, as well as the hope, of my second lecture.

II. DEMOCRATIC ITERATIONS: THE LOCAL,
THE NATIONAL, AND THE GLOBAL

I would like to begin with the following proposition: We are at a point in the political evolution of human communities when the unitary model of citizenship that bundled together residency upon a single territory with the subjection to a common bureaucratic administration of a people perceived to be a more or less cohesive entity is at an end. We are facing today the "disaggregation of citizenship." These are institutional developments that unbundle the three constitutive dimensions of citizenship, namely: collective identity, the privileges of political membership, and the entitlements of social rights and benefits. More and more human beings, and hailing from many parts of the world extending from North America to Europe to South Asia and Latin America, find themselves not sharing in the collective identity of their host countries while enjoying certain rights and benefits as guest workers or permanent residents. The entitlement to social rights, which T. H. Marshall had considered the pinnacle of citizenship, has been dissociated from shared collective identity and political membership.[1]

Part 1 considers the disaggregation of citizenship; building on the promise of "jurisgenerative politics," part 2 develops the concept of "democratic iterations" as offering normative and institutional solutions to the paradoxes of democratic legitimacy. Examining several cases from contemporary European debates about the rights of foreigners and immigrants, parts 3 and 4 illustrate processes of democratic iteration at work. Democratic iterations are complex ways of mediating the will- and opinion-formation of democratic majorities and cosmopolitan norms. In conclusion, I return to the ontological puzzles of cosmopolitan norms outlined in lecture I (part 5).

1. Disaggregation of Citizenship
within the European Union

Within the European Union, in which this disaggregation effect has proceeded most intensively and which I have examined in detail in other writings,[2] the privileges of political membership now accrue to all citi-

---

1. T. H. Marshall, *Citizenship and Social Class and Other Essays.* See also my essay "Transformations of Citizenship: The Case of Contemporary Europe," *Government and Opposition: An International Journal of Comparative Politics* 37, no. 4 (2002): 439–65.

2. See Seyla Benhabib, *The Claims of Culture: Equality and Diversity in the Global Era,* chap. 6; and Benhabib, *The Rights of Others: Aliens, Citizens and Residents,* chap. 4.

zens of member countries of the EU who may be residing in territories other than those of their nationality. It is no longer nationality of origin but EU citizenship that entitles one to these rights. Citizens of the EU can vote and stand for office in local elections in their host countries; they can also participate in elections to the European Parliament. If they are long-term residents in their respective foreign countries, on the whole they are also entitled to an equivalent package of social rights and benefits.

The condition of the EU's third-country nationals, whose countries of origin do not belong to the EU, is of course different. While European Union citizenship makes it possible for all EU citizens to vote and to run for and hold office in local as well as Union-wide elections, this is not the case for third-country nationals. Their entitlement to political rights depends on their national and cultural origins and the political regimes of their host countries. In Denmark, Sweden, Finland, and Holland, third-country nationals can participate in local and regional elections; in Ireland, these rights are granted at the local but not the regional level. In the United Kingdom, Commonwealth citizens can vote in national elections as well.

The most important conclusion to be drawn from these developments is that the entitlement to rights is no longer dependent upon the status of citizenship; legal resident aliens have been incorporated into civil and social rights regimes, as well as being protected by supra- and subnational legislations. The condition of undocumented aliens, as well as of refugees and asylum seekers, however, remains in that murky domain between legality and illegality. Until their applications have been approved, refugees and asylum seekers are not entitled to choose their domicile freely or to accept employment. A resolution to permit those whose application is still in process the right to work after three months of residency has recently been approved by the EU Council of Ministers. In some cases, children of refugees and asylees can attend school; on the whole, asylees and refugees are entitled to certain forms of medical care. Undocumented migrants, by contrast, are cut off from rights and benefits and mostly live and work clandestinely. The conflict between *sovereignty* and *hospitality* has weakened in intensity, but it has by no means been eliminated. In fact, the EU is caught in contradictory currents that move it toward norms of cosmopolitan justice in the treatment of those who are within its boundaries, while leading it to act in accordance with outmoded Westphalian conceptions of unbridled

sovereignty toward those who are on the outside. The negotiation between insider and outsider status has become tense and almost warlike.

The end of the unitary model of citizenship, therefore, does not mean
that its hold upon our political imagination or its normative force in
guiding our institutions has grown obsolete. It does mean that we must
be ready to imagine forms of political agency and subjectivity that anticipate new modalities of political citizenship. In the era of cosmopolitan
norms, new forms of political agency have emerged that challenge the
distinctions between citizens and long-term residents, insiders and outsiders. The spread of cosmopolitan norms, under whose aegis the disaggregation of citizenship proceeds, has led to contestations of the boundaries of the demos. Using the concepts of "jurisgenerative politics" and
"democratic iterations," I would first like to propose an analytical and
normative grid for thinking about these transformations.

2. DEMOCRATIC ITERATIONS

"Iteration" is a term that was introduced into the philosophy of language through Jacques Derrida's work.[3] In the process of repeating a
term or a concept, we never simply produce a replica of the original
usage and its intended meaning: rather, every repetition is a form of
variation. Every iteration transforms meaning, adds to it, enriches it in
ever-so-subtle ways. In fact, there really is no "originary" source of
meaning, or an "original" to which all subsequent forms must conform.
It is obvious in the case of language that an act of original meaning-giving makes no sense, since, as Ludwig Wittgenstein famously reminded
us, to recognize an act of meaning-giving as precisely this act, we would
need to possess language itself.[4] A patently circular notion!

Nevertheless, even if the concept of "original meaning" makes no
sense when applied to language as such, it may not be so ill-placed in
conjunction with documents such as laws and other institutional norms.
Thus, every act of iteration might be assumed to refer to an antecedent
that is taken to be authoritative. The iteration and interpretation of
norms, and of every aspect of the universe of value, however, is never

3. Jacques Derrida, "Signature, Event, Context" [1971], in *Limited Inc.,* pp. 90ff. I am
indebted to the insights of Judith Butler and Bonnie Honig in highlighting the significance
of iterative practices for democratic politics. See Judith Butler, *Excitable Speech: Politics of the
Performative;* Bonnie Honig, *Democracy and the Foreigner;* and Bonnie Honig, "Declarations of
Independence: Arendt and Derrida on the Problem of Founding a Republic," *American Political Science Review* 85, no. 1 (March 1991): 97–113.

4. Ludwig Wittgenstein, *Philosophical Investigations,* trans. G. E. M. Anscombe.

merely an act of repetition. Every iteration involves making sense of an authoritative original in a new and different context. The antecedent thereby is reposited and resignified via subsequent usages and references. Meaning is enhanced and transformed; conversely, when the creative appropriation of that authoritative original ceases or stops making sense, then the original loses its authority upon us as well. Iteration is the reappropriation of the "origin"; it is at the same time its dissolution as the original and its preservation through its continuous deployment.

"Democratic iterations" are linguistic, legal, cultural, and political repetitions-in-transformation, invocations that are also revocations. They not only change established understandings but also transform what passes as the valid or established view of an authoritative precedent. Robert Cover and following him Frank Michelman have made these observations fruitful in the domain of legal interpretation. In *"Nomos* and Narrative," Robert Cover writes:

> . . . there is a radical dichotomy between the social organization of law as power and the organization of law as meaning. This dichotomy, manifest in folk and underground cultures in even the most authoritarian societies, is particularly open to view in a liberal society that disclaims control over narrative. *The uncontrolled character of meaning exercises a destabilizing influence upon power. Precepts must "have meaning," but they necessarily borrow it from materials created by social activity that is not subject to the strictures of provenance that characterize what we call formal lawmaking.* Even when authoritative institutions try to create meaning for the precepts they articulate, they act, in that respect, in an unprivileged fashion. (emphasis added)[5]

I want to suggest that we think of "jurisgenerative politics" as being exemplified in iterative or destabilizing acts through which a democratic people, which considers itself bound by certain guiding norms and principles, reappropriates and reinterprets them, thus showing itself to be not only the *subject* but also the *author of the laws* (Michelman). Whereas natural right doctrines assume that the principles that undergird democratic politics are impervious to transformative acts of popular collective will, and whereas legal positivism identifies democratic legitimacy with the correctly generated legal norms of a sovereign legislature,

5. Robert M. Cover, *"Nomos* and Narrative," *Harvard Law Review* 97, no. 1 (1983): 4–68; here p. 18; Frank Michelman, "Law's Republic," *Yale Law Journal* 97, no. 8 (July 1988): 1493–1537.

jurisgenerative politics signals a space of interpretation and intervention between universal norms and the will of democratic majorities. The rights claims that frame democratic politics, on the one hand, must be viewed as transcending the specific enactments of democratic majorities under specific circumstances; on the other hand, such democratic majorities *reiterate* these principles and incorporate them into democratic will-formation processes through argument, contestation, revision, and rejection.

Since they are dependent on contingent processes of democratic will-formation, not all jurisgenerative politics yields positive results. Thus one ought not make the *validity of cosmopolitan norms* dependent upon jurisgenerative and democratic iterations. This validity must be based on independent normative grounds. But productive or creative jurisgenerative politics results in *the augmentation of the meaning of rights claims* and in *the growth of the political authorship of political actors*, who make these rights their own by democratically deploying them.

Sterile, legalistic, or populistic jurisgenerative processes are also conceivable. In some cases, no normative learning may take place at all, but only a strategic bargaining among the parties may result; in other cases, the political process may simply run into the sandbanks of legalism or the majority of the demos may trample upon the rights of the minority in the name of some totalizing discourse of fear and war.

In the following I focus on two complex legal, political, and cultural phenomena through which democratic iterations have occurred and collective resignifications have emerged.[6] I begin with the "scarf affair," or "l'affaire du foulard," which preoccupied French public opinion and politics throughout the 1990s and still continues to do so. The banning of the wearing of the headscarf by Muslim girls in public schools pitted the right to freedom of conscience, which all French citizens and residents alike are entitled to, against the specific French understanding of the separation of church and state, known as the principle of *laïcité*. This affair led to an intense and unending debate about the meaning of French citizenship in an increasingly multicultural and multifaith society. The extension of a democratic schedule of rights to citizens and residents in a member country of the European Union, such as France, brings in its wake controversy about who precisely the subject of rights is. Can a Muslim woman be a good French citizen and be true to herself?

---

6. For a more extensive version of this argument, see Benhabib, *The Rights of Others*, chap. 5.

And what exactly does it mean to be a "good" French citizen? Who defines the terms here?

On February 10, 2004, the French National Assembly voted by an overwhelming majority of 494 for, 36 against, and with 31 abstentions to ban the wearing of all religious symbols from public schools. Although the new law applies to any ostentatiously displayed religious symbol such as Christian crosses and the yarmulkes of Orthodox Jewish students as well as the headscarves worn by Muslim girls, its main target was Muslim religious attire. To understand the severity of this legislation, which drew criticism even from France's allies in the European Union, such as the British and the Dutch governments, it is important to reconstruct the history of the scarf affair (see 3 below).

Unlike France, Germany until recently had not accepted the naturalization of immigrant children through territorial birthright. The German understanding of citizenship has been less encompassing and republican than the French one and has focused much more on ethnic belonging. This regressive understanding of German citizenship could hardly be reconciled with the realities of modern Germany as a regional and global economic superpower. One of the first challenges to the restrictive German understanding of citizenship came as a request from the city-state of Hamburg and the province of Schleswig-Holstein to permit noncitizen but long-term resident foreigners to vote in municipal and district-wide elections. The German Federal Constitutional Court rejected their request through a resounding declaration on the role of the nation and national belonging in a democracy. Although the Maastricht Treaty (1993), to which Germany is party, has since then overridden this decision by granting all nationals of EU member states who are residents of Germany the right to vote in and run for municipal elections, the earlier decision remains one of the most philosophically interesting, even if conceptually troubling, interpretations of democratic sovereignty and the identity of the demos.

3. "L'Affaire du Foulard" (The Scarf Affair)

A consequence of the transformation of citizenship is the long- and short-term coexistence of individuals and groups of distinct, and often quite contradictory, cultures, mores, and norms in the same public space.[7] If globalization brings with it the ever-rapid movement of peoples and

---

7. Parts of this discussion have previously appeared in Benhabib, *The Claims of Culture,* pp. 94–100.

goods, information and fashion, germs and news across state boundaries, one consequence of these trends is their multidirectionality. Globalization does not simply mean the spread of multinational, and usually American-, British-, or Japanese-run corporations, around the globe. Benjamin Barber's phrase "Jihad vs. McWorld" certainly captures a partial truth.[8] There is also the phenomenon of "reverse globalization," through which the peoples of the poorer regions of the world hailing from the Middle East, Africa, and South-Eastern Asia flock to global cities, such as London and Paris, Toronto and Rome, Madrid and Amsterdam. These groups, a good number of whom originally came to Western countries as guest workers and immigrants, have seen their numbers multiply in the last decades through the entry of refugees and asylum seekers from other regions of the world. The most spectacular examples of multicultural conflict that have recently occupied public consciousness, such as the Salman Rushdie affair in Great Britain, the affair over the "foulard" (headscarf) in French schools, and scandals around the practice of female circumcision, have concerned new ethno-cultural groups, as they have sought to adapt their religious and cultural beliefs to the legal and cultural environment of secular, but mostly Protestant, Catholic, or Anglican, liberal democratic states.

"L'affaire du foulard" refers to a long and drawn-out set of public confrontations that began in France in 1989,[9] with the expulsion from their school in Creil (Oise) of three scarf-wearing Muslim girls, and continued

---

8. Benjamin Barber, *Jihad vs. McWorld.*

9. A note of terminological clarification first: the practice of veiling among Muslim women is a complex institution that exhibits great variety across many Muslim countries. The terms *chador, hijab, niqab,* and *foulard* refer to distinct items of clothing that are worn by Muslim women coming from different Muslim communities: for example, the *chador* is essentially Iranian and refers to the long black robe and headscarf worn in a rectangular manner around the face; the *niqab* is a veil that covers the eyes and the mouth and leaves only the nose exposed; it may or may not be worn in conjunction with the *chador.* Most Muslim women from Turkey are likely to wear either long overcoats and a *foulard* (a headscarf) or a *çarşaf* (a black garment that most resembles the *chador*). These items of clothing have a symbolic function within the Muslim community itself: women coming from different countries signal to one another their ethnic and national origins through their clothing, as well as signifying their distance from or proximity to tradition in doing so. The brighter the colors of their overcoats and scarves—bright blue, green, beige, lilac as opposed to brown, gray, navy, and, of course, black—and the more fashionable their cuts and material by Western standards, the more we can assume the distance from Islamic orthodoxy of the women who wear them. Seen from the outside, however, this complex semiotic of dress codes gets reduced to one or two items of clothing, which then assume the function of crucial symbols in the complex negotiation among Muslim religious and cultural identities and Western cultures.

to the mass exclusion of twenty-three Muslim girls from schools in November 1996 upon the decision of the Conseil d'Etat.[10] The affair, referred to as a "national drama,"[11] or even a "national trauma,"[12] occurred in the wake of France's celebration of the second centennial of the French Revolution and seemed to question the foundations of the French educational system and its philosophical principle, *laïcité.* This concept is hard to translate in terms like the "separation of church and state" or even "secularization": at its best, it can be understood as the public and manifest neutrality of the state toward all kinds of religious practices, institutionalized through a vigilant removal of sectarian religious symbols, signs, icons, and items of clothing from official public spheres. Yet within the French Republic the balance between respecting the individual's right to freedom of conscience and religion, on the one hand, and maintaining a public sphere devoid of all religious symbolisms, on the other, was so fragile that it only took the actions of a handful of teenagers to expose this fragility. The ensuing debate went far beyond the original dispute and touched upon the self-understanding of French republicanism for the left as well as the right, on the meaning of social and sexual equality, and on liberalism vs. republicanism vs. multiculturalism in French life.

The affair began when on October 19, 1989, M. Ernest Chenière, headmaster of the college Gabriel-Havez of Creil, forbade three girls—Fatima, Leila, and Samira—to attend classes with their heads covered. The three had appeared in class that morning wearing their scarves, despite a compromise reached between their headmasters and their parents encouraging them to go unscarfed. The three girls has apparently decided to wear the scarf once more upon the advice of M. Daniel Youssouf Leclerq, the head of an organization called Integrité and the ex-president of the National Federation of Muslims in France (FNMF).

Although hardly noted in the press, the fact that the girls had been in touch with M. Leclerq indicates that wearing the scarf was a conscious political gesture on their part, a complex act of identification and defiance.

---

10. My discussion of these incidents relies primarily upon two sources: *Le Foulard et la République,* by Françoise Gaspard and Farhad Khosrokhavar, and an excellent seminar paper by Marianne Brun-Rovet, "A Perspective on the Multiculturalism Debate: 'L'Affaire Foulard' and *Laïcité* in France, 1989–1999."

11. Gaspard and Khosrokhavar, *Le Foulard et la République,* p. 11.

12. Brun-Rovet, "Perspective on the Multiculturalism Debate," p. 2.

In doing so, Fatima, Leila, and Samira, on the one hand, claimed to exercise their freedom of religion as French citizens; on the other hand, they exhibited their Muslim and North African origins in a context that sought to envelop them within an egalitarian, secularist ideal of republican citizenship as students of the nation. In the years to come, the girls and their followers and supporters forced what the French state wanted to view as a private symbol—an individual item of clothing—into the shared public sphere, thus challenging the boundaries between the public and the private. Ironically, they used the freedom given to them by French society and French political traditions, not the least of which is the availability of free and compulsory public education for all children on French soil, to transpose an aspect of their private identity into the public sphere. They problematized the school as well as the home: they no longer treated the school as a neutral space of French acculturation but brought their cultural and religious differences into open manifestation. They used the symbol of the home to gain entry into the public sphere by retaining the modesty required of them by Islam in covering their heads; yet at the same time, they left the home to become public actors in a civil public space in which they defied the state. Those who saw in the girls' actions simply an indication of their oppression were just as blind to the symbolic meaning of their deeds as those who defended their rights simply on the basis of freedom of religion.

The French sociologists Françoise Gaspard and Farhad Khosrokhavar capture this set of complex symbolic negotiations as follows:

> [The veil] mirrors in the eyes of the parents and the grandparents the illusions of continuity, whereas it is a factor of discontinuity; it makes possible the transition to otherness (modernity), under the pretext of identity (tradition); it creates the sentiment of identity with the society of origin, whereas its meaning is inscribed within the dynamic of relations with the receiving society. ...it is the vehicle of the passage to modernity within a promiscuity that confounds traditional distinctions, of an access to the public sphere that was forbidden to traditional women as a space of action and the constitution of individual autonomy. ...[13]

13. Gaspard and Khosrokhavar, *Le Foulard et la République*, pp. 44–45 (my translation).

The complexity of the social and cultural negotiations hidden behind the simple act of veiling elicited an equally ambiguous and complex decision by the French Conseil d'Etat. On November 4, 1989, the French minister of education, Lionel Jospin, took the matter to the Conseil d'Etat. The Conseil responded by citing France's adherence to constitutional and legislative texts and to international conventions and invoked from the outset the necessity of doing justice to two principles: that the *laïcité* and neutrality of the state be retained in the rendering of public services and that the liberty of conscience of the students be respected. All discrimination based upon the religious convictions or beliefs of the students would be inadmissible. The Conseil then concluded:

> ...the wearing by students, in the schools, of signs whereby they believe to be manifesting their adherence to one religion is itself not incompatible with the principle of laïcité, since it constitutes the exercise of their liberty of expression and manifestation of their religious beliefs; but this liberty does not permit students to exhibit [*d'arborer*] signs of religious belonging that, by their nature, by the conditions under which they are worn individually or collectively, or by their ostentatious or combative [*revendicatif*] character, would constitute an act of pressure, provocation, proselytizing, or propaganda, threatening to the dignity or liberty of the student or to the other members of the educational community, compromising their health or their security, disturbing the continuation of instructional activities or the educational role of the instructors, in short, [that] would disturb proper order in the establishment or the normal functioning of public service.[14]

This Solomonic judgment attempted to balance the principles of *laïcité* and freedom of religion and conscience. Yet instead of articulating some clear guidelines, the Conseil left the proper interpretation of the meaning of wearing of these signs up to the judgment of the school authorities. Not the individual students' own beliefs about what a religious scarf (or for that matter yarmulke) meant to them but its interpretation by the school authorities, and whether or not such articles could be seen as signs of provocation, confrontation, or remonstration, became

---

14. Ruling of the Conseil d'Etat, November 27, 1989 (my translation).

the decisive factors in curtailing the students' freedom of religion. It is not difficult to see why this judgment encouraged both sides in the conflict to pursue their goals further and led to further repression through the promulgation on September 10, 1994, of the Bayrou Guidelines, issued by Minister of Education François Bayrou. Lamenting the ambiguities of the judgment of the Conseil for conveying an impression of "weaknesses" vis-à-vis Islamicist movements, the minister declared that students had the right to wear discreet religious symbols, but that the veil was not among them.[15]

"L'affaire du foulard" eventually came to stand for all dilemmas of French national identity in the age of globalization and multiculturalism: how is it possible to retain French traditions of *laïcité,* republican equality, and democratic citizenship in view of France's integration into the European Union on the one hand and the pressures of multiculturalism generated through the presence of second- and third-generation immigrants from Muslim countries on French soil on the other hand? Would the practices and institutions of French citizenship be flexible and generous enough to encompass multicultural differences within an ideal of republican equality? Clearly, and despite the decision of the French Parliament to pass a law forbidding the wearing of all religious items of clothing in public schools, this affair is by no means over; and as European integration and multiculturalist pressures continue, France will have to discover new models of legal, pedagogical, social, and cultural institutions to deal with the dual imperatives of liberal democracies to preserve freedom of religious expression and the principles of secularism.[16]

We appear to have a paradoxical situation here in which the French state intervenes to dictate more autonomy and egalitarianism in the public sphere than the girls themselves wearing the headscarves seem to wish for. What exactly is the meaning of the girls' actions? Is this an act of religious observance and subversion, or one of cultural defiance, or of adolescent acting out to gain attention and prominence? Are the girls acting out of fear, out of conviction, or out of narcissism? It is not hard to

---

15. *Le Monde,* September 12, 1994, p. 10.

16. For an assessment of the intensity of the debate and the polarization caused by it, see "Derrière la Voile," *Le Monde Diplomatique* 599 (February 2004): 6–9. Among the organizations opposing this legislation were the League for Human Rights and the Movement against Racism and for Friendship among Peoples (MRAP), as well as the United Syndical Federation (FSU) and the Federation of Parents' Councils (FCPE).

imagine that their actions may involve all these elements and motives. The girls' voices are not heard in this heated debate; although there was a genuine public discourse in the French public sphere and a soul-searching on the questions of democracy and difference in a multicultural society, as the sociologists Gaspard and Khosrokhavar pointed out, until they carried out their interviews, the girls' own perspectives were hardly listened to. Even if the girls involved were not adults and in the eyes of the law were still under the tutelage of their families, it is reasonable to assume that at the ages of fifteen and sixteen they could account for themselves and their actions. Had their voices been heard and listened to,[17] it would have become clear that the meaning of wearing the scarf itself was changing from being a religious act to one of cultural defiance and increasing politicization. Ironically, it was the very egalitarian norms of the French public educational system that brought these girls out of the patriarchal structures of the home and into the French public sphere and gave them the confidence and the ability to *resignify the wearing of the scarf.* Instead of penalizing and criminalizing their activities, would it not have been more plausible to ask these girls to account for their actions and doings at least to their school communities, and to encourage discourses among the youth about what it means to be a Muslim citizen in a laic French Republic? Unfortunately, the voices of those whose interests were most vitally affected by the norms prohibiting the wearing of the scarf under certain conditions were silenced.

I am not suggesting that legal norms should originate through collective discursive processes and outside the framework of legal institutions: the legitimacy of the law is not at stake in this example; rather it is the *democratic legitimacy* of a lawful but, in my view, unwise and unfair decision that is at stake. It would have been both more democratic and fairer if the meaning of their act were not simply dictated to these girls by their school authorities, and if they were given more public say in the interpretation of their own actions. Would or should this have changed the Conseil d'Etat's decision? Maybe not, but the clause that permitted the prohibition of "ostentatiously" and "demonstratively" displayed religious symbols should have been reconsidered. There is sufficient evidence in the sociological literature that in many other parts of the world as well Muslim women are using the veil as well as the chador to cover

17. A recent publication tries precisely to let the girls speak for themselves. See *Alma et Lila Levy: Des Filles comme les Autres—Au-delà du Foulard*, interviews by Véronique Giraud and Yves Sintomer.

up the paradoxes of their own emancipation from tradition.[18] To assume that the meaning of their actions is purely one of religious defiance of the secular state constrains these women's own capacity to write the meaning of their own actions and, ironically, reimprisons them within the walls of patriarchal meaning from which they are trying to escape.

Learning processes would have to take place on the part of the Muslim girls as well: while the larger French society would have to learn not to stigmatize and stereotype as "backward and oppressed creatures" all those who accept to wear what appears at first glance to be a religiously mandated piece of clothing, the girls themselves and their supporters, in the Muslim community and elsewhere, have to learn to give a justification of their actions with "good reasons in the public sphere." In claiming respect and equal treatment for their religious beliefs, they have to clarify how they intend to treat the beliefs of *others* from different religions, and how, in effect, they would institutionalize the separation of religion and the state within Islamic tradition.

Despite the harshness of the recent legislation banning the scarf by the French National Assembly, a moderate French Islam may be emerging. On April 14, 2003, the *New York Times* reported the formation of an official Muslim Council to represent the five million Muslims of France. Among other issues, the council will deal with the rights of Muslim women in the workplace. Thus, Karima Debza, an Algerian-born mother of three, is reported as saying, "I cannot find work here because of my head scarf.... But my head scarf is part of me. I won't take it off. We have to educate the state about why the scarf is so important"; and she added, "and why there should be no fear of it."[19]

What Debza is asking for is no less than a process of democratic iteration and cultural resignification. While she is urging her French co-citizens to reconsider the strict doctrine of laicism, which precludes her from appearing in public places with a symbol that bears religious meaning, she herself is resignifying the wearing of the scarf in terms that involve what some have called a "Protestantization" of Islam. The covering of one's head, which in Islam as well as Judaism is an aspect of women's modesty and also, more darkly, an aspect of the repression of female sexuality that is viewed as threatening, is now reinterpreted as a

18. Nilüfer Gole, *The Forbidden Modern: Civilization and Veiling.*

19. Elaine Sciolino, "French Islam Wins Officially Recognized Voice," *New York Times,* April 14, 2003, sec. A, p. 4.

private act of faith and conscience. In presenting the wearing of the scarf as an aspect of her identity and her self-understanding as a Muslim, Debza is transforming these traditional connotations and is pleading for reciprocal recognition from others of her right to wear the scarf, as long as doing so does not infringe upon the rights of others. "Because wearing the scarf," she is saying, "is so fundamental to who I am" (her own words are "it is a part of me"), "you should respect it as long as it does not infringe on your rights and liberties." The wearing of the scarf is resignified as expressing an act of conscience and moral freedom.

Her point can be summarized thus: the protection of the equal right to religious freedom of all citizens and residents of France (a right also protected by the European Convention for the Protection of Human Rights and Fundamental Freedoms) should be considered more fundamental—in Ronald Dworkin's terms, should "trump"—the clause concerning the specific separation of religion and state that France practices, namely, laicism. In this process, Debza states, "we have to educate the state not to fear us"—a marvelous thought coming from an immigrant Muslim woman vis-à-vis the daunting traditions of French republicanism!

The challenge posed to French traditions of *laïcité* cannot be underestimated, and the French legislators' recent decision to ban the wearing of all religious symbols, except those that are very small and hardly visible publicly, in public schools signals a hardening of the fronts. But the clause of the separation of religion and state, while being a cornerstone of liberal democracies, also permits significant democratic variation. Thus the United Kingdom has a Church of England, while Germany subsidizes the three officially recognized denominations—Protestant, Catholic, and Jewish—through an indirect "church tax" known as *Kirchensteuer.* It would be no exaggeration to add that the First Amendment to the U.S. Constitution concerning the separation of church and state is periodically contested and democratically reiterated. Its significance is never frozen in time; rather, it is repeatedly the site of intense public battles. By contrast, emerging out of the historical experience of intense anticlericalism and antagonism toward the institutions of the Catholic church, the French republican tradition finds itself faced today with an unprecedented challenge: how can it accommodate demands for religious diversity in the context of global trends toward increasingly multicultural societies? Is the republican public sphere, cherished by French traditions, really defaced when individuals of different races, colors, and faiths want to function in this very public sphere carrying the signs and symbols of their private faiths and identities? Should their self-presentation through their particular identities be viewed as a threat to French understandings of citizenship?

In an explicit acknowledgment of the "changing face of France," in both the literal and figurative senses, in August 2003 thirteen women (eight of them of North African Muslim origin, and the rest African immigrants or the children of immigrants) were chosen to represent "Marianne," the icon of the Revolution, painted in 1830 by Eugène Delacroix, bare-chested and storming the barricades. Continuing the contentious national dialogue about the separation of church and state, these women wore the ancient Phrygian cap, a symbol of the French Revolution, rather than the Islamic veil or other ethnic or national headdress.[20] Yet, paradoxically, the political body that has decided to honor these women as a countersymbol to others like Debza who insist upon wearing the headscarf has also empowered them to challenge the overwhelmingly white, male, and middle-aged French Assembly, where only 12 percent of the members are women. One of them is quoted as saying: "These Mariannes have made visible something that has been the reality of the last twenty years. Look at the National Assembly. It's all white, rich, male and well educated. Now we have entered their space. We exist."[21]

Culture matters; cultural evaluations are deeply bound up with interpretations of our needs, our visions of the good life, and our dreams for the future. Since these evaluations run so deep, as citizens of liberal democratic polities, we have to learn to live with what Michael Walzer has called "liberalism and the art of separation."[22] We have to learn to live with the otherness of others whose ways of being may be deeply threatening to our own. How else can moral and political learning take place, except through such encounters in civil society? The law provides the framework within which the work of culture and politics goes on. The laws, as the ancients knew, are the walls of the city, but the art and passions of politics occur within those walls; and very often politics leads

---

20. Elaine Sciolino, "Paris Journal—Back to Barricades: Liberty, Equality, Sisterhood," *New York Times*, August 1, 2003, sec. A, p. 4.

21. Ibid.

22. Michael Walzer, "Liberalism and the Art of Separation," *Political Theory* 12 (August 1984): 315–30.

to the breaking down of these barriers or at least to assuring their permeability.

There is a dialectic between constitutional essentials and the actual politics of political liberalism. Rights, and other principles of the liberal democratic state, need to be periodically challenged and rearticulated in the public sphere in order to retain and enrich their original meaning. It is only when new groups claim that they belong within the circles of addressees of a right from which they have been excluded in its initial articulation that we come to understand the fundamental limitedness of every rights claim within a constitutional tradition as well as its context-transcending validity. The democratic dialogue and also the legal hermeneutic one are enhanced through the repositioning and rearticulation of rights in the public spheres of liberal democracies. The law sometimes can guide this process, in that legal reform may run ahead of popular consciousness and may raise popular consciousness to the level of the constitution; the law may also lag behind popular consciousness and may need to be prodded along to adjust itself to it. In a vibrant liberal multicultural democracy, cultural-political conflict and learning through conflict should not be stifled through legal maneuvers. The democratic citizens themselves have to learn the art of separation by testing the limits of their overlapping consensus.

While the intervention of French authorities to ban the wearing of the veil in the schools at first seemed like the attempt of a progressive state bureaucracy to modernize the "backward-looking" customs of a group, this intervention cascaded into a series of democratic iterations. These ranged from the intense debate among the French public about the meaning of wearing the veil, to the self-defense of the girls involved and the rearticulation of the meaning of their actions, to the encouragement of other immigrant women to wear their headscarves into the workplace, and finally to the very public act of resignifying the face of "Marianne," via having immigrant women from Arab countries as well as Africa represent her.

I do not want to underestimate, however, the extent of public dissatisfaction with and significant xenophobic resentment toward France's Muslim population. Democratic iterations can lead to processes of public self-reflection as well as generating public defensiveness. The mobilization of many right-wing parties throughout Europe is intensifying: in France, the Netherlands, the United Kingdom, Denmark, Germany, and elsewhere, we see well that the status of Europe's migrants, and particularly of its Muslim population, remains an incendiary issue. Nevertheless, it is clear that all future struggles with respect to the rights of Muslim and other immigrants will be fought for within the framework created by the universalistic principles of Europe's commitment to human rights on the one hand and the exigencies of democratic self-determination on the other.[23]

4. Who Can Be a German Citizen?
Redefining the Nation

On October 31, 1990, the German Constitutional Court ruled against a law passed by the provincial assembly of Schleswig-Holstein on February 21, 1989, that changed the qualifications for participating in local municipal (*Bezirk*) and district-wide (*Kreis*) elections (BVerfG, vol. 83, II, Nr. 3, p. 37; the following translations from the German are all mine).[24] According to Schleswig-Holstein's election laws in effect since May 31, 1985, all those who were defined as German in accordance with

---

23. In recent years, the German public and the courts have dealt with a challenge quite akin to the scarf affair in France. An elementary school teacher in Baden-Württemberg, Fereshda Ludin, of Afghani origin and German citizenship, insisted on being able to teach her classes with her head covered. The school authorities refused to permit her to do so. The case ascended all the way to the German Constitutional Court (BVerfG), and on September 30, 2003, the court decided as follows. Wearing a headscarf, in the context presented to the court, expresses that the claimant belongs to the "Muslim community of faith" (*die islamische Religionsgemeinschaft*). The court concluded that to describe such behavior as lack of qualification (*Eignungsmangel*) for the position of a teacher in elementary and middle schools clashed with the right of the claimant to equal access to all public offices in accordance with Article 33, Paragraph 2, of the Basic Law (*Grundgesetz*), and also clashed with her right to freedom of conscience, as protected by Article 4, Paragraphs 1 and 2, of the Basic Law, without, however, providing the required and sufficient lawful reasons for doing so (BVerfG, 2BvR, 1436/02, IVB 1 and 2). While acknowledging the fundamental rights of Fereshda Ludin, the court nevertheless ruled against the claimant and transferred the final say on the matter to the democratic legislatures. "The responsible provincial legislature is nevertheless free to create the legal basis [to refuse to permit her to teach with her head covered], by determining anew within the framework set by the constitution the extent of religious articles to be permitted in the schools. In this process, the provincial legislature must take into consideration the freedom of conscience of the teacher as well as of the students involved, and also the right to educate their children on the part of parents as well as the obligation of the state to retain neutrality in matters of world-view and religion" (BVerfG, 2BvR, 1436/02, 6; my translation). This case is discussed more extensively in Benhabib, *The Rights of Others*, chap. 5.

24. A similar change in its election laws was undertaken by the free state of Hamburg to enable its foreign residents at least eighteen years old to participate in the election of local municipal assemblies (*Bezirkversammlungen*). Since Hamburg is not a federal province (*Land*) but a free city-state, with its own constitution, some of the technical aspects of this decision are not parallel to those in the case of Schleswig-Holstein. I chose to focus on the latter case alone. It is nonetheless important to note that the federal government, which had opposed Schleswig-Holstein's electoral reforms, supported those of Hamburg. See BVerfG 83, 60, II, Nr. 4, pp. 60–81.

Article 116 of the Basic Law, who had reached the age of eighteen, and who had resided in the electoral district for at least three months were eligible to vote. The law of February 21, 1989, proposed to amend this as follows: all foreigners residing in Schleswig-Holstein for at least five years who possessed a valid permit of residency or who were in no need of one, and who were citizens of Denmark, Ireland, the Netherlands, Norway, Sweden, and Switzerland, would be able to vote in local and district-wide elections. The choice of these six countries was made on the grounds of reciprocity. Since these countries permitted their foreign residents to vote in local, and in some cases regional, elections, the German provincial legislators considered it appropriate to reciprocate.

The claim that the new election law was unconstitutional was brought by 224 members of the German Parliament, all of them members of the conservative CDU/CSU (Christian Democratic and Christian Social Union) Party; it was supported by the Federal Government of Germany. The court justified its decision with the argument that the proposed change of the electoral law contradicted "the principle of democracy," as laid out in Articles 20 and 28 of Germany's Basic Law, and according to which "All state-power [*Staatsgewalt*] proceeds from the people" (BVerfG 83, 37, Nr. 3, p. 39). Furthermore:

> The people [*das Volk*], which the Basic Law of the Federal Republic of Germany recognizes to be the bearer of the authority [*Gewalt*] from which issues the constitution, as well as the people that is the subject of the legitimation and creation of the state, is the German people. Foreigners do not belong to it. Membership in the community of the state [*Staatsverband*] is defined through the right of citizenship.... Citizenship in the state [*Staatsangehörigkeit*] constitutes a fundamentally indissoluble personal right between the citizen and the state. The vision [or image: *Bild*] of the people of the state [*Staatsvolkes*], which underlies this right of belonging to the state, is the political community of fate [*die politische Schicksalsgemeinschaft*], to which individual citizens are bound. Their solidarity with and their embeddedness in [*Verstrickung*] the fate of their home country, which they cannot escape [*sich entrinnen können*], are also the justification for restricting the vote to citizens of the state. They must bear the consequences of their decisions. By contrast, foreigners, regardless of however long they may have resided in the territory of the state, can always return to their homeland. (BVerfG 83, 37, Nr. 3, pp. 39–40)

This resounding statement by the court can be analyzed into three components: first, a disquisition on the meaning of *popular sovereignty* (all power proceeds from the people); second, a *procedural* definition of how we are to understand *membership* in the state; third, a philosophical explication of the nature of the bond between the state and the individual, based on the vision of a "political community of fate." The court argued that, according to the principle of popular sovereignty, there needed to be a "congruence" between the principle of democracy, the concept of the people, and the main guidelines for voting rights, at all levels of state power—namely, federal, provincial, district, and communal. Different conceptions of popular sovereignty could not be employed at different levels of the state. Permitting long-term resident foreigners to vote would imply that popular sovereignty would be defined in different fashion at the district-wide and communal levels than at the provincial and federal levels. In an almost direct repudiation of the Habermasian discursive democracy principle, the court declared that Article 20 of Germany's Basic Law does not imply that "the decisions of state órgans must be legitimized through those whose interests are affected [*Betroffenen*] in each case; rather their authority must proceed from the people as a group bound to each other as a unity [*das Volk als eine zur Einheit verbundene Gruppe von Menschen*]" (BVerfG 83, 37, II, Nr. 3, p. 51).

The provincial parliament of Schleswig-Holstein challenged the court's understanding and argued that neither the principle of democracy nor that of the people excludes the rights of foreigners to participate in elections: "The model underlying the Basic Law is the construction of a democracy of human beings, and not that of the collective of the nation. This basic principle does not permit that one distinguish in the long run between the people of the state [*Staatsvolk*] and an association of subservients [*Untertanenverband*]" (BVerfG, 83, 37, II, p. 42).

The German Constitutional Court eventually resolved this controversy about the meaning of popular sovereignty by upholding a unitary and functionally undifferentiated version of it; but it did concede that the sovereign people, through its representatives, could change the definition of citizenship. Procedurally, "the people" simply means all those who have the requisite state membership. If one is a citizen, one has the right to vote; if not, one does not. "So the Basic Law... leaves it up to the legislator to determine more precisely the rules for the acquisition and loss of citizenship and thereby also the criteria of belonging to the people. The law of citizenship is thus the site at which the legislator can do justice to the transformations in the composition of the population of the Federal Republic of Germany." This can be accomplished by expediting the acquisition of citizenship by all those foreigners who are long-term permanent residents of Germany (BVerfG 83, 37, II, Nr. 3, p. 52).

The court here explicitly addresses what I have called "the paradox of democratic legitimacy" in the first lecture, namely, that those whose rights to inclusion or exclusion from the demos are being decided upon will not themselves be the ones to decide upon these rules. The democratic demos can change its self-definition by altering the criteria for admission to citizenship. The court still holds to the classical model of citizenship according to which democratic participation rights and nationality are strictly bundled together; but by signaling the procedural legitimacy of changing Germany's naturalization laws, the court also acknowledges the power of the democratic sovereign to alter its self-definition such as to accommodate the changing composition of the population. The line separating citizens and foreigners can be renegotiated by the citizens themselves.

Yet the procedural democratic openness signaled by the court stands in great contrast to the conception of the democratic people, also adumbrated by it, according to which the people is viewed as "a political community of fate," held together by bonds of solidarity in which individuals are embedded (*verstrickt*). Here the democratic people is viewed as an *ethnos*, as a community bound together by the power of shared fate, memories, solidarity, and belonging. Such a community does not permit free entry and exit. Perhaps marriage with members of such a community may produce some integration over generations; but, by and large, membership in an ethnos—in a community of memory, fate, and belonging—is something that one is born into, although as an adult one may renounce this heritage, exit it, or wish to alter it. To what extent should one view liberal democratic polities as communities based on ethnos? Despite its emphatic evocation of the nation as "a community of fate," the court also emphasizes that the democratic legislator has the prerogative to transform the meaning of citizenship and the rules of democratic belonging. Such a transformation of citizenship may be necessary to do justice to the changed nature of the population. The demos and the ethnos do not simply overlap.

In retrospect this decision of the German Constitutional Court, written in 1990, is a swan song to a vanishing ideology of nationhood. In 1993 the Treaty of Maastricht, or the Treaty on the European Union, established European citizenship, which granted voting rights and rights to run for office for all members of the fifteen signatory states residing in the territory of other member countries. Of the six countries to whose citizens Schleswig-Holstein wanted to grant reciprocal voting rights—Denmark, Ireland, the Netherlands, Norway, Sweden, and Switzerland—only Norway and Switzerland remained nonbeneficiaries of the Maastricht Treaty since they were not EU members.

In the following years, an intense process of democratic iteration unfolded in the now-unified Germany, during which the challenge of bringing the definition of citizenship in line with the composition of the population posed by the German Constitutional Court to the democratic legislator was taken up, rearticulated, and reappropriated. The city-state of Hamburg, in its parallel plea to alter its local election laws, stated this very clearly. "The Federal Republic of Germany has in fact become in the last decades a country of immigration. Those who are affected by the law that is being attacked here are thus not strangers but cohabitants [*Inländer*], who only lack German citizenship. This is especially the case for those foreigners of the second and third generation born in Germany" (BVerfG 83, 60, II, Nr. 4, p. 68). The demos is not an ethnos, and those living in our midst who do not belong to the ethnos are not strangers either; they are rather "cohabitants," or, as later political expressions would have it, "our co-citizens of foreign origin [*Ausländische Mitbürger*]." Even these terms, which may sound odd to ears not accustomed to any distinctions besides those of citizens, residents, and nonresidents, suggest the transformations of German public consciousness in the 1990s.

This intense and soul-searching public debate finally led to an acknowledgment of the *fact* as well as the *desirability* of immigration. The need to naturalize second- and third-generation children of immigrants was recognized, and the new German citizenship law was passed in January 2000. Ten years after the German Constitutional Court turned down the election law reforms of Schleswig-Holstein and the city-state of Hamburg on the grounds that resident foreigners were not citizens, and were thus ineligible to vote, Germany's membership in the European Union led to the disaggregation of citizenship rights. Resident members of EU states can vote in local as well as EU-wide elections; furthermore, Germany now accepts that it is a country of immigration; immigrant children become German citizens according to *jus soli* and keep dual nationality until the age of twenty-four, at which point they must choose either German citizenship or that of their country of birth. Furthermore, long-term residents who are third-country nationals can naturalize if they wish to do so.

With the cases of the scarf affair and German voting laws, I have sought to elucidate processes of democratic iteration that attest to a dialectic of rights and identities. In such processes, both the identities involved and the very meaning of rights claims are reappropriated, resignified, and imbued with new and different meaning. Political agents, caught in such public battles, very often enter the fray with a present understanding of who they are and what they stand for; but the process itself frequently alters these self-understandings. Thus, in the scarf affair in France, we witness the increasing courage, maybe even militancy, of a group of women usually considered to be "docile subjects," in Michel Foucault's sense.[25] Traditional Muslim girls and women are not supposed to appear in the public sphere at all; ironically, precisely the realities of Western democracies with their more liberal and tolerant visions of women's role permit these girls and women to be educated in public schools, to enter the labor force, and, in the case of Fereshda Ludin, even to become a German teacher with the status of a civil servant. They are transformed from "docile bodies" into "public selves." Although their struggle at first is a struggle to retain their *traditional identities,* whether they choose it or not, as women they also become empowered in ways they may not have anticipated. They learn to *talk back to the state.* My prediction is that it is a matter of time before these women, who are learning to talk back to the state, will also engage and contest the very meaning of the Islamic traditions that they are now fighting to uphold. Eventually, these public battles will initiate private gender struggles about the status of women's rights within the Muslim tradition.[26]

---

25. Michel Foucault, *Discipline and Punish: The Birth of the Prison,* trans. Alan Sheridan.

26. The French scarf affair is being followed very closely in Turkey, a secular, multiparty democracy, the majority of whose population is Muslim. Throughout the 1980s and 1990s, Turkey confronted its own version of the scarf affair as the Islamist parties increased their power in Parliament and unprecedented numbers of Turkish Islamist women began attending the universities. From the standpoint of Turkish state authorities, the scarf is seen as a violation of the principle of *laiklik* (laïcité) articulated by Kemal Atatürk, the founder of the Republic. The Turkish Constitutional Court decided in 1989 against the use of scarves as well as turbans in universities. Students and the Islamist organizations representing them appealed to Article 24 of the Turkish Constitution, which guarantees freedom of religious expression, and to Article 10, which prohibits discrimination due to religious belief and differences in language, ethnicity, and gender. Their appeals were rejected. While officially the

These cases also show that outsiders are not only at the borders of the polity, but also within. In fact the very binarism between nationals and foreigners, citizens and migrants, is sociologically inadequate; the reality is much more fluid, since many citizens are of migrant origin, and many nationals themselves are foreign-born. The practices of immigration and multiculturalism in contemporary democracies flow into one another.27 While the scarf affair both in France and in Germany challenges the vision of the "homogeneity" of the people, the German Constitutional Court's decision shows that there may often be an incongruity between those who have the formal privilege of democratic citizenship and others who are members of the population but who do not formally belong to the demos. In this case, the challenge posed by the German court to the democratic legislature of adjusting the formal definition of German citizenship to reflect the changing realities of the population was taken up, and the citizenship law was reformed. The democratic people can reconstitute itself through such acts of democratic iteration so as to enable the extension of democratic voice. Aliens can become residents, and residents can become citizens. Democracies require porous borders.

The constitution of "we, the people" is a far more fluid, contentious, contested, and dynamic process than either Rawlsian liberals or decline-of-citizenship theorists would have us believe. The Rawlsian vision of peoples as self-enclosed moral universes is not only empirically but also normatively flawed.28 This vision cannot do justice to the dual identity of a people as an ethnos (as a community of shared fate, memories, and moral sympathies), on the one hand, and as the demos (as the democratically enfranchised totality of all citizens, who may or may not belong to the same ethnos), on the other. All liberal democracies that are modern nation-states exhibit these two dimensions. The politics of peoplehood consists in their negotiation. The people is not a self-enclosed and self-sufficient entity. The presence of so many migrants from Algeria, Tunisia, and Morocco, as well as from central Africa, testifies to France's imperial past and conquests, just as the presence of so many *Gastarbeiter*

---

wearing of the "turban" (a form of headscarf worn by observant Muslim women) is banned, many faculty members as well as administrators tolerate it when they can. See Benhabib, *The Claims of Culture*, p. 203.

27. See ibid., pp. 165–77.

28. John Rawls, *The Law of Peoples*, pp. 23–35, and my critique in Benhabib, *The Rights of Others*, chap. 3.

in Germany is a reflection of the economic realities of Germany since World War II. Some would even argue that, without their presence, the post–World War II German miracle would not have been conceivable.[29] Peoplehood is dynamic and not a static reality.

Decline-of-citizenship theorists, such as Michael Walzer and David Jacobson,[30] are just as wrong as Rawlsian liberals, in conflating the ethnos and the demos. The presence of others who do not share the dominant culture's memories and morals poses a challenge to the democratic legislatures to rearticulate the meaning of democratic universalism. Far from leading to the disintegration of the culture of democracy, such challenges reveal the depth and the breadth of the culture of democracy. Only polities with strong democracies are capable of such universalist rearticulation, through which they refashion the meaning of their own peoplehood. Will French political traditions be less strong if they are now carried forth and reappropriated by Algerian women or women from the Cote d'Ivoire? Will German history be less confusing and puzzling if it is taught by an Afghani-German woman, as in the Fereshda Ludin case? Rather than the decline of citizenship, I see in these instances the reconfiguration of citizenship through democratic iterations.

5. COSMOPOLITAN RIGHTS AND REPUBLICAN SELF-DETERMINATION

I began these lectures with a puzzle, the first articulations of which I attributed to Hannah Arendt and Karl Jaspers. After the capture of Eichmann by Israeli agents in 1960, Arendt and Jaspers initiated a series of reflections on the status of international law and norms of cosmopolitan justice. I summarized their queries in terms of three questions: (1) What is the ontological status of cosmopolitan norms in a postmetaphysical universe? (2) What is the authority of norms that are not backed by a sovereign with the power of enforcement? (3) How can we reconcile cosmopolitan norms with the fact of a divided humankind? I promised that I would begin by answering the last question first and then proceeding to the others.

---

29. James F. Hollifield, *Immigrants, Markets, and States: The Political Economy of Postwar Europe.*

30. Michael Walzer, *Spheres of Justice: A Defense of Pluralism and Equality;* David Jacobson, *Rights across Borders: Immigration and the Decline of Citizenship.*

In regard to question 3—how to reconcile cosmopolitanism with the unique legal, historical, and cultural traditions and memories of a people—we must respect, encourage, and initiate multiple processes of democratic iteration. Not all such processes are instances of jurisgenerative politics. Jurisgenerative politics are cases of legal and political contestation when the meaning of rights and other fundamental principles are reposited, resignified, and reappropriated by new and excluded groups, or by the citizenry in the face of unprecedented hermeneutic challenges and meaning constellations. I have tried to illustrate such cases of "rights at work," in instances when cosmopolitan norms that apply to the rights of residents or immigrant foreigners are rearticulated by constituted democratic legislatures. The French scarf affair and the German Constitutional Court's decision concerning the voting rights of resident foreigners are cases in which democratic majorities contested and redeployed cosmopolitan norms.

As we see in the French scarf affair, processes of democratic iteration do not invariably and necessarily result in political outcomes that we may want to endorse. It is clear that with the passing of legislation banning the wearing of all religious symbols in the schools, the French state has heightened the confrontation with its observant populations, Jewish and Muslim alike. It is also clear that future battles will take place inside and outside France. The Iraq War has already produced restiveness among France's Muslim population. It is likely to be a matter of time before some group brings charges against the actions of the French National Assembly in front of the European Court of Human Rights. Along with the debate that is unfolding in the new Europe about the separation of church and state within the EU Constitution, France's strict understanding of laicism, deplored even by its closest neighbors, will itself be challenged at the highest levels of jurisgenerative politics. This is the peculiarity of cosmopolitan justice: precisely because France is a signatory to the European Convention for the Protection of Human Rights and Fundamental Freedoms as well as to the European Charter of Human Rights, even the actions and decisions of its National Assembly are not immune to future juridical challenges.

Such controversies reenact in practice the theoretical dilemma of discursive scope: universalist norms are mediated by the self-understanding of local communities. The availability of cosmopolitan norms, however, increases the threshold of justification to which formerly exclusionary practices are now submitted. Exclusions take place, but the threshold for justifying them is now higher. This higher threshold also heralds an increase in democratic reflexivity. It becomes increasingly more difficult to justify practices of exclusion by democratic legislatures simply because they express the will of the people; such decisions are now subject to constitutional checks and balances not only in domestic law but in the international arena as well.

The French courts and politicians find it necessary to ban the wearing of religious symbols only on the basis of grounds that can be generalized for all: it is the future well-being and integrity of French society, as a society of *all* its citizens, that is appealed to. Reflexive grounds must be justifiable through reasons that would be valid for all. This means that such grounds can themselves be recursively questioned for failing to live up to the threshold set in their own very articulation.

In regard to Arendt's and Jaspers's question as to the authority of cosmopolitan norms, my answer is: *the democratic power of global civil society*. Of course, the global human rights regime by now has its agencies of negotiation, articulation, observation, and monitoring. In addition to processes of naming, shaming, and sanctions that can be imposed upon sovereign nations in the event of egregious human rights violations, the use of power by the international community, as authorized by the UN Security Council and the General Assembly, remains an option.

Finally, I come to the first question: what is the ontological status of cosmopolitan norms in a postmetaphysical universe? Briefly, such norms and principles are morally constructive: they create a universe of meaning, values, and social relations that had not existed before by changing the normative constituents and evaluative principles of the world of "objective spirit," to use Hegelian language. They found a new order— a *novus ordo saeculorum*. They are thus subject to all the paradoxes of revolutionary beginnings. Their legitimacy cannot be justified through appeal to antecedents or to consequents: it is the fact that there was no precedent for them that makes them unprecedented, and likewise we can only know their consequences once they have been adopted and enacted. The act that "crimes against humanity" has come to name and to interdict was itself unprecedented in human history—that is, the mass murder of a human group on account of race through an organized state power with all the legal and technological means at its disposal. Certainly, massacres, group murder, and tribal atrocities were known and practiced throughout human history. But the full mobilization of state power, with all the means of a scientific-technological civilization at its disposal, in order to extinguish a human group on account of their claimed racial characteristics was wholly novel. Once we name "genocide" as the supreme crime against humanity, we move into a new normative universe. I would even dare say that we move into a universe that now contains a new moral fact—"Thou shalt not commit genocide and perpetrate crimes against humanity." It is precisely because we as humankind have learned from the memories of genocide that we can name it as the supreme crime. Cosmopolitan norms, of which the prohibition against "crimes against humanity" is the most significant, create such new moral facts by opening novel spaces for signification, meaning, and rearticulation in human relations.

Let me end by turning to Arendt once more. Although she was skeptical that international criminal law would ever be formulated and reinforced, Arendt in fact praised and commended the judges who sought to extend existing categories of international law to the criminal domain. She wrote:

> ...that the unprecedented, once it has appeared, may become a precedent for the future, that all trials touching upon "crimes against humanity" must be judged according to a standard that is today still an "ideal." If genocide is an actual possibility of the future, then no people on earth...can feel reasonably sure of its continued existence without the help and the protection of international law. Success or failure in dealing with the hitherto unprecedented can lie only in the extent to which this dealing may serve as a valid precedent on the road to international penal law.... in consequence of this as yet unfinished nature of international law, it has become the task of ordinary trial judges to render justice without the help of, or beyond the limitation set upon them through, positive, posited laws.[31]

However fragile their future may be, cosmopolitan norms have evolved beyond the point anticipated and then problematized by Hannah Arendt. An International Criminal Court exists, although the oldest democracy in the world, the United States, has refused to sign the Rome Treaty legitimizing it. It is this paradox that these lectures have sought to understand—and, I hope, to transcend. The spread of cosmopolitan norms, from interdictions of war crimes, crimes against humanity, and

---

31. Hannah Arendt, *Eichmann in Jerusalem: A Report on the Banality of Evil,* pp. 273–74.

genocide to the increasing regulations of cross-border movements through the Geneva Conventions and other accords, has yielded a new political condition: the local, the national, and the global are all imbricated in one another. Future democratic iterations will make their interconnections and interdependence deeper and wider. Rather than seeing this situation as a challenge to democratic sovereignty, we can view it as promising the emergence of new political struggles and forms of agency.

BIBLIOGRAPHY

Alma et Lila Levy: Des Filles comme les Autres—Au-delà du Foulard. Interviews by Véronique Giraud and Yves Sintomer. Paris: La Découverte, 2004.

Arendt, Hannah. *Eichmann in Jerusalem: A Report on the Banality of Evil* [1963]. Revised and enlarged ed. New York: Penguin Books, 1994.

———. *The Human Condition.* Chicago: University of Chicago Press, 1958.

———. *The Origins of Totalitarianism.* New ed. with added prefaces. Rpt. New York: Harcourt Brace Jovanovich, 1979. (1st ed. published in 1951; new ed. published in 1966.)

Barber, Benjamin. *Jihad vs. McWorld.* New York: Times Books, 1995.

Benhabib, Seyla. *The Claims of Culture: Equality and Diversity in the Global Era.* Princeton: Princeton University Press, 2002.

———. *Reclaiming Universalism: Democracy and Cosmopolitanism.* With comments by Jeremy Waldron, Bonnie Honig, and Will Kymlicka and a reply. Oxford: Oxford University Press, forthcoming.

———. *The Rights of Others: Aliens, Citizens and Residents.* The John Seeley Memorial Lectures. Cambridge: Cambridge University Press, 2004.

———. "Transformations of Citizenship: The Case of Contemporary Europe." *Government and Opposition: An International Journal of Comparative Politics* 37, no. 4 (2002): 439–65.

Bohman, James. "The Public Spheres of the World Citizen." In *Perpetual Peace: Essays on Kant's Cosmopolitan Ideal,* edited by James Bohman and Matthias Lutz-Bachmann, pp. 179–201. Boston: MIT Press, 1997.

Brun-Rovet, Marianne. "A Perspective on the Multiculturalism Debate: '*L'Affaire Foulard*' and *Laïcité* in France, 1989–1999" (on file with author).

Buchanan, Allen. "From Nuremberg to Kosovo: The Morality of Illegal International Legal Reform." *Ethics* 111 (July 2001): 673–705.

Butler, Judith. *Excitable Speech: Politics of the Performative.* New York and London: Routledge, 1997.

Cover, Robert M. "*Nomos* and Narrative." *Harvard Law Review* 97, no. 1 (1983): 4–68.

Derrida, Jacques. "Signature, Event, Context" [1971]. In *Limited Inc.,* pp. 90ff. Evanston, Ill.: Northwestern University Press, 1988.

"Derrière la Voile." *Le Monde Diplomatique* 599 (February 2004): 6–9.

Doyle, Michael. "The New Interventionism." In *Global Justice,* edited by Thomas W. Pogge, pp. 219–42. Oxford: Basil Blackwell, 2001.

Foucault, Michel. *Discipline and Punish: The Birth of the Prison.* Translated by Alan Sheridan. New York: Pantheon Books, 1997.

Friedman, James. "Arendt in Jerusalem, Jackson at Nuremberg: Presuppositions of the Nazi War Crimes Trials." *Israel Law Review* 28, no. 4 (1994): 601–25.

Gaspard, Françoise, and Farhad Khosrokhavar. *Le Foulard et la République.* Paris: Découverte, 1995.

Gole, Nilüfer. *The Forbidden Modern: Civilization and Veiling.* Ann Arbor: University of Michigan Press, 1996.

Habermas, Jürgen. "The European Nation-State: On the Past and Future of Sovereignty and Citizenship." In *The Inclusion of the Other: Studies in Political Theory,* edited by Ciaran Cronin and Pablo De Greiff, pp. 105–29. Cambridge, Mass.: MIT Press, 1998.

————. "Kant's Idea of Perpetual Peace, with the Benefit of Two Hundred Years' Hindsight." In *Perpetual Peace: Essays on Kant's Cosmopolitan Ideal,* edited by James Bohman and Matthias Lutz-Bachmann, pp. 113–55. Boston: MIT Press, 1997.

Hannah Arendt–Karl Jaspers Correspondence: 1926–1969. Edited by Lotte Kohler and Hans Saner. Translated by Robert and Rita Kimber. New York: Harcourt Brace Jovanovich, 1992.

Hardt, Michael, and Antonio Negri. *Empire.* Cambridge, Mass.: Harvard University Press, 2000.

Held, David. "Cosmopolitan Democracy and the Global Order: A New Agenda." In *Perpetual Peace: Essays on Kant's Cosmopolitan Ideal,* edited by James Bohman and Matthias Lutz-Bachmann, pp. 235–53. Boston: MIT Press, 1997.

————. *Democracy and the Global Order: From the Modern State to Cosmopolitan Governance.* Cambridge: Polity Press, 1995.

———— "Law of States, Law of Peoples: Three Models of Sovereignty." *Legal Theory* 8 (2002): 1–44.

Hobbes, Thomas. *Leviathan* [1651]. Edited and with an introduction by C. B. McPherson. London: Penguin Books, 1968.

Hollifield, James F. *Immigrants, Markets, and States: The Political Economy of Postwar Europe.* Cambridge and London: Harvard University Press, 1992.

Honig, Bonnie. "Declarations of Independence: Arendt and Derrida on the Problem of Founding a Republic." *American Political Science Review* 85, no. 1 (March 1991): 97–113.

————. *Democracy and the Foreigner.* Princeton: Princeton University Press, 2001.

Ignatieff, Michael. *Human Rights as Politics and Idolatry.* With commentary by K. Anthony Appiah, David Hollinger, Thomas W. Laquer, and Diane F. Orentlicher. Princeton: Princeton University Press, 2001.

Jacobson, David. *Rights across Borders: Immigration and the Decline of Citizenship.* Baltimore and London: Johns Hopkins University Press, 1997.

Jaspers, Karl. *The Origin and Goal of History.* Translated by Michael Bullock. New Haven: Yale University Press, 1953.

Kant, Immanuel. *The Metaphysics of Morals.* Translated and edited by Mary Gregor. Cambridge: Cambridge University Press, 1996.

———. "Die Metaphysik der Sitten in zwei Teilen" [1797]. In *Immanuel Kants Werke,* edited by A. Buchenau, E. Cassirer, and B. Kellermann, pp. 5–309. Berlin: Verlag Bruno Cassirer, 1922.

———. "Perpetual Peace: A Philosophical Sketch" [1795]. Translated by H. B. Nisbet. In *Kant: Political Writings,* edited by Hans Reiss, pp. 93–131. 2nd and enlarged ed. Cambridge: Cambridge University Press, 1994.

———. "Zum Ewigen Frieden: Ein philosophischer Entwurf" [1795]. In *Immanuel Kants Werke (Schriften von 1790–1796),* edited by A. Buchenau, E. Cassirer, and B. Kellermann, pp. 425–74. Berlin: Verlag Bruno Cassirer, 1923.

Koskenniemi, Marti. *The Gentle Civilizer of Nations: The Rise and Fall of International Law, 1870–1960.* Cambridge: Cambridge University Press, 2001.

Marshall, T. H. *Citizenship and Social Class and Other Essays.* London: Cambridge University Press, 1950.

Michelman, Frank. "Law's Republic." *Yale Law Journal* 97, no. 8 (July 1988): 1493–1537.

Le Monde, September 12, 1994, p. 10.

Neuman, Gerald. "Human Rights and Constitutional Rights: Harmony and Dissonance." *Stanford Law Review* 55, no. 5 (May 2003): 1863–1901.

Nussbaum, Martha. "Patriotism and Cosmopolitanism." In *For Love of Country: Debating the Limits of Patriotism,* edited by Joshua Cohen, pp. 3–17. Boston, Mass.: Beacon Press, 1996.

O'Neill, Onora. *Bounds of Justice.* Cambridge: Cambridge University Press, 2000.

Ratner, Steven R., and Jason S. Abrams. *Accountability for Human Rights Atrocities in International Law: Beyond the Nuremberg Legacy* [1997]. New York: Clarendon Press, 2001.

Rawls, John. *The Law of Peoples.* Cambridge, Mass.: Harvard University Press, 1999.

Schabas, William A. *An Introduction to the International Criminal Court.* Cambridge: Cambridge University Press, 2001.

Schmitt, Carl. *The Concept of the Political* [1927]. Translated, introduction, and notes by George Schwab. Chicago: University of Chicago Press, 1996.

Sciolino, Elaine. "French Islam Wins Officially Recognized Voice." *New York Times,* April 14, 2003, sec. A, p. 4.

———. "Paris Journal—Back to Barricades: Liberty, Equality, Sisterhood." *New York Times,* August 1, 2003, sec. A, p. 4.

Tuck, Richard. *The Rights of War and Peace: Political Thought and International Order from Grotius to Kant.* Cambridge: Cambridge University Press, 1999.

U.S. Representatives on the Commission of Responsibilities. *Memorandum of Reservations to the Majority Report,* April 4, 1919. Excerpted in Michael Marrus, *The Nuremberg War Crimes Trial 1945–46: A Documentary History.* New York: Bedford/St. Martin's, 1997.

Waldron, Jeremy. "Minority Cultures and the Cosmopolitical Alternative." In *The Rights of Minority Cultures,* edited by Will Kymlicka, pp. 93–119. Oxford: Oxford University Press, 1995.

———. "What Is Cosmopolitan?" *Journal of Political Philosophy* 8, no. 2 (2000): 227–43.

Walzer, Michael. "Liberalism and the Art of Separation." *Political Theory* 12 (August 1984): 315–30.

———. *Spheres of Justice: A Defense of Pluralism and Equality.* New York: Basic Books, 1983.

Wittgenstein, Ludwig. *Philosophical Investigations.* Translated by G. E. M. Anscombe. Oxford: Blackwell, 1953.

I. *Taking Ourselves Seriously*
II. *Getting It Right*

THE TANNER LECTURES ON HUMAN VALUES

Delivered at

Stanford University
April 14–16, 2004

HARRY G. FRANKFURT is Professor Emeritus of Philosophy at Princeton University. He was educated at Johns Hopkins University, where he received his Ph.D. He has held positions at Ohio State University, the State University of New York at Binghamton, Rockefeller University, and at Yale. He was also a visiting fellow at All Souls College, Oxford. He is a fellow of the American Academy of Arts and Sciences. He has written more than 50 scholarly articles, essays, and reviews and is the author of three books: *Demons, Dreamers and Madmen: The Defense of Reason in Descartes' Meditations* (1970); *The Importance of What We Care About* (1988); and *Necessity, Volition and Love* (1999); and the editor of *Leibniz: A Collection of Critical Essays* (1972).

I. TAKING OURSELVES SERIOUSLY

I suppose some of you must have noticed that human beings have a tendency to be heavily preoccupied with thinking about themselves. Blind rollicking spontaneity is not exactly the hallmark of our species. We put very considerable effort into trying to get clear about what we are really like, trying to figure out what we are actually up to, and trying to decide whether anything can be done about this. The strong likelihood is that no other animal worries about such matters. Indeed, we humans seem to be the only things around that are even *capable* of taking themselves seriously.

Two features of our nature are centrally implicated in this: our rationality and our ability to love. Reason and love play critical roles in determining what we think and how we are moved to conduct ourselves. They provide us with decisive motivations, and also with rigorous constraints, in our careers as self-conscious and active creatures. They have a great deal to do, then, with the way we live and with what we are.

We are proud of the human abilities to reason and to love. This makes us prone to rather egregious ceremonies and excursions of self-congratulation when we imagine that we are actually making use of those abilities. We often pretend that we are exercising one or the other—that we are following reason, or that we are acting out of love—when what is truly going on is something else entirely. In any case, each of the two is emblematic of our humanity, and each is generally acknowledged to merit a special deference and respect. Both are chronically problematic, and the relation between them is obscure.

Taking ourselves seriously means that we are not prepared to accept ourselves just as we come. We want our thoughts, our feelings, our choices, and our behavior to make sense. We are not satisfied to think that our ideas are formed haphazardly, or that our actions are driven by transient and opaque impulses or by mindless decisions. We need to direct ourselves—or at any rate to *believe* that we are directing ourselves—in thoughtful conformity to stable and appropriate norms. We want to get things right.

It is reason and love—the directives of our heads and of our hearts—that we expect to equip us most effectively to accomplish this. Our lives are naturally pervaded, therefore, by an anxious concern to recognize what they demand and to appreciate where they lead. Each has, in its own way, a penetrating and resonant bearing upon our basic condition—the condition of persons, attempting to negotiate the environments of their internal as well as of their external worlds.

Sometimes, to be sure, we energetically resist what reason or love dictates. Their commands strike us as too burdensome, or as being in some other way unwelcome. So we recoil from them. Perhaps, finally, we reject them altogether. Even then, however, we ordinarily allow that they do possess a genuine and compelling authority. We understand that what they tell us really does count. Indeed, we have no doubt that it counts a great deal—even if, in the end, we prefer not to listen.

Among my aims in these lectures is to explore the roles of reason and of love in our active lives, to consider the relation between them, and to clarify their unmistakable normative authority. In my judgment, as you will see, the authority of practical reason is less fundamental than that of love. In fact, I believe, its authority is grounded in and derives from the authority of love. Now love is constituted by desires, intentions, commitments, and the like. It is essentially—at least as I construe it—a *volitional* matter. In my view, then, the ultimate source of practical normative authority lies not in reason but in the will.

I hope that you will find my analyses and arguments at least more or less convincing. I also hope, of course, that they will be clear. In this connection, I must confess to being a bit unsettled by a rather mordant piece of advice that comes (I understand) from the quantum physicist Nils Bohr. He is said to have cautioned that one should never *speak* more clearly than one can *think.* That must be right; but it is rather daunting. In any event, here goes.

2

What is it about human beings that makes it possible for us to take ourselves seriously? At bottom it is something more primitive, more fundamental to our humanity, and more inconspicuous than either our capacity for reason or our capacity to love. It is our peculiar knack of separating from the immediate content and flow of our own consciousness and introducing a sort of division within our minds. This elementary maneuver establishes an inward-directed, monitoring oversight. It puts in place an elementary reflexive structure, which enables us to focus our attention directly upon ourselves.

When we divide our consciousness in this way, we *objectify* to ourselves the ingredient items of our ongoing mental life. It is this self-objectification that is particularly distinctive of human mentality. We are unique (probably) in being able simultaneously to be engaged in whatever is going on in our conscious minds, to detach ourselves from it, and to observe it—as it were—from a distance. We are then in a position to form reflexive or higher-order responses to it. For instance, we may approve of what we notice ourselves feeling, or we may disapprove; we may want to remain the sort of person we observe ourselves to be, or we may want to be different. Our division of ourselves situates us to come up with a variety of supervisory desires, intentions, and interventions that pertain to the several constituents and aspects of our conscious life. This has implications of two radically opposed kinds.

On the one hand, it generates a profound threat to our well-being. The inner division that we introduce impairs our capacity for untroubled spontaneity. This is not merely a matter of spoiling our fun. It exposes us to psychological and spiritual disorders that are nearly impossible to avoid. These are not only painful; they can be seriously disabling. Facing ourselves, in the way that internal separation enables us to do, frequently leaves us chagrined and distressed by what we see, as well as bewildered and insecure concerning who we are. Self-objectification facilitates both an inhibiting uncertainty or ambivalence and a nagging general dissatisfaction with ourselves. Except in their most extreme forms, these disorders are too commonplace to be regarded as pathological. They are so integral to our fundamental experience of ourselves that they serve to define, at least in part, the inescapable human condition.

On the other hand, however, this very capacity to divide and to objectify ourselves provides the foundational structure for several particularly cherished features of our humanity. It accounts for the fact that we possess such a thing as practical reason; it equips us to enjoy a significant freedom in the exercise of our will; and it creates for us the possibility of going beyond simply wanting various things, and of coming instead to care about them, to regard them as important to ourselves, and to love them. The same structural configuration that makes us vulnerable to disturbing and potentially crippling disabilities also immeasurably enhances our lives by offering us—as I will try to explain—opportunities for practical rationality, for freedom of the will, and for love.

3

When we begin attending to our own feelings and desires, to our attitudes and motives, and to our dispositions to behave in certain ways, what we confront is an array of—so to speak—psychic raw material. If we are to amount to more than just biologically qualified members of a certain animal species, we cannot remain passively indifferent to these materials. Developing higher-order attitudes and responses to oneself is fundamental to achieving the status of a responsible person.

To remain wantonly unreflective is the way of nonhuman animals and of small children. They do whatever their impulses move them most insistently to do, without any self-regarding interest in what sort of creature that makes them. They are one-dimensional, without the inner depth and complexity that render higher-order responses to oneself possible. Higher-order responses need not be especially thoughtful, or even entirely overt. However, we become responsible persons—quite possibly on the run and without full awareness—only when we disrupt ourselves from an uncritical immersion in our current primary experience, take a look at what is going on in it, and arrive at some resolution concerning what we think about it or how it makes us feel.

Some philosophers have argued that a person becomes responsible for his own character insofar as he shapes it by voluntary choices and actions that cause him to develop habits of discipline or indulgence and hence that make his character what it is. According to Aristotle, no one can help acting as his virtuous or vicious character requires him to act; but in some measure a person's character is nonetheless voluntary, because "we are ourselves...part-causes of our state of character" (*Nicomachean Ethics* III.5, 1114.b22). In other words, we are responsible for what we are to the extent that we have caused ourselves—by our voluntary behavior—to become that way.

I think Aristotle is wrong about this. Becoming responsible for one's character is not essentially a matter of *producing that character* but of *taking responsibility for it*. This happens when a person selectively identifies with certain of his own attitudes and dispositions, whether or not it was he that caused himself to have them. In identifying with them, he incorporates those attitudes and dispositions into himself and makes them his own. What counts is our current effort to define and to manage ourselves, and not the story of how we came to be in the situation with which we are now attempting to cope.

Even if we *did* cause ourselves to have certain inclinations and tendencies, we can decisively rid ourselves of any responsibility for their continuation by renouncing them and struggling conscientiously to prevent them from affecting our conduct. We will still be responsible, of course, for having brought them about. That cannot be changed. However, we will no longer be responsible for their *ongoing* presence in our psychic history, or for any conduct to which that may lead. After all, if they do persist, and if they succeed in moving us to act, it will now be only against our will.

4

When we consider the psychic raw materials with which nature and circumstance have provided us, we are sometimes more or less content. They may not exactly please us, or make us proud. Nevertheless, we are *willing* for them to represent us. We *accept* them as conveying what we really feel, what we truly desire, what we do indeed think, and so on. They do not arouse in us any determined effort to dissociate ourselves from them. Whether with a welcoming approval, or in weary resignation, we consent to having them and to being influenced by them.

This willing acceptance of attitudes, thoughts, and feelings transforms their status. They are no longer merely items that happen to appear in a certain psychic history. We have taken responsibility for them as authentic *expressions of ourselves.* We do not regard them as disconnected from us, or as alien intruders by which we are helplessly beset. The fact that we have adopted and sanctioned them makes them intentional and legitimate. Their force is now our force. When they move us, we are therefore not *passive.* We are *active,* since we are being moved just by ourselves.

Being identified with the contents of one's own mind is a very elementary arrangement. It is so ubiquitous, so intimately familiar, and so indispensable to our normal experience, that it is not easy to bring it into sharp focus. It is so natural to us, and as a rule it comes about so effortlessly, that we generally do not notice it at all. In very large measure, it is simply the default condition.

5

Of course, the default condition does not always prevail. Sometimes we do not participate actively in what goes on in us. It takes place, somehow, but we are just bystanders to it. There are obsessional thoughts, for instance, that disturb us but that we cannot get out of our heads; there are peculiar reckless impulses that make no sense to us, and upon which we could never think of acting; there are hot surges of anarchic emotion that assault us from out of nowhere and that have no recognizable warrant from the circumstances in which they erupt.

These are psychic analogues of the seizures and spasmodic movements that occur at times in our bodies. The fact is that we are susceptible to mental tics, twitches, and convulsions, as well as to physical ones. These are things that *happen to us*. When they occur, we are not participating agents, who are expressing what we really think or want or feel. Just as various bodily movements occur without the body being moved by the person whose body it is, so various thoughts, desires, and feelings enter a person's mind without being what that person truly thinks or feels or wants.

Needless to say, however dystonic and disconnected from us these mental events may be, they do occur in *our* minds—just as the analogous physical events occur nowhere else but in our bodies. They are, at least in a gross literal sense, our thoughts, our feelings, and our desires. Moreover, they often provide important indications of what else is going on in our minds. Uncontrollably spasmodic movements of the limbs are likely to be symptomatic of some deeper and otherwise hidden physical condition. Similarly, the fact that I have an obsessional thought that the sun is about to explode, or a wild impulse to jump out the window, may reveal something very significant about what is going on in my unconscious. Still, that is not what I really think about the sun; nor does the impulse to jump express something that I really want to do.

6

What a person finds in himself may not just seem oddly disconnected from him. It may be dangerously antithetical to his intentions and to his conception of himself. Some of the psychic raw material that we confront may be so objectionable to us that we cannot permit it to determine our attitudes or our behavior. We cannot help having that dark side. However, we are resolved to keep it from producing any direct effect upon the design and conduct of our lives.

These unacceptable intruders arouse within us, then, an anxious disposition to resist. By a kind of psychic immune response—which may be mobilized without our even being aware of it—we push them away, and we introduce barriers of repression and inhibition between them and ourselves. That is, we dissociate ourselves from them and seek to prevent them from being at all effective. Instead of incorporating them, we *externalize* them.

This means that we deny them any entitlement to supply us with motives or with reasons. They are outlawed and disenfranchised. We refuse to recognize them as grounds for deciding what to think or what to do. Regardless of how insistent they may be, we assign their claims no place whatever in the order of preferences and priorities that we establish for our deliberate choices and acts. The fact that we continue to be powerfully moved by them gives them no rational claim. Even if an externalized desire turns out to be irresistible, its dominion is merely that of a tyrant. It has, for us, no legitimate authority.

Some philosophers maintain that, just by virtue of having a desire, a person *necessarily* has a reason for trying to satisfy it. The reason may not be a very strong one; there may be much better reasons to perform another action instead. Nevertheless, it counts for *something*. The very fact that a person wants to do something always means, on this view, that there is at least that much of a reason in favor of his doing it.

However, the mere fact that a person has a desire does not give him a reason. What it gives him is a *problem*. He has the problem of whether to identify with the desire and thus validate it as eligible for satisfaction, or whether to dissociate himself from it, treat it as categorically unacceptable, and try to suppress it or rid himself of it entirely. If he identifies with the desire, he acknowledges that satisfying it is to be assigned *some* position—however inferior—in the order of his preferences and priorities. If he externalizes the desire, he determines to give it no position in that order at all.

7

Reflexivity and identification have fundamental roles in the constitution of practical reason. Indeed, it is only by virtue of these elementary maneuvers that we *have* such a thing as practical reason. Without their intervention, we could not regard any fact as giving us a reason for performing any action.

When does a fact give us a reason for performing an action? It does so when it suggests that performing the action would help us reach one or another of our goals. For example, the fact that it is raining gives me a reason for carrying an umbrella insofar as doing that would be helpful as a means to my goal of keeping dry.

Having a goal is not the same, however, as simply being moved by a desire. Suppose I have a desire to kill someone, and that firing my pistol at him would be an effective way to accomplish this. Does that mean I have a reason to fire my pistol at him? In fact, I have a reason for doing that *only* if killing the man is not just an outcome for which a desire happens to be occurring in me. The desire must be one that I accept and with which I identify. The outcome must be one that I really want.

Suppose that the man in question is my beloved son, that our relationship has always been a source of joy for me, and that my desire to kill him has no evident connection to anything that has been going on. The desire is wildly exogenous; it comes entirely out of the blue. No doubt it signifies God knows what unconscious fantasy, which is ordinarily safely repressed. In any case, it instantly arouses in me a massive and wholehearted revulsion. I do whatever I can to distance myself from it, and to block any likelihood that it will lead me to act.

The murderous inclination is certainly real. I do have that lethal desire. However, it is not true that I want to kill my son. I don't really want to kill him. Therefore, I don't have any reason to fire my pistol at him. It would be preposterous to insist that I do have at least a weak reason to shoot him—a reason upon which I refrain from acting only because it is overridden by much stronger reasons for wanting him to remain alive. The fact that shooting him is likely to kill him gives me *no reason at all* to shoot him, even though it is true that I have a desire to kill him and that shooting him might do the trick. Since the desire is one with which I do not identify, my having it does not mean that killing my son is actually among my goals.

8

Practical reasoning is, in part, a procedure through which we determine what we have most reason to do in order to reach our goals. There could be no deliberative exercise of practical reason if we were related to our desires only in the one-dimensional way that animals of nonreflective species are related to whatever inner experience they have. Like them, we would be mutely immersed in whatever impulses happen at the moment to be moving us; and we would act upon whichever of those impulses happened to be most intense. We would be no more able than they are to decide what we have reason to do because, like them, we would be unable to construe anything as being for us an end or a goal.

In fact, without reflexivity we could not make decisions at all. To make a decision is to make up one's mind. This is an inherently reflexive act, which the mind performs upon itself. Subhuman animals cannot perform it because they cannot divide their consciousness. Since they cannot take themselves apart, they cannot put their minds back together. If we lacked our distinctive reflexive and volitional capacities, making decisions would be impossible for us too.

That would not alter the fact that, like all animals in some degree, we would be capable of behaving *intelligently.* Being intelligent and being rational are not the same. When I attempt to swat an insect, the insect generally flies or scurries rapidly away to a place that is more difficult for me to reach. This behavior reduces the likelihood that it will die. The insect's self-preservative movements are not structured in detail by *instinct.* They are not inflexibly *modular* or *tropistic.* They are continuously adjusted to be effective in the particular, and often rapidly changing, circumstances at hand. In other words, the insect—although it does not deliberate or reason—behaves intelligently. Even if we too were unable to reason or to deliberate, we too would nevertheless often still be able—by appropriately adaptive adjustments in our behavior—to find our way intelligently to the satisfaction of our desires.

9

Let us suppose that a certain motive has been rejected as unacceptable. Our attempt to immunize ourselves against it may not work. The resistance we mobilize may be insufficient. The externalized impulse or desire may succeed, by its sheer power, in defeating us and forcing its way. In that case, the outlaw imposes itself upon us without authority, and against our will. This suggests a useful way of understanding what it is for a person's will to be free.

When we are doing exactly what we want to do, we are acting freely. A free act is one that a person performs simply because he wants to perform it. Enjoying freedom of action consists in maintaining this harmonious accord between what we do and what we want to do.

Now sometimes, similarly, the desire that motivates a person as he acts is precisely the desire by which he wants to be motivated. For instance, he wants to act from feelings of warmth and generosity; and in fact he *is* warm and generous in what he does. There is a straightforward parallel here between a free action and a free will. Just as we act freely when what we do is what we want to do, so we will freely when what we want is what we want to want—that is, when the will behind what we do is exactly the will by which we want our action to be moved. A person's will is free, on this account, when there is in him a certain volitional unanimity. The desire that governs him as he is acting is in agreement with a higher-order volition concerning what he wants to be his governing desire.

Of course, there are bound to be occasions when the desire that motivates us when we act is a desire by which we do *not* want to be motivated. Instead of being moved by the warm and generous feelings that he would prefer to express, a person's conduct may be driven by a harsh envy, of which he disapproves but which he has been unable to prevent from gaining control. On occasions like that, the will is not free.

But suppose that we are doing what we want to do, that our motivating first-order desire to perform the action is exactly the desire by which we want our action to be motivated, and that there is no conflict in us between this motive and any desire at any higher order. In other words, suppose we are thoroughly wholehearted both in what we are doing and in what we want. Then there is no respect in which we are being violated or defeated or coerced. Neither our desires nor the conduct to which they lead are imposed upon us without our consent or against our will. We are acting just as we want, and our motives are just what we want them to be. Then so far as I can see, we have on that occasion all the freedom for which finite creatures can reasonably hope. Indeed, I believe that we have as much freedom as it is possible for us even to conceive.

10

Notice that this has nothing to do with whether our actions, our desires, or our choices are causally determined. The widespread conviction among thoughtful people that there is a radical opposition between free will and determinism is, on this account, a red herring. The possibility that everything is necessitated by antecedent causes does not threaten our freedom. What it threatens is our power. Insofar as we are governed by causal forces, we are not omnipotent. That has no bearing, however, upon whether we can be free.

As finite creatures, we are unavoidably subject to forces other than our own. What we do is, at least in part, the outcome of causes that stretch back indefinitely into the past. This means that we cannot design our lives from scratch, entirely unconstrained by any antecedent and external conditions. However, there is no reason why a sequence of causes, outside our control and indifferent to our interests and wishes, might not happen to lead to the harmonious volitional structure in which the free will of a person consists. That same structural unanimity might also conceivably be an outcome of equally blind chance. Whether causal determinism is true or whether it is false, then, the wills of at least some of us may at least sometimes be free. In fact, this freedom is clearly not at all uncommon.

11

In the Scholium to Proposition 52 in Part IV of his *Ethics,* Baruch Spinoza declares that "the highest good we can hope for" is what he refers to
as "acquiescentia in se ipso." Various translators render this Latin phrase
into English as "self-contentment," as "self-esteem," or as "satisfaction
with oneself." These translations are a little misleading. The good to
which Spinoza refers is certainly not to be confused with the contentment or pride or satisfaction that people sometimes award themselves
because of what they think they have accomplished, or because of the tal-
ents or other personal gifts with which they believe they are endowed. It
is not Spinoza's view that the highest good for which we can hope has to
do either with successful achievement or with vanity or pride.

There is something to be said for a bluntly literal construction of his
Latin. That would have Spinoza mean that the highest good consists in
acquiescence to oneself—that is, in acquiescence to being the person that
one is, perhaps not enthusiastically but nonetheless with a willing
acceptance of the motives and dispositions by which one is moved in
what one does. This would amount to an inner harmony that comes to
much the same thing as having a free will. It would bring with it the
natural satisfaction—or the contentment or self-esteem—of being just
the kind of person one wants to be.

Unquestionably, it is a very good thing to be in this sense contented
with oneself. Spinoza does not say that it is the *best* thing one can hope for;
he doesn't say even that it is enough to make life good. After all, it may be
accompanied by terrible suffering, disappointment, and failure. So why
say, as he does, that it is the highest thing for which one can hope?

Perhaps because it resolves the *deepest* problem. In our transition
beyond naive animality, we separate from ourselves and disrupt our original unreflective spontaneity. This puts us at risk for varieties of inner
fragmentation, dissonance, and disorder. Accepting ourselves reestab-
lishes the wholeness that was undermined by our elementary constitutive maneuvers of division and distancing. When we are acquiescent to
ourselves, or willing freely, there is no conflict within the structure of
our motivations and desires. We have successfully negotiated our distinctively human complexity. The unity of our self has been restored.

12

The volitional unity in which freedom of the will consists is purely
structural. The fact that a person's desire is freely willed implies nothing

as to *what* is desired or as to whether the person actually cares in the least about it. In an idle moment, we may have an idle inclination to flick away a crumb; and we may be quite willing to be moved by that desire. Nonetheless, we recognize that flicking the crumb would be an altogether inconsequential act. We want to perform it, but performing it is of no importance to us. We really don't care about it at all.

What this means is not that we assign it a very low priority. To regard it as truly of *no* importance to us is to be willing to give up having any interest in it whatever. We have no desire, in other words, to *continue* wanting to flick away the crumb. It would be all the same to us if we completely ceased wanting to do that. When we do care about something, we go beyond wanting it. We want to *go on* wanting it, at least until the goal has been reached. Thus, we feel it as a lapse on our part if we neglect the desire, and we are disposed to take steps to refresh the desire if it should tend to fade. The caring entails, in other words, a commitment to the desire.

Willing freely means that the self is at that time harmoniously integrated. There is, within it, a *synchronic* coherence. Caring about something implies a *diachronic* coherence, which integrates the self across time. Like free will, then, caring has an important structural bearing upon the character of our lives. By our caring, we maintain various thematic continuities in our volitions. We engage ourselves in guiding the course of our desires. If we cared about nothing, we would play no active role in designing the successive configurations of our will.

The fact that there are things that we do care about is plainly more basic to us—more constitutive of our essential nature—than what those things are. Nevertheless, *what* we care about—that is, what we consider important to ourselves—is obviously critical to the particular course and to the particular quality of our lives. This naturally leads people who take themselves seriously to wonder how to get it right. It leads them to confront fundamental issues of normativity. How are we to determine what, if anything, we *should* care about? What *makes* something genuinely important to us?

13

Some things are important to us only because we care about them. Who wins the American League batting title this year is important to me if I am the kind of baseball fan who cares about that sort of thing, but probably not otherwise. My close friends are especially important to me; but if I did not actually care about those individuals, they would be no more important to me than anyone else.

Of course, many things are important to people even though they do not actually care about them. Vitamins were important to the ancient Greeks, who could not have cared about them since they had no idea that there were such things. Vitamins are, however, indispensable to health; and the Greeks did care about that. What people do not care about may nonetheless be quite important to them, obviously, because of its value as a means to something that they do in fact care about.

In my view, it is *only* in virtue of what we actually care about that anything is important to us.[1] The world is everywhere infused for us with importance; many things are important to us. That is because there are many things that we care about just for themselves, and many that stand in pertinent instrumental relationships to those things. If there were nothing that we cared about—if our response to the world were utterly and uniformly flat—there would be no reason for us to care about anything.

14

Does this mean that it is all simply up to us—that what is truly important to us depends just upon what goes on in our minds? Surely there are certain things that are *inherently* and *objectively* important and worth caring about, and other things that are not. Regardless of what our own desires or attitudes or other mental states may happen to be, surely there are some things that we *should* care about, and others that we certainly should *not* care about. Is it not unmistakably apparent that people should at least care about adhering to the requirements of morality, by which all of us are inescapably bound no matter what our individual inclinations or preferences may be?

Some philosophers believe that the authority of morality is as austerely independent of personal contingencies as is the authority of logic. Indeed, their view is that moral principles are grounded in the same fundamental rationality as logically necessary truths. For instance, one advocate of this moral rationalism says: "Just as there are rational requirements on thought, there are rational requirements on action"; and since "the requirements of ethics are rational requirements..., the

---

1. I will not discuss whether this needs to be modified to refer also to what we *would* care about if we were properly acquainted with it. In any case, the modification could readily be absorbed into the voluntaristic account of practical normativity that I am developing.

motive for submitting to them must be one which it would be contrary to reason to ignore."[2] On this account, failure to submit to the moral law is irrational. The authority of the moral law is the authority of reason itself.

The normative authority of reason, however, cannot be what accounts for the normative authority of morality. There must be some other explanation of why we should be moral. For one thing, our response to immoral conduct is very different from our response to errors in reasoning. Contradicting oneself or reasoning fallaciously is not, as such, a *moral* lapse. People who behave immorally incur a distinctive kind of opprobrium, which is quite unlike the normal attitude toward those who reason poorly. Our response to sinners is not the same as our response to fools.

Moreover, if it *were* possible for people to justify their conduct strictly by reason (i.e., with rigorous proofs demonstrating that acting otherwise would be irrational) that would provide no advantage to morality. In fact, it would render the claims of morality far less compelling, because it would take people off the hook. After all, being convinced by proofs does not implicate any of a person's individual preferences or predilections. Reason necessitates assent and leaves no room for individual choice. It is entirely impersonal. It does not reveal character.

Construing the basis of morality rationalistically misses the whole point of moral norms. Morality is essentially designed to put people *on* the hook. Whether or not a person adheres to the moral law is not supposed to be independent of the kind of person he is. It is presumed to reveal something about him deeper and more intimate than his cognitive acuity. Moral principles cannot rest, therefore, simply upon rational requirements. There must be something behind the authority of the moral law besides reason.

15

Let us assume, then, that moral authority cannot be satisfactorily established by invoking just the bloodless support of strict rationality. Is there not a sufficient basis of some other kind for recognizing that moral requirements (and perhaps normative requirements of various other types as well) are genuinely important in themselves, regardless of any-

2. Thomas Nagel, *The Possibility of Altruism* (Oxford: Oxford University Press, 1970), p. 3.

one's beliefs or feelings or inclinations? In my judgment, there is not. There can be no rationally warranted criteria for establishing anything as *inherently* important.

Here is one way to see why. Nothing is important if everything would be exactly the same with it as without it. Things are important only if they make a difference. However, the fact that they do make a difference is not enough to show that they are important. Some differences are too trivial. A thing is important only if it makes an *important* difference. Thus, we cannot know whether something is important until we already know how to tell whether the difference it makes is important.

The unlimited regress to which this leads is clearly unacceptable. If it were possible for attributions of inherent importance to be rationally grounded, they would have to be grounded in something besides other attributions of inherent importance. The truth is, I believe, that it is possible to ground judgments of importance only in judgments concerning what people care about. Nothing is truly important to a person unless it makes a difference that he actually cares about. Importance is never inherent. It is always dependent upon the attitudes and dispositions of the individual. Unless a person knows what he *already* cares about, therefore, he cannot determine what he has reason to care about.

The most fundamental question for anyone to raise concerning importance cannot be the *normative* question of what he *should* care about. That question can be answered only on the basis of a prior answer to a question that is not normative at all, but straightforwardly *factual:* namely, the question of what he actually does care about.[3] If he attempts to suspend all of his convictions, and to adopt a stance that is conscientiously neutral and uncommitted, he cannot even begin to inquire methodically into what it would be reasonable for him to care about. No one can pull himself up by his own bootstraps.

16

What we care about has to do with our particular interests and inclinations. If what we *should* care about depends upon what we *do* care about, any answer to the normative question must be derived from considerations that are manifestly subjective. This may make it appear that what we should care about is indeed up to us, and that it is therefore likely to vary from one person to another and to be unstable over time.

---

3. If the modification mentioned in note 1 above is adopted, the pertinent question (concerning what the person *would* care about) will still be straightforwardly factual.

Answers to the normative question are certainly up to us in the sense that they depend upon what we care about. However, what we care about is not always up to us. Our will is not invariably subject to our will. We cannot have, simply for the asking, whatever will we want. There are some things that we cannot *help* caring about. Our caring about them consists of desires and dispositions that are not under our immediate voluntary control. We are committed in ways that we cannot directly affect. Our volitional character does not change just because we wish it to change, or because we resolve that it do so. Insofar as answers to the normative question depend upon carings that we cannot alter at will, what we should care about is not up to us at all.

Among the things that we cannot help caring about are the things that we love. Love is not a voluntary matter. It may at times be possible to contrive arrangements that make love more likely or that make it less likely. Still, we cannot bring ourselves to love, or to stop loving, by an act of will alone—that is, merely by choosing to do so. And sometimes we cannot affect it by any means whatsoever.

The actual causes of love are various, and often difficult to trace. It is sometimes maintained that genuine love can be aroused only by the perceived value of the beloved object. The *value* of the beloved is what captivates the lover and moves him to love. If he were not responsive to its value, he would not love it. I do not deny that love may be aroused in this way. However, love does not *require* a response by the lover to any real or imagined value in what he loves. Parents do not ordinarily love their children so much, for example, because they perceive that their children possess exceptional value. In fact, it is the other way around: the children seem to the parents to be valuable, and they are valuable to the parents, only because the parents love them. Parents have been known to love— quite genuinely—children that they themselves recognize as lacking any particular inherent merit.

As I understand the nature of love, the lover does not depend for his loving upon reasons of any kind. Love is not a conclusion. It is not an outcome of reasoning, or a consequence of reasons. It *creates* reasons. What it *means* to love is, in part, to take the fact that a certain action would serve the good of the beloved as an especially compelling reason for performing that action.

17

We care about many things only for their instrumental value. They are intermediate goals for us, which we pursue as means to other things. Conceivably, a person's goals might all be intermediate: whatever he wants, he wants just for the sake of another thing; and he wants that other thing just in order to obtain something else; and so on. That sort of life could certainly keep a person busy. However, running endlessly from one thing to another, with no conclusive destinations, could not provide any full satisfaction because it would provide no sense of genuine achievement. We need *final* ends, whose value is not merely instrumental. I believe that our final ends are provided and legitimated by love.

Love is paradigmatically personal. What people love differs and may conflict. There is often, unfortunately, no way to adjudicate such conflicts. The account of normativity that I have been giving may therefore seem excessively skeptical. Many people are convinced that our final ends and values—most urgently our moral values—must be impregnably secured by reason, and must possess an inescapable authority that is altogether independent of anyone's personal desires and attitudes. What we should care about, they insist, must be determined by a reality entirely other than ourselves. My account is likely to strike them as radically neglectful of these requirements. They will have the idea that it is unacceptably noncognitive and relativistic. I think that idea is wrong, and I will try to correct it in my next lecture.

II. GETTING IT RIGHT

I

Suppose you are trying to figure out how to live. You want to know what goals to pursue and what limits to respect. You need to get clear about what counts as a good reason in deliberations concerning choice and action. It is important to you to understand what is important to you.

In that case, your most fundamental problem is not to understand how to identify what is valuable. Nor is it to discover what the principles of morality demand, forbid, and permit. You are concerned with how to make specific concrete decisions about what to aim at and how to behave. Neither judgments of value in general nor moral judgments in particular can settle this for you.

From the fact that we consider something to be valuable, it does not follow that we need to be concerned with it. There are many objects, activities, and states of affairs that we acknowledge to be valuable but in which we quite reasonably take no interest because they do not fit into our lives. Other things, perhaps even of lesser value, are more important to us. What we are actually to care about—what we are to regard as really important to us—cannot be based simply upon judgments concerning what has the most value.

In a similar way, morality too fails to get down to the bottom of things. The basic concern of morality is with how to conduct ourselves in our relations with other people. Now why should *that* be, always and in all circumstances, the most important thing in our lives? No doubt it is important; but, so far as I am aware, there is no convincing argument that it must invariably override everything else. Even if it were entirely clear what the moral law commands, it would remain an open question how important it is for us to obey those commands. We would still have to decide how much to care about morality. Morality itself cannot satisfy us about that.

What a person really needs to know, in order to know how to live, is what to care about and how to measure the relative importance to him of the various things about which he cares. These are the deepest as well as the most immediate normative concerns of our active lives. To the extent that we succeed in resolving them, we are able to identify and to order our goals. We possess an organized repertoire of final ends. That puts us in a position to determine, both in general and in particular instances, what we have reason to do. It is our understanding of what to care about, then, that is the ultimate touchstone and basis of our practical reasoning.

2

So, what *are* we to care about? This is not a matter that we can settle arbitrarily, or by deploying some shallow and unstable measure. In designing and committing our lives, we cannot rely upon casual impulse. Our deliberations and our actions must be guided by procedures and standards in which it is appropriate for us to have a mature confidence. The final ends by which we govern ourselves require authentication by some decisive rational warrant.

There is a famous passage in David Hume's *Treatise of Human Nature* that appears to rule out the possibility of providing any rational basis for deciding what we are to care about. Even the most grotesque pre-

ferences, Hume insists, are not irrational. He declares, for instance, that
" 'tis not *contrary* to *reason* to prefer the destruction of the whole world to
the scratching of my finger."[1]

Now it is true that this preference involves no purely *logical* mistake.
So far as logic alone is concerned, it is unobjectionable. Someone who
chooses to protect his finger from a trivial injury at the cost of unlimited
destruction elsewhere is not thereby guilty of any contradiction or faulty
inference. In this purely formal sense of rationality, his choice is not at all
irrational.

But what would we say of someone who made that choice? We would
say he must be *crazy.* In other words, despite the unassailability of his
preference on logical grounds, we would consider both it and him to be
wildly irrational. Caring more about a scratched finger than about
"destruction of the whole world" is not just an unappealing personal
quirk. It is *lunatic.* Anybody who has that preference is *inhuman.*

3

When we characterize the person in Hume's example as "crazy," or as
"lunatic," or as "inhuman," these epithets do not function as mere vitu-
perative rhetoric. They are literal denials that the person is a rational
creature. There is a familiar mode of rationality, then, that is not exclu-
sively defined by *a priori,* formal necessities. Hume's madman may be as
competent as we are in designing valid chains of inference and in distinguishing between what is and what is not logically possible. His irra-
tionality is not fundamentally a *cognitive* deficiency at all. He is *volitionally* irrational. He has a defect of the *will,* which bears upon how he is
disposed to choose and to act.

Our basis for considering him to be volitionally irrational is not that
his preferences happen to be merely very different from ours. It is that
the relative importance to him of protecting his finger and of destroying
the world is altogether *incommensurate* with how much we care about
those things. He is moved to bring about unimaginable destruction for
a reason that strikes us as so inconsequential as hardly to justify incur-
ring any cost at all. An outcome from which we recoil in horror is, to
him, positively attractive. The critical point has to do with possibilities:
he is prepared to implement voluntarily a choice that we *could* not, under
any circumstances, *bring ourselves* to make.

---

1. David Hume, *A Treatise of Human Nature,* edited by L. A. Selby-Bigge (Oxford:
Oxford University Press, 1888), book II, part III, section III, p. 416 (emphasis added).

4

There are structural analogues between the requirements of volitional rationality and the strictly formal, *a priori* requirements of pure reason. Both modes of rationality limit what is possible, and each imposes a corresponding necessity. The boundaries of formal rationality are defined by the necessary truths of logic, to which no alternatives are conceivable. The boundaries of volitional rationality are defined by contingencies that effectively constrain the will. They limit what it is in fact possible for us to care about, what we can accept as reasons for action, and what we can actually bring ourselves to do. Violations of volitional rationality are not *inconceivable*. Rather, what stands in their way is that they are *unthinkable*.

Being volitionally rational is not just a matter of the choices that a person actually makes. It involves being *incapable*, under any circumstances, of making certain choices. If someone attempts to reach a cool and balanced judgment about whether it would be a good idea to destroy the entire world in order to avoid being scratched on his finger, that is not a demonstration of sturdy rationality. Even if he finally concludes that destroying the world to protect his finger is after all *not* such a good idea, the fact that he had to deliberate about this would make it clear that something is wrong with him.

Rationality does not *permit* us to be open-minded and judicious about everything. It requires that certain choices be utterly out of the question. Just as a person transgresses the boundaries of formal reason if he supposes of some self-contradictory state of affairs that it might really be possible, so he transgresses the boundaries of volitional rationality if he regards certain choices as genuine options.

A rational person cannot bring himself to do various things that, so far as his power and skill are concerned, he would otherwise be entirely capable of doing. He may think that a certain action is appropriate, or even mandated; but, when the chips are down, he finds that he just cannot go through with it. He cannot mobilize his will to implement his judgment. No reasons are good enough to move him actually to carry out the action. He cannot bring himself to destroy the world in order to avoid a scratch on his finger. In virtue of the necessities by which his will is constrained, making that choice is not among his genuine options. It is simply unthinkable.

5

What makes it unthinkable? Why are we unable to bring ourselves to do certain things? What accounts for our inability, or our inflexible refusal, to include among our alternatives various actions that we are otherwise quite capable of performing? What is the ground of the constraints upon our will that volitional rationality entails?

One view is that these volitional necessities are responses to an independent normative reality. On this account, certain things are *inherently* important. They therefore provide incontrovertible reasons for acting in certain ways. This is not a function of our attitudes or beliefs or desires, or of subjective factors of any kind. It does not depend in any way upon the condition of our will, or upon what we happen to regard as reasons for acting. In virtue of their unequivocal objectivity, moreover, these reasons possess an inescapable normative authority. It is the natural authority of the real, to which all rational thought and conduct must seek to conform.

In some way—just how is commonly left rather obscure—the independent reality of these reasons becomes apparent to us. We recognize, with a vivid clarity, that various things are inherently important. Then we cannot help accepting the authority of the reasons that they provide. It is impossible for us to deny, or to hold back from acknowledging, the importance that is—so to speak—right before our eyes. Seeing is believing. Thus, our will comes to be constrained by the forceful immediacy of reality.

This is the doctrine of "normative realism." It holds that there are objective reasons for us to act in various ways, whether we know them, or care about them, or not. If we fail to appreciate and to accept those reasons, we are making a mistake. Some philosophers presume that normative realism is implicitly supported by the presumption that, as Robert Adams puts it, "keeping an eye out for possible corrections of our views is an important part of the seriousness of normative discourse."[2] In their view, our concern to avoid mistakes—our belief that we need to get our normative judgments and attitudes *right*—"strongly favors" the supposition that the importance of reasons is inherent in them and that practical reason is therefore securely grounded in the independent reality of its governing norms.

2. Robert M. Adams, *Finite and Infinite Goods* (Oxford: Oxford University Press, 1999), p. 18.

6

My own view is different. I do not believe that anything is inherently important. In my judgment, normativity is not a feature of a reality that is independent of us. The standards of volitional rationality and of practical reason are grounded, so far as I can see, only in ourselves. More particularly, they are grounded only in what we cannot help caring about and cannot help considering important.

Our judgments concerning normative requirements can certainly get things wrong. There is indeed an objective normative reality, which is not up to us and to which we are bound to conform. However, this reality is not objective in the sense of being entirely outside of our minds. Its objectivity consists just in the fact that it is outside the scope of our voluntary control.

Normative truths require that we submit to them. What makes them inescapable, however, is not that they are grounded in an external and independent reality. They are inescapable because they are determined by volitional necessities that we cannot alter or elude. In matters concerning practical normativity, the demanding objective reality that requires us to keep an eye out for possible correction of our views is a reality that is within ourselves.

7

Let me begin to illustrate and to explain this by considering what I suppose everyone will agree is a clear paradigm of something that is genuinely important to us.

Except perhaps under very extraordinary conditions, the fact that an action would protect a person's life is universally acknowledged to be a reason for that person to perform the action. He may have a better reason for doing something else instead. There may even be entirely convincing reasons for him to prefer to die. However, self-defense is rarely (if ever) either thought to be a wholly *irrelevant* consideration in the evaluation of alternatives or thought to be in itself a reason *against* performing an action. Generally it is acknowledged without reserve to be at least a reason *in favor of* performing any action that contributes to it.

As a source of reasons for acting, our interest in staying alive has enormous scope and resonance. There is no area of human activity in which it does not generate reasons—sometimes weaker, sometimes stronger—for doing certain things or for doing things in a certain way. Self-preservation is perhaps the most commanding, the most protean, and the least questioned of our final ends. Its importance is recognized by everyone, and it radiates everywhere. It infuses importance into innumerable objects and activities, and it helps to justify innumerable decisions. Practical reason could hardly get along without it.

8

How come? What accounts for the fact that we are always at least minimally attentive to the task of protecting our lives? What is it about survival that makes it at all important to us? What warrants our invariable acceptance of self-preservation as a reason that supports preferring one course of action over another?

Many people claim to believe that every human life is intrinsically valuable, regardless of how it is lived. Some individuals profess that what *they* are doing with *their* lives, or what they are likely to do with them, gives their lives a special importance. However, even when people have ideas like these about the value or importance of human life, that is ordinarily not the sole or even the primary explanation of why they are determined to go on living. It is not what really accounts for the fact that, in making decisions concerning what to do, they regard preserving their lives as a significant justifying consideration. Someone who acts in self-defense is universally conceded to have a pertinent reason for doing what he does, regardless of how he or others may evaluate his life.

Another view purports to identify reasons for living that do not require any assumption concerning the value of our lives. One of the best recent moral philosophers, the late Bernard Williams, suggests that it is a person's ambitions and plans—what he calls the person's "projects"— that provide "the motive force [that] propels [the person] into the future, and gives him a reason for living." These projects are "a condition of his having any interest in being around" in the world at all. Unless we have projects that we care about, Williams insists, "it is unclear why [we] should go on."[3] In other words, we have a reason to do what it takes to go on living if we have projects that require our survival, but not otherwise.

That can't be right. It seems to me that what Williams says pertains just to people who are seriously depressed. The individuals he describes have no natural vitality. Their lives are inert, lacking any inherent momentum or flow. The movement from one moment to the next does

---

3. These quotations are from "Persons, Character, and Morality," in Bernard Williams, *Moral Luck* (Cambridge: Cambridge University Press, 1981), pp. 12–14.

not come to these people in the usual way—as a matter of course. They need a special push. They will move willingly into the future only if they are "propelled" into doing so. Unless they can supply themselves with an effectively propulsive fuel—"projects"—they will conclude that there is no reason for them to go on at all, and they will lose interest in being around.

Surely Williams has it backward. Our interest in living does *not* commonly depend upon our having projects that we desire to pursue. It's the other way around: we are interested in having worthwhile projects because we do intend to go on living, and we would prefer not to be bored. When we learn that a person has acted to defend his own life, we do not need to inquire whether he had any projects in order to recognize that he had a reason for doing whatever it was that he did.

9

What ordinarily moves us to go on living, and also to accept our desire to continue living as a legitimate reason for acting, is not that we think we have reasons of *any* kind for wanting to survive. Our desire to live and our readiness to invoke this desire as generating reasons for performing actions that contribute to that end are not themselves based on reasons. They are based on love. They derive from and express the fact that, presumably as an outcome of natural selection, we love life. That is, we love living.

This does not mean that we especially enjoy it. Frequently we do not. Many people willingly put up with a great deal of suffering simply in order to stay alive. It is true, of course, that some people are so very miserable that they do really want to die. But this hardly shows that they do not love life. It only shows that they hate misery. What they would certainly prefer, if only they could arrange it, is not to end their lives but just to end the misery.

The desire to go on living is not only universal. It is irreducible. It is only if our prerational urge to preserve our lives has somehow become drastically attenuated that we demand reasons for preserving them. Otherwise, we do not require reasons at all. Our interest in self-preservation is a lavishly fecund source of reasons for choice and for action. However, it is not itself grounded in reasons. It is grounded in love.

10

In addition to their interest in staying alive, people generally have various other similarly primitive and protean concerns as well, which also provide them with reasons for acting. For instance, we cannot help caring about avoiding crippling injury and illness, about maintaining at least some minimal contact with other human beings, and about being free from chronic suffering and endlessly stupefying boredom. We love being intact and healthy, being satisfied, and being in touch. We cannot bring ourselves to be wholly indifferent to these things, much less categorically opposed to them. To a considerable degree, moreover, it is our concerns for them that give rise to the more detailed interests and ambitions that we develop in response to the specific content and course of our experience.

These fundamental necessities of the will are not transient creatures of social prescription or of cultural habit. Nor are they constituted by peculiarities of individual taste or judgment. They are solidly entrenched in our human nature from the start. Indeed, they are elementary constituents of volitional reason itself. It is conceivable, of course, that someone might actually not care a bit about these presumptively universal final ends. There is no logical barrier to rejecting them altogether or to being devoted to their opposites. Loving death, or incapacity, or isolation, or continuously vacant or distressing experience involves no contradiction. If a person did love those things, however, we would be unable to make sense of his life.

It is not terribly difficult to understand that a sensible person might regard certain states of affairs as giving him sufficient reason to commit suicide, or to incur crippling injuries, or to seek radical and permanent isolation, or to accept endless boredom or misery. What *would* be unintelligible is someone pursuing those things for their own sakes, rather than just to attain other goals that he cared about more. We could not empathize with, or expect ourselves to be understood by, someone who loves death or disability or unhappiness. We would be unable to grasp how he could possibly be drawn to what we cannot help being so naturally driven to avoid. His preferences, his deliberations, and his actions are guided by final ends that to us would be flatly incomprehensible. It makes no sense to us that anyone could love them.

11

What is at stake here is not a matter of avoiding mistakes and getting things right. The volitionally irrational lover of death or disability or suffering has not overlooked something, or misunderstood something, or miscalculated, or committed *any* sort of error. From our point of view, his will is not so much in error as it is deformed. His attitudes do not depend upon beliefs that might be demonstrated by cogent evidence or argument to be false. It is impossible to reason with him meaningfully concerning his ends, any more than we could reason with someone who refuses to accept any proposition unless it is self-contradictory.

Many philosophers believe that an act is right only if it can be justified to other rational beings. For this to be plausible, it is not enough that the rationality of the others be merely of the formal variety. Those whom we seek to convince must be volitionally rational as well. If they are not, then their practical reasoning—however formally correct it may be—builds upon a foundation that is in radical opposition to ours. What justifies something to us will, to them, serve only to condemn it. We can therefore do no more with them than to express the bewilderment and revulsion that are inspired in us by the grotesque ends and ideals that they love.

12

So what is love? My conception does not aim at encompassing every feature of the hopelessly inchoate set of conditions that people think of as instances of love. The phenomenon that I have in mind includes only what is, for my purposes, philosophically indispensable. Most especially, it is not to be confused with romantic love, infatuation, dependency, obsession, lust, or similar varieties of psychic turbulence.

As I construe it, love is a particular mode of caring. It is an involuntary, nonutilitarian, rigidly focused, and—as is any mode of caring—self-affirming concern for the existence and the good of what is loved. The object of love can be almost anything—a life, a quality of experience, a person, a group, a moral ideal, a nonmoral ideal, a tradition, whatever. The lover's concern is *rigidly focused* in that there can be no equivalent substitute for its object, which he loves in its sheer particularity and not as an exemplar of some general type. His concern is *nonutilitarian* in that he cares about his beloved for its own sake, rather than only as a means to some other goal.

It is in the nature of the lover's concern that he is *invested* in his beloved. That is, he benefits when his beloved flourishes; and he suffers when it is harmed. Another way of putting it is that the lover *identifies himself* with what he loves. This consists in the lover accepting the interests of his beloved as his own. Love does not necessarily include a desire for union of any other kind. It does not entail any interest in reciprocity or symmetry in the relationship between lover and beloved. Moreover, since the beloved may be entirely unaware of the love, and may be entirely unaffected by it, loving entails no special obligation to the beloved.

Loving is risky. Linking oneself to the interests of another, and exposing oneself to another's vicissitudes, warrants a certain prudence. We can sometimes take steps that inhibit us from loving, or steps that stimulate us to love; more or less effective precautions and therapies may be available, by means of which a person can influence whether love develops or whether it lasts. Love is nonetheless *involuntary,* in that it is not under the immediate control of the will. We cannot love—or stop loving— merely by deciding to do so.

The causes of love are multifarious, and frequently obscure. In any event, love is not essentially a matter of judgment or of reasoned choice. People often think of what causes them to love something as giving them reasons to love it. However, loving is not the rationally determined outcome of even an implicit deliberative or evaluative process. Parmenides said that love is "the first-born offspring of necessity."[4] We come to love because we cannot help loving. Love *requires* no reasons, and it can have *anything* as its cause.

However, love is a powerful *source* of reasons. When a lover believes that an action will benefit his beloved, he does not need to wonder whether there is a reason for him to perform it. Believing that the action will have that effect means that he already has a reason. Insofar as a person loves something, he *necessarily* counts its interests as giving him reasons to serve those interests. The fact that his beloved needs his help is in itself a reason for him to provide that help—a reason that takes precedence, other things being equal, over reasons for being comparably helpful to something that he does not love. That is part of what it means to love. Loving thus *creates* the reasons by which the lover's acts of devotion to his beloved are dictated and inspired.

---

4. J. Burnet, *Early Greek Philosophy* (London: A. & C. Black, 1948), p. 177 (fragment 13).

13

Love entails two closely related volitional necessities. First, a person cannot help loving what he loves; and second, he therefore cannot help taking the expectation that an action would benefit his beloved as a powerful and often decisively preemptive reason for performing that action. Through loving, then, we acquire final ends to which we cannot help being bound; and by virtue of having those ends, we acquire reasons for acting that we cannot help but regard as particularly compelling.

It is not essential to love that it be accompanied by any particular feelings or thoughts. The heart of the matter is not affective or cognitive, but strictly volitional. The necessities of love, which drive our conduct and which circumscribe our options, are necessities of the will. Their grip means that there are certain considerations by which we cannot help being moved to act, and which we cannot help counting as reasons for action. What is essential to love is just these constrained dispositions to reason and to act out of concern for the beloved.

To be sure, the necessities that configure the lover's will are often associated with extravagant passion, and also with representations of the beloved as exceptionally worthy or attractive. It is not difficult to understand why. Love commits us to significant requirements and limitations. These are boundaries that delineate the substance and the structure of our wills. That is, they define what—as active beings—we most intimately and essentially are. Accordingly, love is not only risky. It profoundly shapes our personal identities and the ways in which we experience our lives.

Therefore, it is only natural that loving tends to arouse strong feelings in us. It is also only natural that we may hold ourselves away from loving until we are satisfied that it will be worth the anxieties, distractions, and other costs that it is likely to bring. Thus, love is often accompanied both by vivid enthusiasms and by reassuring characterizations of the beloved. These may be very closely related to loving, but the relationship is only contingent. They are not conceptually indispensable elements of love.

14

It is important to appreciate the difference between the necessities of love and various other deeply entrenched constraints upon the will, which are due to unwelcome and more or less pathological conditions such as compulsions, obsessions, addictions, and the like. These conditions do not involve what I understand by the term "volitional necessity." The necessities that they do involve may be even more urgent and more relentless than those of love; and their influence upon our lives may be no less pervasive and profound. However, they differ fundamentally from the volitional necessities of love in that we only submit to them unwillingly—that is, because they force us to do so. They are generated and sustained from outside the will itself. Their power over us is external, and merely coercive. The power of love, in contrast, is not like that.

Unfortunately, in attempting to explain the difference, it is easy to get lost in a thicket of complexities and qualifications. The trouble is that people are maddeningly nuanced and equivocal. It is impossible to grasp them accurately in their full depth and detail. They are too subtle, too fluid, and too mixed up, for sharp and decisive analysis. So far as love is concerned, people tend to be so endlessly ambivalent and conflicted that it generally cannot be asserted entirely without caveat either that they do love something or that they don't. Frequently, the best that can be said is that part of them loves it and part of them does not.

In order to keep my discussion here fairly simple, I therefore propose just to *stipulate* that a lover is never troubled by conflict, or by ambivalence, or by any other sort of instability or confusion. Lovers do not waver or hold back. Their love, I shall assume, is always robustly wholehearted, uninhibited, and clear.

Now the necessities of wholehearted love may be irresistible, but they are not coercive. They do not prevail upon the lover against his will. On the contrary, they are constituted and confirmed by the fact that he *cannot help* being wholeheartedly behind them. The lover does not passively submit to the grip of love. He is fully identified with and responsible for its necessities. There is no distance or discrepancy between what a lover is constrained to will and what he cannot help wanting to will. The necessities of love are imposed upon him, then, by himself. It is by his own will that he does what they require. That is why love is not coercive. The lover may be unable to resist the power it exerts, but it is his own power.

Moreover, the wholehearted lover cannot help being wholehearted. His wholeheartedness is no more subject to the immediate control of his will than is his loving itself. There may be steps that would cause his love to falter and to fade; but someone whose love is genuinely wholehearted cannot bring himself to take those steps. He cannot deliberately try to stop himself from loving. His wholeheartedness means, by definition,

that he has no reservations or conflicts that would move him to initiate
or to support such an attempt. There is nothing within him that tends to
undermine his love, or that gives him any interest in freeing himself
from it. If the situation were otherwise, that would show either that his
love had already somehow been undermined or that it had never been
truly wholehearted to begin with.

15

The volitional necessities that I have been considering are absolute and
unconditional. No rational person ever aims at death or disability or
misery purely for their own sakes. In no possible circumstances could a
rational person choose those things as final ends, or consider the likelihood that an action would achieve them as being in itself a reason for
performing the action. Those judgments and choices are out of the question no matter what. They are precluded by volitional constraints that
cannot be eluded and that never change.

Are these constraints "objective"? Well, in one sense they are obviously *not* objective. They derive from our attitudes; they are grounded
nowhere but in the character of our own will. That evidently means that
they are subjective. On the other hand, we cannot help having the dispositions that control the actions, choices, and reasons at issue. The character of our will could conceivably be different from what it is. However,
its actual contingent necessities are rigorous and stable; and they are
outside our direct voluntary control. This warrants regarding them as
objective, despite their origin within us.

It seems to me that what the principles of morality essentially
accomplish is that they elaborate and elucidate universal and categorical
necessities that constrain the human will. They develop a vision that
inspires our love. Our moral ideals define certain qualities and conditions of life to which we are lovingly devoted. The point of the moral law
is to codify how personal and social relationships must reasonably be
ordered by people who cannot help caring about the final ends that are
most fundamental in the lives of all fully rational beings.

It is sensible to insist that moral truths are, and must be, stringently
objective. After all, it would hardly do to suppose that the requirements
of morality depend upon what we happen to want them to be, or upon
what we happen to think they are. So far as I can see, all the objectivity
required by the moral law is provided by the real necessities of our volitionally rational will. There is no need to look elsewhere to explain how

moral judgments can be objective. In any case, there is really nowhere else to look.

The truths of morality do not appear to be merely contingent. The appearance that they are necessary truths is, I believe, a reflection or a projection of the volitional necessities from which morality derives. We are aware that we have no choice, and we locate this inescapability in the object instead of in its actual source, which is within ourselves. If we suppose that the moral law is timeless and unalterable, that is because we suppose—rightly or wrongly—that the most fundamental volitional features of human nature are not susceptible to change.

The particular mode of opprobrium that is characteristic of our response to immorality is easy to account for when we recognize that our moral beliefs promote a vision of ideal personal and social relationships that has inspired our love. Attributing moral blame is distinctively a way of being angry at the wrongdoer. The anger is itself a kind of punishment. This is perhaps most transparent when a person directs his anger inward and suffers the lacerations of self-imposed feelings of guilt. What makes moral anger understandable and appropriate is that the transgression of an immoral agent consists in his willfully rejecting and impeding the realization of our moral ideal. In other words, he deliberately injures something that we love. That is enough to make anyone angry.

16

Needless to say, many of our volitional necessities and final ends are far from universal. The fact that I care about various specific individuals, groups, and ways of doing things is not a function simply of generic human nature. It arises from my particular makeup and experience. Some of the things that I happen to love are also loved by others; but some of my loves are shared only by, at most, a small number of people. The very fact that these more personal volitional necessities are not universal implies that they depend upon variable conditions. Naturally, we cannot change them at will; but they can be changed. Even within the life of a single individual, love comes and it goes.

This certainly does *not* mean that loving one thing is as good as loving another. It is true that nothing is *inherently* either worthy or unworthy of being loved, independently of what we are and what we care about. The ground of normativity is relative in part to the common nature of human beings and in part to individual experience and character. Still, despite this relativity, there are plenty of ways that our loving can go absolutely wrong. There is plenty of room for demonstrating the seriousness of our normative discourse, in the way that counts so much for Adams and other normative realists, by "keeping an eye out for possible corrections of our views."

We may need to correct our views concerning what is important to us because our love for one thing conflicts with our love for another. Perhaps we care about worldly success and also about peace of mind, and then it comes to our attention that pursuing the one tends to interfere with attaining the other. Determining which of the two we love more is likely to be facilitated by increasing our understanding of them. As we learn more about what each is and what it entails, it will often become clear that one arouses in us a more substantial interest and concern than the other.

Even when we are not aware of any conflict among our goals, it is only reasonable for us to be alert to the possibility that we do not understand the people and the ideals and the other things that we love well enough. Getting to know them better may reveal conflicts that previously were unnoticed. Our loving may turn out to have been misguided because its objects are not what we thought they were, or because the requirements and consequences of loving them differ from what we had supposed. In love, no less than in other matters, it is helpful to be clear about what we are getting into and what that lets us in for.

In addition to the fact that our understanding of the things we love may require correction, there is also the fact that we often do not understand ourselves very well. It is not so easy for people to know what they really care about or what they truly love. Our motives and our dispositions are notoriously uncertain and opaque, and we often get ourselves wrong. It is hard to be sure what we can bring ourselves to do, or how we will behave when the chips are down. The will is a thing as real as any reality outside us. The truth about it does not depend upon what we think it is, or upon what we wish it were.

17

Once we have learned as much as possible about the natural characteristics of the things we care about, and as much as possible about ourselves, there are no further substantive corrections that can be made. There is really nothing else to look for, so far as the normativity of final ends is concerned. There is nothing else to get right.

The legitimacy and the worthiness of our final ends are not susceptible to being demonstrated by impersonal considerations that all rational
agents would accept as appropriately controlling. Sometimes normative
disagreements cannot be rationally resolved. It may even be true that
other people are required by what they care about to harm or to destroy
what we love. Our love may be inspired by an endearing vision of how
relationships between individuals might ideally be arranged; but other
people may be driven by what they care about to struggle against
arranging things in that way. There may be no convincing basis for
regarding either them or ourselves as rationally defective or as having
made some sort of mistake.

So far as reason goes, the conflict between us may be irreducible.
There may be no way to deal with it, in the end, other than to separate or
to slug it out. This is a discouraging outcome, but it does not imply a
deficiency in my theory. It is just a fact of life.[5]

18

Wholehearted love definitively settles, for each of us, issues concerning
what we are to care about. It expresses what we, as active individuals,
cannot help being. We have no recourse other than to accept its dictates.
Moreover, wholehearted love expresses—beyond that—what we cannot
help wholeheartedly *wanting* to be. This means that we accept its authority not merely as inescapable, but as legitimate too. It is the only legitimate authority upon which, for each of us, our normative attitudes and
convictions can properly and finally rely.

Even after we have recognized what it is that we love, and acquiesced
to it as establishing the defining necessities of our volitional nature,
problems do of course remain. We can fail what we love, through igno-
rance or ineptitude; and we can betray what we love, and thereby betray
ourselves as well, through a shallow indulgence that leads us to neglect
its interests and hence also to neglect our own. These problems have to
do with competence and character.

On the other hand, for normative guidance in understanding what
we should want or what we should do, there can be no authority superior
to the welcome necessities of our own nature. As in the realm of politics,

---

5. There may be similarly irreducible conflicts within a single person, for whom there
will then be no alternatives but to separate one part of himself radically from the other or to
endure tumultuous inner conflict.

the legitimacy of authority here can derive only from the will of the governed. A rational acquiescence to this authority requires a clear self-understanding and a wholehearted acceptance of the essential requirements and boundaries of our will. This amounts to finding a mature confidence, which is not vulnerable to destruction of the self's integrity by familiar varieties of hyper-rationalistic skepticism.

This confidence, in which the authority of our norms of conduct is grounded, is a confidence in what we cannot help being. That provides us with the deepest and most secure foundation for practical reason. Without it, we could not even know where the exercise of practical rationality ought to begin. Without this confidence, in fact, there is no point in trying to become confident about anything else at all.[6]

6. It is worth noticing that Descartes found it impossible to rely confidently upon theoretical reason without first acquiring—through his argument that God could not have made him so defective as to be misled by the clear and distinct perceptions that he could not help accepting—a firm confidence in the necessities of his own cognitive nature. My argument about the ground of practical normativity is, I believe, significantly analogous to his argument about the ground of theoretical reason.

THE TANNER LECTURERS

1976–77

OXFORD Bernard Williams, Cambridge University

MICHIGAN Joel Feinberg, University of Arizona
"Voluntary Euthanasia and the Inalienable Right to Life"

STANFORD Joel Feinberg, University of Arizona
"Voluntary Euthanasia and the Inalienable Right to Life"

1977–78

OXFORD John Rawls, Harvard University

MICHIGAN Sir Karl Popper, University of London
"Three Worlds"

STANFORD Thomas Nagel, Princeton University

1978–79

OXFORD Thomas Nagel, Princeton University
"The Limits of Objectivity"

CAMBRIDGE C. C. O'Brien, London

MICHIGAN Edward O. Wilson, Harvard University
"Comparative Social Theory"

STANFORD Amartya Sen, Oxford University
"Equality of What?"

UTAH Lord Ashby, Cambridge University
"The Search for an Environmental Ethic"

UTAH STATE R. M. Hare, Oxford University
"Moral Conflicts"

1979–80

OXFORD Jonathan Bennett, University of British Columbia
"Morality and Consequences"

CAMBRIDGE Raymond Aron, Collège de France
"Arms Control and Peace Research"

HARVARD George Stigler, University of Chicago
"Economics or Ethics?"

MICHIGAN Robert Coles, Harvard University
"Children as Moral Observers"

STANFORD Michel Foucault, Collège de France
"Omnes et Singulatim: Towards a Criticism of 'Political Reason'"

UTAH Wallace Stegner, Los Altos Hills, California
*"The Twilight of Self-Reliance: Frontier Values and
Contemporary America"*

1980–81

OXFORD   Saul Bellow, University of Chicago
"A Writer from Chicago"

CAMBRIDGE   John Passmore, Australian National University
"The Representative Arts as a Source of Truth"

HARVARD   Brian M. Barry, University of Chicago
"Do Countries Have Moral Obligations? The Case of World Poverty"

MICHIGAN   John Rawls, Harvard University
"The Basic Liberties and Their Priority"

STANFORD   Charles Fried, Harvard University
"Is Liberty Possible?"

UTAH   Joan Robinson, Cambridge University
"The Arms Race"

HEBREW
UNIV.   Solomon H. Snyder, Johns Hopkins University
"Drugs and the Brain and Society"

1981–82

OXFORD   Freeman Dyson, Princeton University
"Bombs and Poetry"

CAMBRIDGE   Kingman Brewster, President Emeritus, Yale University
"The Voluntary Society"

HARVARD   Murray Gell-Mann, California Institute of Technology
"The Head and the Heart in Policy Studies"

MICHIGAN   Thomas C. Schelling, Harvard University
"Ethics, Law, and the Exercise of Self-Command"

STANFORD   Alan A. Stone, Harvard University
"Psychiatry and Morality"

UTAH   R. C. Lewontin, Harvard University
"Biological Determinism"

AUSTRALIAN
NATL. UNIV.   Leszek Kolakowski, Oxford University
"The Death of Utopia Reconsidered"

1982–83

OXFORD   Kenneth J. Arrow, Stanford University
"The Welfare-Relevant Boundaries of the Individual"

CAMBRIDGE   H. C. Robbins Landon, University College, Cardiff
"Haydn and Eighteenth-Century Patronage in Austria and Hungary"

HARVARD   Bernard Williams, Cambridge University
"Morality and Social Justice"

STANFORD   David Gauthier, University of Pittsburgh
"The Incompleat Egoist"

UTAH   Carlos Fuentes, Princeton University
"A Writer from Mexico"

JAWAHARLAL
NEHRU UNIV. Ilya Prigogine, Université Libre de Bruxelles
            "Only an Illusion"

1983–84

OXFORD   Donald D. Brown, Johns Hopkins University
            "The Impact of Modern Genetics"

CAMBRIDGE   Stephen J. Gould, Harvard University
            "Evolutionary Hopes and Realities"

MICHIGAN   Herbert A. Simon, Carnegie-Mellon University
            "Scientific Literacy as a Goal in a High-Technology Society"

STANFORD   Leonard B. Meyer, University of Pennsylvania
            "Music and Ideology in the Nineteenth Century"

UTAH   Helmut Schmidt, former Chancellor, West Germany
            "The Future of the Atlantic Alliance"

HELSINKI   Georg Henrik von Wright, Helsinki
            "Of Human Freedom"

1984–85

OXFORD   Barrington Moore, Jr., Harvard University
            "Authority and Inequality under Capitalism and Socialism"

CAMBRIDGE   Amartya Sen, Oxford University
            "The Standard of Living"

HARVARD   Quentin Skinner, Cambridge University
            "The Paradoxes of Political Liberty"
            Kenneth J. Arrow, Stanford University
            "The Unknown Other"

MICHIGAN   Nadine Gordimer, South Africa
            "The Essential Gesture: Writers and Responsibility"

STANFORD   Michael Slote, University of Maryland
            "Moderation, Rationality, and Virtue"

1985–86

OXFORD   Thomas M. Scanlon, Jr., Harvard Univesity
            "The Significance of Choice"

CAMBRIDGE   Aldo Van Eyck, The Netherlands
            "Architecture and Human Values"

HARVARD   Michael Walzer, Institute for Advanced Study
            "Interpretation and Social Criticism"

MICHIGAN   Clifford Geertz, Institute for Advanced Study
            "The Uses of Diversity"

STANFORD   Stanley Cavell, Harvard University
            "The Uncanniness of the Ordinary"

UTAH   Arnold S. Relman, Editor, New England Journal of Medicine
            "Medicine as a Profession and a Business"

1986–87

OXFORD   Jon Elster, Oslo University and the University of Chicago
              "Taming Chance: Randomization in Individual and Social Decisions"

CAMBRIDGE   Roger Bulger, University of Texas Health Sciences Center,
              Houston
              *"On Hippocrates, Thomas Jefferson, and Max Weber: The
              Bureaucratic, Technologic Imperatives and the Future of
              the Healing Tradition in a Voluntary Society"*

HARVARD   Jürgen Habermas, University of Frankfurt
              "Law and Morality"

MICHIGAN   Daniel C. Dennett, Tufts University
              "The Moral First Aid Manual"

STANFORD   Gisela Striker, Columbia University
              "Greek Ethics and Moral Theory"

UTAH   Laurence H. Tribe, Harvard University
              "On Reading the Constitution"

1987–88

OXFORD   F. Van Zyl Slabbert, University of the Witwatersrand,
              South Africa
              "The Dynamics of Reform and Revolt in Current South Africa"

CAMBRIDGE   Louis Blom-Cooper, Q.C., London
              "The Penalty of Imprisonment"

HARVARD   Robert A. Dahl, Yale University
              "The Pseudodemocratization of the American Presidency"

MICHIGAN   Albert O. Hirschman, Institute for Advanced Study
              *"Two Hundred Years of Reactionary Rhetoric: The Case of the
              Perverse Effect"*

STANFORD   Ronald Dworkin, New York University and University College,
              Oxford
              "Foundations of Liberal Equality"

UTAH   Joseph Brodsky, Russian poet, Mount Holyoke College
              "A Place as Good as Any"

CALIFORNIA   Wm. Theodore de Bary, Columbia University
              "The Trouble with Confucianism"

BUENOS AIRES Barry Stroud, University of California, Berkeley
              "The Study of Human Nature and the Subjectivity of Value"

MADRID   Javier Muguerza, Universidad Nacional de Educatión a
              Distancia, Madrid
              "The Alternative of Dissent"

WARSAW   Anthony Quinton, British Library, London
              "The Varieties of Value"

1988–89

OXFORD Michael Walzer, Institute for Advanced Study
"Nation and Universe"

CAMBRIDGE Albert Hourani, Emeritus Fellow, St. Antony's College, and
Magdalen College, Oxford
"Islam in European Thought"

MICHIGAN Toni Morrison, State University of New York at Albany
*"Unspeakable Things Unspoken: The Afro-American Presence in
American Literature"*

STANFORD Stephen Jay Gould, Harvard University
"Unpredictability in the History of Life"
*"The Quest for Human Nature: Fortuitous Side, Consequences, and
Contingent History"*

UTAH Judith Shklar, Harvard University
"Amerian Citizenship: The Quest for Inclusion"

CALIFORNIA S. N. Eisenstadt, The Hebrew University of Jerusalem
*"Cultural Tradition, Historical Experience, and Social Change:
The Limits of Convergence"*

YALE J. G. A. Pocock, Johns Hopkins University
"Edward Gibbon in History: Aspects of the Text in The History
of the Decline and Fall of the Roman Empire*"*

CHINESE
UNIVERSITY OF
HONG KONG Fei Xiaotong, Peking University
"Plurality and Unity in the Configuration of the Chinese People"

1989–90

OXFORD Bernard Lewis, Princeton University
"Europe and Islam"

CAMBRIDGE Umberto Eco, University of Bologna
"Interpretation and Overinterpretation: World, History, Texts"

HARVARD Ernest Gellner, Kings College, Cambridge
"The Civil and the Sacred"

MICHIGAN Carol Gilligan, Harvard University
"Joining the Resistance: Psychology, Politics, Girls, and Women"

UTAH Octavio Paz, Mexico City
"Poetry and Modernity"

YALE Edward N. Luttwak, Center for Strategic and International
Studies
"Strategy: A New Era?"

PRINCETON Irving Howe, writer and critic
"The Self and the State"

1990–91

OXFORD   David Montgomery, Yale University
              "Citizenship and Justice in the Lives and Thoughts of Nineteenth-
              Century American Workers"

CAMBRIDGE   Gro Harlem Brundtland, Prime Minister of Norway
              "Environmental Challenges of the 1990s: Our Responsibility
              toward Future Generations"

HARVARD   William Gass, Washington University
              "Eye and Idea"

MICHIGAN   Richard Rorty, University of Virginia
              "Feminism and Pragmatism"

STANFORD   G. A. Cohen, All Souls College, Oxford
              "Incentives, Inequality, and Community"
              János Kornai, University of Budapest and Harvard University
              "Market Socialism Revisited"

UTAH   Marcel Ophuls, international filmmaker
              "Resistance and Collaboration in Peacetime"

YALE   Robertson Davies, novelist
              "Reading and Writing"

PRINCETON   Annette C. Baier, Pittsburgh University
              "Trust"

LENINGRAD   János Kornai, University of Budapest and Harvard University
              "Transition from Marxism to a Free Economy"

1991–92

OXFORD   R. Z. Sagdeev, University of Maryland
              "Science and Revolutions"

CALIFORNIA
LOS ANGELES   Václav Havel, former President, Republic of Czechoslovakia
              (Untitled lecture)

BERKELEY   Helmut Kohl, Chancellor of Germany
              (Untitled lecture)

CAMBRIDGE   David Baltimore, former President of Rockefeller University
              "On Doing Science in the Modern World"

MICHIGAN   Christopher Hill, seventeenth-century historian, Oxford
              "The Bible in Seventeenth-Century English Politics"

STANFORD   Charles Taylor, Professor of Philosophy and Political Science,
              McGill University
              "Modernity and the Rise of the Public Sphere"

UTAH   Jared Diamond, University of California, Los Angeles
              "The Broadest Pattern of Human History"

PRINCETON   Robert Nozick, Professor of Philosophy, Harvard University
              "Decisions of Principle, Principles of Decision"

1992–93

MICHIGAN   Amos Oz, Israel
"The Israeli-Palestinian Conflict: Tragedy, Comedy, and Cognitive Block—A Storyteller's Point of View"

CAMBRIDGE   Christine M. Korsgaard, Harvard University
"The Sources of Normativity"

UTAH   Evelyn Fox Keller, Massachusetts Institute of Technology
"Rethinking the Meaning of Genetic Determinism"

YALE   Fritz Stern, Columbia University
"Mendacity Enforced: Europe, 1914–1989"
"Freedom and Its Discontents: Postunification Germany"

PRINCETON   Stanley Hoffmann, Harvard University
"The Nation, Nationalism, and After: The Case of France"

STANFORD   Colin Renfrew, Cambridge University
"The Archaeology of Identity"

1993–94

MICHIGAN   William Julius Wilson, University of Chicago
"The New Urban Poverty and the Problem of Race"

OXFORD   Lord Slynn of Hadley, London
"Law and Culture—A European Setting"

HARVARD   Lawrence Stone, Princeton University
"Family Values in a Historical Perspective"

CAMBRIDGE   Peter Brown, Princeton University
"Aspects of the Christianisation of the Roman World"

UTAH   A. E. Dick Howard, University of Virginia
"Toward the Open Society in Central and Eastern Europe"

Jeffrey Sachs, Harvard University
"Shock Therapy in Poland: Perspectives of Five Years"

UTAH   Adam Zagajewski, Paris
"A Bus Full of Prophets: Adventures of the Eastern-European Intelligentsia"

PRINCETON   Alasdair MacIntyre, Duke University
"Truthfulness, Lies, and Moral Philosophers: What Can We Learn from Mill and Kant?"

CALIFORNIA   Oscar Arias, Costa Rica
"Poverty: The New International Enemy"

STANFORD   Thomas Hill, University of North Carolina at Chapel Hill
"Basic Respect and Cultural Diversity"
"Must Respect Be Earned?"

UC
SAN DIEGO   K. Anthony Appiah, Harvard University
"Race, Culture, Identity: Misunderstood Connections"

1994–95

YALE   Richard Posner, United States Court of Appeals
                  "Euthanasia and Health Care: Two Essays on the Policy Dilemmas
                  of Aging and Old Age"

MICHIGAN   Daniel Kahneman, University of California, Berkeley
                  "Cognitive Psychology of Consequences and Moral Intuition"

HARVARD   Cass R. Sunstein, University of Chicago
                  "Political Conflict and Legal Agreement"

CAMBRIDGE   Roger Penrose, Oxford Mathematics Institute
                  "Space-time and Cosmology"

PRINCETON   Antonin Scalia, United States Supreme Court
                  "Common-Law Courts in a Civil-Law System: The Role of the United
                  States Federal Courts in Interpreting the Constitution and Laws"

UC
SANTA CRUZ   Nancy Wexler, Columbia University
                  "Genetic Prediction and Precaution Confront Human Social Values"

OXFORD   Janet Suzman, South Africa
                  "Who Needs Parables?"

STANFORD   Amy Gutmann, Princeton University
                  "Responding to Racial Injustice"

UTAH   Edward Said, Columbia University
                  "On Lost Causes"

1995–96

PRINCETON   Harold Bloom, Yale University
                  I. *"Shakespeare and the Value of Personality,"* and
                  II. *"Shakespeare and the Value of Love"*

OXFORD   Simon Schama, Columbia University
                  "Rembrandt and Rubens: Humanism, History, and the Peculiarity
                  of Painting"

CAMBRIDGE   Gunther Schuller, Newton Center, Massachusetts
                  I. *"Jazz: A Historical Perspective,"* II. *"Duke Ellington,"* and
                  III. *"Charles Mingus"*

UC
RIVERSIDE   Mairead Corrigan Maguire, Belfast, Northern Ireland
                  "Peacemaking from the Grassroots in a World of Ethnic Conflict"

HARVARD   Onora O'Neill, Newham College, Cambridge
                  "Kant on Reason and Religion"

STANFORD   Nancy Fraser, New School for Social Research
                  "Social Justice in the Age of Identity Politics: Redistribution,
                  Recognition, and Participation"

UTAH   Cornell West, Harvard University
                  "A Genealogy of the Public Intellectual"

YALE   Peter Brown, Princeton University
                  "The End of the Ancient Other World: Death and Afterlife between
                  Late Antiquity and the Early Middle Ages"

1996–97

TORONTO	Peter Gay, Emeritus, Yale University *"The Living Enlightenment"*
MICHIGAN	Thomas M. Scanlon, Harvard University *"The Status of Well-Being"*
HARVARD	Stuart Hampshire, Emeritus, Stanford University *"Justice Is Conflict: The Soul and the City"*
CAMBRIDGE	Dorothy L. Cheney, University of Pennsylvania *"Why Animals Don't Have Language"*
PRINCETON	Robert M. Solow, Massachusetts Institute of Technology *"Welfare and Work"*
CALIFORNIA	Marian Wright Edelman, Children's Defense Fund *"Standing for Children"*
YALE	Liam Hudson, Balas Copartnership *"The Life of the Mind"*
STANFORD	Barbara Herman, University of California, Los Angeles *"Moral Literacy"*
OXFORD	Francis Fukuyama, George Mason University *"Social Capital"*
UTAH	Elaine Pagels, Princeton University *"The Origin of Satan in Christian Traditions"*

1997–98

UTAH	Jonathan D. Spence, Yale University *"Ideas of Power: China's Empire in the Eighteenth Century and Today"*
PRINCETON	J. M. Coetzee, University of Cape Town *"The Lives of Animals"*
MICHIGAN	Antonio R. Damasio, University of Iowa *"Exploring the Minded Brain"*
CHARLES UNIVERSITY	Timothy Garton Ash, Oxford University *"The Direction of European History"*
HARVARD	M. F. Burnyeat, Oxford University *"Culture and Society in Plato's Republic"*
CAMBRIDGE	Stephen Toulmin, University of Southern California *"The Idol of Stability"*
UC IRVINE	David Kessler, Yale University *"Tobacco Wars: Risks and Rewards of a Major Challenge"*
YALE	Elaine Scarry, Harvard University *"On Beauty and Being Just"*
STANFORD	Arthur Kleinman, Harvard University *"Experience and Its Moral Modes: Culture, Human Conditions, and Disorder"*

1998–99

MICHIGAN   Walter Burkert, University of Zurich
              "Revealing Nature Amidst Multiple Cultures: A Discourse with
              Ancient Greeks"

UTAH   Geoffrey Hartman, Yale University
              "Text and Spirit"

YALE   Steven Pinker, Massachusetts Institute of Technology
              "The Blank Slate, the Noble Savage, and the Ghost in the Machine"

STANFORD   Randall Kennedy, Harvard University
              "Who Can Say 'Nigger'?...and Other Related Questions"

UC DAVIS   Richard White, Stanford University
              "The Problem with Purity"

OXFORD   Sidney Verba, Harvard University
              "Representative Democracy and Democratic Citizens: Philosophical
              and Empirical Understandings"

PRINCETON   Judith Jarvis Thomson, Massachusetts Institute of Technology
              "Goodness and Advice"

HARVARD   Lani Guinier, Harvard University
              "Rethinking Powers"

1999–2000

YALE   Marina Warner, London
              "Spirit Visions"

MICHIGAN   Helen Vendler, Harvard University
              "Poetry and the Mediation of Value: Whitman on Lincoln"

HARVARD   Wolf Lepenies, Free University, Berlin
              "The End of 'German Culture'"

CAMBRIDGE   Jonathan Lear, University of Chicago
              "Happiness"

OXFORD   Geoffrey Hill, Boston University
              "Rhetorics of Value"

PRINCETON   Michael Ignatieff, London
              "Human Rights as Politics" and "Human Rights as Idolatry"

UNIVERSITY
OF UTAH   Charles Rosen, New York
              "Tradition without Convention: The Impossible Nineteenth-
              Century Project"

STANFORD   Jared Diamond, UCLA Medical School
              "Ecological Collapses of Pre-industrial Societies"

2000–2001

MICHIGAN   Partha Dasgupta, Cambridge University
              "Valuing Objects and Evaluating Policies in Imperfect Economies"

HARVARD	Simon Schama, Columbia University *"Random Access Memory"*
UC SANTA BARBARA	William C. Richardson, The Kellogg Foundation *"Reconceiving Health Care to Improve Quality"*
OXFORD	Sir Sydney Kentridge, Q.C., London *"Human Rights: A Sense of Proportion"*
UTAH	Sarah Blaffer Hrdy, University of California at Davis *"The Past and Present of the Human Family"*
UC BERKELEY	Joseph Raz, Columbia University *"The Practice of Value"*
PRINCETON	Robert Pinsky, poet, Boston University *"American Culture and the Voice of Poetry"*
YALE	Alexander Nehamas, Princeton University *"A Promise of Happiness: The Place of Beauty in a World of Art"*
CAMBRIDGE	Kwame Anthony Appiah, Harvard University *"Individuality and Identity"*
STANFORD	Dorothy Allison, novelist *"Mean Stories and Stubborn Girls"* and *"What It Means to Be Free"*

2001–2002

MICHIGAN	Michael Fried, Johns Hopkins University *"Roger Fry's Formalism"*
UC BERKELEY	Sir Frank Kermode, Cambridge, England *"Pleasure, Change, and the Canon"*
HARVARD	Kathleen Sullivan, Stanford University *"War, Peace, and Civil Liberties"*
YALE	Salman Rushdie, New York *"Step Across this Line"*
CAMBRIDGE	Seamus Heaney, Harvard University *"Homiletic Elegy: Beowulf and Wilfrid Owens," "On Pastoral:* *Starting from Virgil," and "On Pastoral: Eclogues in extremis"*
UTAH	Benjamin Barber, University of Maryland *"Democratic Alternatives to the Mullahs and the Malls:* *Citizenship in an Age of Global Anarchy"*
STANFORD	Paul Krugman, Princeton University *"Intractable Slumps" and "Currency Crises"*
PRINCETON	T. J. Clark, University of California Berkeley *"Painting at Ground Level"*
OXFORD	Laurence H. Tribe, Harvard University *"The Constitution in Crisis: From Bush v. Gore to* *the War on Terrorism"*

2002–2003

MICHIGAN   Claude Steele, Stanford University
             "The Specter of Group Image: The Unseen Effects on Human
             Performance and the Quality of Life in a Diverse Society"

UC BERKELEY Derek Parfit, Oxford University
             "What We Could Rationally Will"

HARVARD   Lorraine Daston, Max Planck Institute, Berlin
             "The Morality of Natural Orders: The Power of Medea"
             "Nature's Customs versus Nature's Laws"

AUSTRALIAN
NAT. UNIV.
and   Martha C. Nussbaum, University of Chicago
CAMBRIDGE   *"Beyond the Social Contract: Toward Global Justice"*

PRINCETON   Jonathan Glover, King's College London
             "Towards Humanism in Psychology"

STANFORD   Mary Robinson, New York
             "Human Rights and Ethical Globalization"
             "The Challenge of Human Rights Protection in Africa"

YALE   Garry L. Wills, Northwestern University
             "Henry Adams: The Historian as Novelist"

OXFORD   David M. Kennedy, Stanford University
             "The Dilemma of Difference in Democratic Society"

2003–2004

UTAH   Sebastião Salgado, Paris
             "Art, Globalism and Cultural Instability"

PRINCETON   Frans de Waal, Emory University
             "Morality and the Social Instincts: Continuity with the
             Other Primates"

HARVARD   Richard Dawkins, University of Oxford
             "The Science of Religion" and *"The Religion of Science"*

MICHIGAN   Christine M. Korsgaard, Harvard University
             "Fellow Creatures: Kantian Ethics and Our Duties to Animals"

CAMBRIDGE   Neil MacGregor, The British Museum
             "The Meanings of Things"

UC BERKELEY Seyla Benhabib, Yale University
             "Reclaiming Universalism: Negotiating Republican Self-Determination
             and Cosmopolitan Norms"

YALE   Oliver Sacks, Albert Einstein College of Medicine, New York
             "Journey Into Wonder: Reflections on a Chemical Boyhood" and
             "Awakenings Revisited"

STANFORD   Harry Frankfurt, Princeton University
             "Taking Ourselves Seriously" and *"Getting It Right"*

OXFORD   Joseph Stiglitz, Columbia University
             "Ethical Dimensions of Globalization"